WHOLE NUMBERS
AND HALF TRUTHS

'Rukmini has been a trailblazer in data-based journalism in India. Her pioneering achievements also result from courage, persistence, and the willingness to speak truth to power. This terrific book showcases these many rich qualities.' —**Arvind Subramanian**, Senior Fellow, Brown University, Watson Institute for International and Public Affairs; former Chief Economic Adviser, Government of India

'Governments are always using numbers to obfuscate. People quote a number with such confidence that it becomes more powerful than the truth. In today's journalism, no journalist can last without the ability to understand these numbers. Only a person who understands data well will understand politics well. It is essential to understand where these numbers come from, when do they come and when do they not, if they do come then how are they to be analysed. Rukmini's book should be in the toolkit of anyone who wants to understand India.' —**Ravish Kumar**, Senior Journalist and Writer, Senior Executive Editor (NDTV)

'Engaging and clear, Rukmini's book shows what in and how India is changing. She explores a range of areas to dispel widely held opinions about Indian society, its behaviour and potential pace of change. As the shape of social interactions transform, independent measurement and interpretation are critical for understanding emerging trends, and Rukmini delivers a fizzy, readable book brimming with insights.' —**Dr Gagandeep Kang**, Professor of Microbiology, Division of Gastrointestinal Sciences, Christian Medical College, Vellore; Fellow of the Royal Society (London)

'This is not a book about data—it's jargon-free, equation-free, econ-speak-free. Neither is it a book about Indian statistics. We meet the organisations and people behind the numbers but they are not the book's central focus. This is a book about modern India, the story of India told through the lens of its data. Through its narration and choice of questions, the book reveals both the power and limitations of data journalism.' —*Mint*

'In our diverse country, nothing is what it seems and the reality is messy. For anybody who wants to understand and unite the country, *Whole Numbers and Half Truths* is essential reading.' —*The Hindu*

'The book draws you in, slowly, as it lays bare a wide array of numbers and percentages, while also explaining the sheer lack of information about the real state of elections, jobs, population growth, urbanisation, migration, healthcare, and death in contemporary India…. [For] those who want to understand India's strange data architecture or think about what missing data can tell about us as a society, *Whole Numbers* might serve as a good starting point.' —*Telegraph*

'Every chapter is chock-full of insights and excellent reportage, weaving the data with human interest stories. The charts are well done and are thoughtfully designed to tell their story in Black & White—an important factor in comprehending them in a B & W book, and often overlooked.' —*The Hindu BusinessLine*

'The author, a data journalist, provides a detailed and eye-opening view on several issues that we take for granted, or probably are not aware of. In fact, when she talks of marriages and customs, the revelations are quite startling…. *Whole Numbers* is a must-read book for everyone as it lays out in stark numbers what happens around us. It also explains why often things don't change, and we remain a conservative society that prefers not to upset status quo.' —*Financial Express*

'Rukmini makes a passionate argument in her book *Whole Numbers and Half Truths* … that there is a wealth of data in India but many times we overlook it. She says that other times we do have the data but we don't look at the context [and] thereby we skew the interpretation. I found this book fascinating.' —**Dhanya Rajendran, *The News Minute***

'Written as a "tool-kit for India" by data journalism pioneer Rukmini Shrinivasan, it shatters the country's warm notions about itself through cold official statistics about everything from love to food and marriage to elections. —**Sharmila Ganesan,** *Times of India*

'A wonderful new book by one of India's pioneering data journalist Rukmini. The book paints a detailed, even surprising in some measure, picture of modern India and who we are as a people. In *Whole Numbers and Half Truths*, Rukmini marshals data from multiple sources to interrogate some widely held beliefs and narratives of what Indians think and believe.' —**Smitha Nair, Your Weekly Fix,** *Scroll.in*

'The book uses rigorous data to take a good hard look at our multitudes. The chapter titles themselves indicate the sweep of the book, what India thinks, feels and believes, how India really votes. How India works. how India is growing, aging and so on. What makes this book so enlightening is Rukmini's approach. She gets into every issue without preconceptions or biases. She is open to letting the data speak for itself even when it indicates patterns that make her uncomfortable. The result is a book that contains many truths that seem counterintuitive to us. That fly in the face of received wisdom.' —**Amit Varma,** *The Seen and the Unseen*

'The book is stuffed with information but it is even for somebody who knows nothing about statistics. It kind of gives you an idea of where we are headed and the consequences of these statistics and this data.' —**Manjula Narayan,** *HT Smartcast*

'*Whole Numbers* ... is not a mathematical exercise full of hard facts and statistics. It is a nuanced and complete look at how you can use available data—from reliable sources which includes government and private efforts—to understand what's happening around you. It explains how instant polls and pat conclusions can be both dangerous and ultimately pointless because they blank out the truth and deal in shadows. And more importantly, how not having enough data leaves too many questions unaskable and therefore unanswered.' —**Ranjona Banerji,** *The Asian Age*

WHOLE
NUMBERS
AND HALF
TRUTHS

What Data Can and Cannot
Tell Us About Modern India

RUKMINI S.

cntxt

First published by Context, an imprint of Westland Publications Private Limited, in 2021

Published by Context, an imprint of Westland Books, a division of Nasadiya Technologies Private Limited, in 2022

No. 269/2B, First Floor, 'Irai Arul', Vimalraj Street, Nethaji Nagar, Allappakkam Main Road, Maduravoyal, Chennai 600095

Westland, the Westland logo, Context and the Context logo are the trademarks of Nasadiya Technologies Private Limited, or its affiliates.

ISBN: 9789395073004

10 9 8 7 6 5 4 3 2

Typeset by SÜRYA, New Delhi

Printed at Manipal Technologies Limited, Manipal

For Thatha (VVS), Nilavan and Kanali—the three greatest lovers of books that I have known.

CONTENTS

than those in the south. But beyond this lies a surprising world of nuance—women are actually having their children earlier than ever on average, 'family planning' is having some terrifying unintended consequences, and stereotypes about Muslim families miss most of the story.

Urbanisation and migration were supposed to be the big stories of the last decade. Looking at where and how India lives shows that neither played out the way it was supposed to, but planners don't seem to have caught on to this.

Who gets sick in India, of what, where do they go to get better and how does treatment work? We think we know the answers, but a lot of what we think we know about illness, doctor abilities and health costs is actually false and a result of polarised activism and news reporting. The COVID pandemic provides a special impetus to getting the answers right.

What can we then say that we really know about India from the data, how could we go about getting the data to do a better job of capturing the country, and is there a way out of the Left/ Right binary?

INTRODUCTION

How do the nuts and bolts of Indian democracy work? It would seem that we have all the answers to that question. Newspapers and nightly TV shows are full of experts explaining to you what Indians think, feel and do; you can hardly take an Uber pool or an overnight train without someone reeling off their pet theory about what Indians are really like. The problem is most of these established 'narratives' are pure fiction masquerading as fact.

India's statistical architecture is vast and impressive. Since the early part of the twentieth century, Census enumerators have fanned out across the country with the grand objective of capturing every single Indian (see chapter 9), National Statistical Office surveyors head out with forms to capture the exact number of eggs that every household in their massive national sample has eaten in the last week (see chapter 6), the National Crime Records Bureau aggregates every single First Information Report from every police station in the country, and the National Family Health Survey tries to discreetly ask women if they have ever been assaulted, even if they never reported it to the police (see chapter 1). The Civil Registration System can capture births and deaths and tell us how many children women are having in Kerala compared to Bihar (chapter 8), as well as how many Indians die every year, how many deaths go uncounted and how many excess deaths COVID might have caused (see chapter 10).

Private research organisations like the National Council for Applied Economic Research conduct massive surveys that allow us to check if the government is getting its data right and answer questions that the government never asks, like how much money Indians make (see chapter 5) or who they choose to marry (see chapter 4). Organisations like the Centre for the Study of Developing Societies with fifty years of opinion polling experience conduct world-class surveys about voter intentions and electoral decisions (see chapter 3). Newer private surveyors like the Centre for the Monitoring of the Indian Economy can provide high-frequency panel data on the economy and employment even during a national lockdown to create an early-alert system in times of crisis (see chapter 7). Private organisations like the Lok Foundation invest significant money into large surveys that give us never-before insights into how Indians think about working women, about people from other castes, about the future of liberalism and even democracy (see chapter 2).

Yet, even with this wealth of data, people build inaccurate narratives around how India works, either without looking at the data or because of bad data. They assume there are vote-banks where none exist. They assume people vote for reasons that don't actually guide their decisions. They decide they are middle class with little basis. They imagine urban explosions and migrant floods with little reason. These narratives, repeated enough times, become 'fact' and political fodder.

Part of the problem is that statistics can be unintelligible, out of date, hard to find and harder still to communicate. But the other part is that statistics alone don't tell us everything. They need context, interpretation that's free from ideological spin, and to be held up to the light.

I have reported on stories small and big from the ground

across the country since 2004 and worked on Indian socio-economic data for over a decade now, and I finally see the connections—how the processes and people I encountered on the ground aggregate into statistics, what these numbers mean in terms of actual lived experience, what the numbers are either failing to capture or are obfuscating, and how to fix these gaps in our understanding.

Numbers enlighten, empower, elevate. Numbers can help us make sense of modern India. Numbers can help us anticipate the future. But numbers do not exist in a rarefied space. The push and pull of political and social forces around the world don't leave numbers unaffected.

This is a country of wonder and beauty, of idealism and sacrifice, of extraordinary leaps of faith, and people who move mountains. Numbers, far from being cold and unintelligible, can capture much of this nuance, this humanity, that pre-packaged narratives sometimes flatten out. If Indian statistics have seemed impenetrable, that is a failing of the community that produces data and works with it. Everyone should hear the stories numbers tell, and then make up their own minds about the country.

The last few years have seen a vicious polarisation colour not only most news reporting, but also the world of data. Part of the reason people find it hard to make sense of the world using numbers is because they first need to turn the tin upside down to check on the manufacturer before opening it. They need to know who produced it, what it missed, and what the other side is saying before they can be sure this is the whole truth. Democracy is best served by those who engage with it critically. But blanket suspicion is problematic and harmful. Knowing how to engage critically with data will only help strengthen democracy. This book is a toolkit.

A NOTE ON THE DATA

All assertions in this book, except where stated as an opinion, are backed with footnoted data. In all cases, the most recently available data has been used and the year of the Census, survey, or study clearly mentioned. Where official data is available, the book uses official sources. The book relies heavily on data from the Census, National Statistical Office, National Family Health Survey, National Crime Records Bureau, Election Commission of India, National Health Mission, Civil Registration System and Sample Registration System.

The only private sources used are high-quality, well-regarded sources with transparent methodology that are for the most part publicly available. These include the India Human Development Surveys, the Lokniti-CSDS surveys, the Lok Survey with the University of Oxford and the Centre for the Monitoring of the Indian Economy, the CMIE's Consumer Pyramids Household Survey and the Social Attitudes Research survey. No small-size sample surveys, online surveys, or surveys where the raw data was not available for review have been used.

Except where mentioned, data refers to nationally representative data. In cases where the data has flaws or needs additional interpretation, this is clearly mentioned in the main text of the book—there are no hidden caveats or loopholes that are kept from the reader.

I

HOW INDIA TANGLES WITH
COPS AND COURTS

Relying on police statistics and media reporting of police reports has created a distorted picture about the reality of crime in India, and perverse incentives for the police force.

In January 2013, Seema*, who had moved to Delhi from rural Bihar, went to a small temple on Delhi's Panchkuian Road with nineteen-year-old Sameer*. He drew a streak of red through her neatly parted hair, the couple embraced and now married in their own eyes, they ran away to Sameer's native village in Samastipur, Bihar. By May, Seema, pregnant, was in a court-mandated shelter home for young women, and Sameer had been placed in custody, accused of kidnapping and assaulting his young love.

In India's official statistics, their tragic story added to the growing number of reported rapes, while Sameer's eventual acquittal in court added to what is criticised as an 'abysmally low conviction rate' for sexual crime. Beneath India's crime statistics lies a complicated world of true crime, but also corruption, laws both underpowered and over-powered, power and pride—and even love. Yet, taken at face value, as they are in both Indian and international media, these statistics create a deeply distorted picture of what crime, punishment and life itself look like in India.

Official statistics often misreport non-criminal activity as crime, intentionally use wrong sections of the law to book some crimes, and significantly undercount a vast range of typically non-violent crime.

Moving Cars and 'Cold Drink' Bottles

India's only official source of statistics on crime is the National Crime Records Bureau (NCRB). The NCRB's annual *Crime In India* report is a slim volume of many tables and little context, published every year since 1950. This includes the number of offences recorded under various sections of the law, some demographic information about complainants and the accused, and statistics around convictions, acquittals and prison sentences. NCRB data comes from police stations; when a complainant approaches a police station, the police may turn her complaint into a First Information Report (FIR). All FIRs filed in police stations across the country are collected at the state level and then put together at the national level to produce these all-India statistics.

Knowing where, when and against whom crimes occur, and how often, is essential for a democracy. Accurate crime statistics help police forces put in place measures to prevent crime, and understand how better to allocate resources. Comparative crime rates help spotlight regions where there is more or less crime, and can form the foundation for an understanding of why this might be so—the sociological or policing factors that might be driving these differences are vital tools in the hands of citizens and policymakers. Finally, crime statistics help the public form perceptions about a place's relative risks and take actions that might protect them. Young women in Delhi, for instance, are more likely to choose colleges that do not need them to take 'unsafe' bus routes, even if they are of lower quality.[1]

Yet, most people know little about the NCRB's processes and methodology. For instance, the NCRB follows a system known as the 'principal offence rule'. Instead of all the Indian Penal Code (IPC) sections involved in an alleged crime making it to the statistics, the NCRB only picks the 'most heinous' crime from each FIR for their statistics. I stumbled upon this then unknown fact in an off-the-record conversation with an NCRB statistician in the months after the deadly sexual assault of a physiotherapy student in Delhi in December 2012. In the course of that conversation, I learnt that the crime that shook the country would have only made it to the NCRB statistics as a murder, and not as a sexual assault, because murder carries the maximum penalty. This, I was told, was to prevent the crime statistics from being 'artificially inflated': 'If the FIR is for theft, there will be a[n IPC] section for assault also, causing hurt also. If you include all the sections, people will think these are separate crimes and the numbers will seem too huge,' he told me. After I reported this,[2] the NCRB for the first time began to include the 'principal offence rule' in its disclaimer.[3]

Not knowing how the NCRB data is compiled can also lead to unrealistic expectations from it. In 2019, the NCRB's then director Ish Kumar told the media that he had ensured that data on mob lynchings and hate crimes would make it to the report. In the absence of such data, some media organisations had begun to compile news articles to 'track hate', a notoriously imprecise operation, given the biases and pressures under which news reporting operates. By the time the NCRB report was published in October 2019, Kumar had been transferred, and the omission of that data in the report led to an outcry in the media about its 'suppression' by the new Modi government.[4] But the fact is that for the NCRB to be able to put data out, an IPC section needs to exist[5]—just two months later, the government told Parliament that IPC sections on murder were the only legal tools available against mob lynchings.[6] The NCRB cannot be the magic wand that makes data appear; the hard advocacy and political work to create the legal framework for that data needs to happen first.

Not just statistics, most news reporting on crime too emerges from the FIR. Apart from the occasional daring investigation, the standard Indian crime reporter's practice is to faithfully reproduce the contents of an FIR as fact, in part to keep the police establishment happy. This reliance on FIRs is fraught with problems. Alongside acts of great bravery and hard work in trying circumstances, there is also extreme venality in Indian police forces. And, alongside genuine crime, there are also complex sociological forces that drive people into police stations, forces that have little to do with true crime. In short, FIRs alone say too little.

Yet, this is largely how journalists and, as a result, the public, form their sense of sexual crime in the country, and women their sense of safety. The release of the NCRB statistics is usually accompanied by headlines that call a city a 'rape capital' or proclaim that one state is now more unsafe for women than the other. In 2019, for instance, the *Hindu* reported that 'Delhi ranks first in crimes against women'.[7]

In the wake of the December 2012 assault, a long-overdue movement against sexual violence built up across India. Amplifying this outrage was the media, which, partly out of solidarity and partly with a canny eye on audience, began to highlight all reported sexual crimes against women to an extent that it hadn't in the past. Every incident reported became front-page news, and the most horrifying details were highlighted—women pulled into moving cars, given 'sedative-laced cold drinks' in a market, and abducted and assaulted. The international media was awash with stories on India's 'epidemic of rape'.

But the stories that emerge once these cases go to trial reveal the more complex nature of gender relations, sexuality and sexual crime in India. In 2014, I examined every judgement passed in a case involving rape (IPC section 376) in Delhi's seven district courts in 2013—nearly 600 in all.[8] I found that one-fifth of the cases were wound up because the complainant did not appear, turned hostile, insisting that they had never alleged rape, or admitted in court that they had filed a false complaint. While it is likely that some of these were on account of the pressure exerted on women to withdraw complaints—in two cases, the complainants referred to 'community members' intervening in their depositions—in several others, the complainant said that she had filed a false case for money or as a result of a property dispute. Naturally, all of these resulted in acquittals.

Of the 460 cases that were fully argued before the courts, the largest category (189 cases) dealt with cases involving or allegedly involving consenting couples. The majority of these—174 of these 189 cases—involved couples like Seema and Sameer who seemed to have eloped, after which parents, usually of the woman, filed complaints of abduction and rape with the police. Many of them involved inter-caste or inter-religious relationships. (Fig. 1.1)

In two-thirds (107) of these cases, the woman 'complainant' deposed consistently before the police, doctors, magistrate, district judge, and under cross-examination that she had eloped and had sexual relations—and in most cases got married and sometimes had children—with the accused because she was in love with him.

In case after case, as well as in interviews with me, the behaviour of the families of these young consenting women was shocking: they arrived at the hotel or friend's house the couple had eloped to and dragged them home, they beat and even injured the couple (in one case breaking the young woman's spine), they threatened their own daughters and nieces with acid, they forced them to submit to invasive medical tests and in many cases, even to an abortion. Young women deposed about the suffering they faced at the hands of their parents—beatings, confinement, threats, being forced to undergo medical examinations, being forced to undergo abortions—even as they pleaded before the court they be allowed to stay with their husbands. There are undoubtedly crimes taking place against the women here, but not the ones that are being prosecuted by the State.

In most of the remaining sixty-seven cases in Delhi involving alleged elopement, the woman deposed in at least one instance, either in the initial FIR, or during her medical examination, or in her statement to the magistrate, that she was in love with the accused and went away with him of her own will. However, in court she supported her parents' and prosecution's case. 'Once the girl is sent back to her parents,

Figure 1.1: What one year of district court rulings in sexual assault trials showed

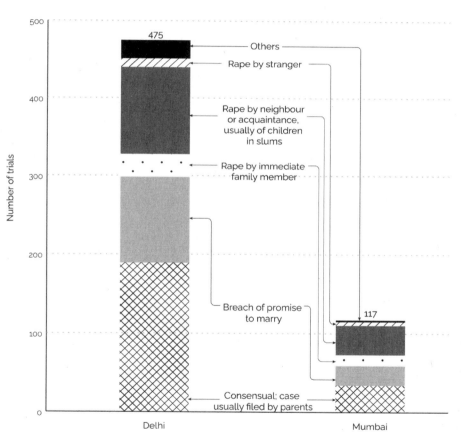

Number of trials

475

Others

Rape by stranger

Rape by neighbour or acquaintance, usually of children in slums

Rape by immediate family member

Breach of promise to marry

117

Consensual; case usually filed by parents

Delhi

Mumbai

Delhi's Conviction Rate: **23%**   Mumbai's Conviction Rate: **37%**

Source: Author's calculations for the *Hindu*, 2014, 2015

there is tremendous pressure on her and she often changes her stance,' lawyer and activist Seema Mishra, who has seen countless such cases in Lucknow as well, told me.

'If the girl is not sent to a shelter once she is picked up by the police, and instead sent home, you can be sure they will brainwash her and she will change her statement in court,' one public prosecutor added. Indeed, in one of the cases, the young woman pleaded before the magistrate that she be allowed to stay with the accused, but the magistrate denied her wish as she was a minor, and forced her to return to her parents' home. In her deposition in the sessions trial, she subsequently changed her stand.

Filing kidnapping cases when couples elope or are in relationships is not a new phenomenon in India. On 23 May 1972, an eighteen-year-old girl, Mathura, was called to the Desaiganj police station in Maharashtra for questioning. There, the woman was raped by two policemen, who were later acquitted by the Supreme Court. The 'Mathura rape case', as it came to be called, galvanised the Indian feminist movement and became the pivot for changes in Indian rape law in 1983,[9] but an often overlooked detail is why the young woman was in that police station at all. Her brother had complained to the police that she had been kidnapped by a young man and his relatives. Mathura was in a relationship with the man, which her brother did not approve of. He filed an FIR against the man and his relatives for 'kidnapping from lawful guardianship' his sister, which had led to the young woman being summoned to the station. What the legal system essentially did was to provide the disapproving brother the capacity to use criminal law to thwart his sister's choices.

This is where the moving cars and the cold drinks from

newspaper headlines come in. To prove that their daughter or sister did not choose to elope with the accused man, the complainant father or brother must demonstrate that she was taken against her will. Cops step in to create moving cars that abduct young women or sedative-laced cold drinks that render the 'victim' unconscious and unable to consent to her own escape.

Going by FIRs alone, most rape cases in Delhi in 2013 involved teenagers who were given intoxicant-laced cold drinks before being abducted and assaulted. Police stations followed an informal script to record sexual assault cases, conversations with police officials and judges revealed. Madhu Mehra, feminist lawyer and executive director of Partners for Law in Development, says that their studies have shown the same. To make the case sound as if the young woman was abducted and did not go with the young man of her own consent—that her consent was 'vitiated' in the eyes of the law—an element of intoxication was added to the FIR, usually a 'cold drink laced with a sedative'. None of this stood up in court. In not one of the 583 cases I looked at was the police able to produce any proof of intoxication; the cold drink bottle was the smoking gun that never appeared.

This situation is about to get much worse. Over the last decade, Hindu nationalist groups in India have floated a theory they call 'love jihad', the belief that Muslim men lure Hindu women into sexual relationships and marriage as a way of spreading their faith. Once laughed at by the Indian mainstream as the talking point of an extremist fringe, the idea has now taken firm hold among India's Hindu right-wing. In 2020, three Indian states ruled by the right-wing Hindu nationalist BJP, which is also in power at the Union, brought in stricter sentences for men found to be 'coercing' women into religious conversion for the purpose of marriage, and also added restrictions on consenting inter-religious couples. Whether these cases stand up in court or not appears to be irrelevant; in the first few months since the new law was passed in India's largest state, Uttar Pradesh, where one-fifth of the population is Muslim, dozens of young Muslim men were arrested for 'offences' that included meeting a Hindu girl for a pizza date. In police statistics, these will go down as kidnappings and rapes and in the media as further 'proof' of growing crimes against women. Once again, there *is* a crime taking place here—just not the one that is being reported.

Tough Times and Bad Laws

Ruling on Seema and Sameer's case in October 2013, Additional Sessions Judge Dharmesh Sharma said, 'The instant case racks [sic] up a perennial problem being faced by all of us on the judicial side: what should be the judicial response to elopement cases like the instant one . . . This life drama is enacted, played and repeated everyday in the Police Stations and Courts . . .' Of the case before him, Judge Sharma noted, 'This case is a teenage love drama where our dysfunctional, cruel society and the justice system have separated the two love birds and have taught them a bitter lesson.' In this instance, Judge Sharma was able to acquit Sameer, since Seema was around eighteen, while the age of consent for sex at the time was sixteen years.

Today, however, Sameer could have been convicted. Faced with massive public anger in the wake of the December 2012 sexual assault in Delhi, the Indian Parliament passed a series of problematic laws. In 2013, the age at which a woman could consent to sexual acts was raised from sixteen to eighteen. A rape charge can now be added to a kidnapping charge in cases brought because of familial objection to relationships, where the woman is a teenager or in her early twenties. Though the couple might subsequently be able to prove in court that the woman was eighteen at the time, the family would have already got the desired outcome—getting the couple separated, the male partner arrested, and the woman either back in her parents' custody or in a state-run shelter home.

The FIRs in most of the Delhi cases stated that the young women were between the ages of fifteen and eighteen, and the court had to decide if they were minors, in which case even a consensual relationship would constitute statutory rape. In ten of these cases, the court agreed that the relationship was consensual and that the couple had got 'married', but convicted the boy anyway as the girl was a minor.

In 2015, I analysed all 142 cases decided by Mumbai's two sessions courts hearing sexual assault cases and reached similar conclusions.[10] One-quarter of all cases involved parents filing cases of kidnap and rape against young men whom their young daughters had eloped with; several of these were inter-caste and inter-religious couples, and many recounted parental opposition to their relationship. These thirty-three cases followed a similar pattern: an FIR would be registered, in which the woman was described as a minor, even though it would eventually be proved in court she was eighteen, or nearly eighteen, the couple would usually be retrieved from another part of the state or even another state by the police, the young man would be arrested and his partner sent to a children's shelter. 'I ran away in the middle of the night with him and we got married and stayed with his relatives in

Assam,' a complainant in one such case said. 'When the police brought us back, I said I am an adult, but they gave me two options—go back to your parents or go to Dongri [state-run children's home]. I went to Dongri but it was such a terrible experience till he was acquitted that if I wasn't strong and already pregnant with our baby, I would have given up.'

Across the system, I found some amount of concern and sympathy for these consenting couples, especially among judges. Some of the judges in Delhi sentenced the men in such cases to the period already served by them in jail, or to a token one week. Such discretion, however, was taken away by another amendment passed in 2013; as a response to public sentiment in the wake of the December 2012 rape that laws were too lax, the courts' discretionary power to reduce sentences by taking into consideration the age difference between the young partners ('age proximity') if the sexual act was consensual was taken away. The move placed young men in romantic relationships with young women in the same category as paedophiles.

In recent years, India has seen growing concern over juvenility and crime—both crimes against children and those allegedly perpetrated by them—especially sexual crime. The number of reported sexual assaults on children rose over the last five years, even while the rates of most other violent crimes fell. But a closer look at the Delhi cases shows that consensual relationships between young people are often reframed as 'rape of a minor' at the FIR stage. The demand for harsher sentences for juvenile offenders too has its roots in a complex interplay of forces. The news that a juvenile was involved in the December 2012 sexual assault, as well as the illegally leaked information that he was Muslim, led to demands that the boy be tried in a regular criminal court and be punished as an adult. Since the law at the time did not allow for this, the government amended India's progressive Juvenile Justice Act to allow children over the age of sixteen who were charged with committing 'heinous' crimes to be tried as adults in a regular criminal court, despite the official age of adulthood in India remaining eighteen. If a seventeen-year-old boy indulges in a consensual sexual act with a fifteen-and-a-half-year-old girl, he can now be tried as an adult for rape and kidnapping in a court which will have no option but to sentence him to a minimum of ten years in prison.

Whose Fault Is a Low Conviction Rate?

Of the 460 rape cases fully argued before the Delhi courts, another 109 dealt with 'breach of promise to marry', cases in which the woman complains that her consent for sex was obtained under a false promise of marriage, following which the man refused to marry her. Even though the law allows them to, courts are increasingly disinclined to convict in such cases, especially if the complainant is educated; only twelve of the 109 cases resulted in convictions, and in most of these, the man was either already married or had conducted a fraudulent marriage with the complainant.

For 'promise of marriage', a different script is deployed: the accused is first described as having committed sexual assault on the complainant anywhere between two and thirteen years before the FIR was filed; subsequently, the FIR says, the complainant asked the accused to marry her, and he continued having sexual relations with her for several years under this promise but ultimately called it off with one last non-consensual encounter. 'We tell the girl that you will have to say that at least the first time and most recent time was without your consent for it to go to court,' one police official said frankly.

The argument used by prosecutors in these cases is that if a woman has sexual relations with a man only under a false promise of marriage, her consent is not free as it was obtained through deceit. However, in most such cases, proving that the accused never intended to marry the complainant becomes hard to do, unless he is already married to someone else and hiding it.

'You might say it is wrong, but when the girl's father comes to the police station and says she has been ruined, a policeman will tend to take the father's side,' one senior Delhi police officer explained. More often than not, he said, the FIR was a way of forcing a man attempting to call off a marriage into going through with it; in a third of such cases, the woman deposed in court that she was now married and hence no longer accused him of rape.

When they analysed 644 cases of sexual assault in Mumbai since 2008 that they had studied or intervened in, the women's rights legal advocacy group Majlis found that 20 per cent involved breach of promise to marry. In a quarter of such cases, the complainant was pregnant, highlighting the vulnerability of her situation.

'Your family discovers you have been having relations with a man for five years and now he has called it off because of pressure from his family,' one complainant who lost her case explained. 'Before you know what is happening, your father and uncle have gone to the police station and you are forced into this. Everyone tells you that if you do not go along with it, you will never get married,' she said.

Judges, prosecutors and police officers tended to be far less sympathetic in discussing these cases. None of it stood up in court either; the only twelve promise of marriage cases that saw convictions in the Delhi trials were ones in which there was clear deceit, such as the accused being already married.

The 162 remaining cases of the nearly 600 heard in Delhi in 2013 dealt with rape as it is most commonly understood. Nearly half of these involved an adult neighbour preying on a minor child of a neighbour or a vulnerable woman sleeping outdoors or alone at home, most took place in slums, and had a conviction rate of over 75 per cent. 'Mothers like me have to work all day and are not able to keep an eye on our children,' one mother who secured a conviction in the rape of her three-year-old by a neighbour said, in tears. The medical investigation and courtroom terrified her, the woman said, but her family supported her.

Just twelve cases involved strangers and all resulted in convictions. These tended to be opportunistic crimes in which a man or group of men preyed on a vulnerable woman—one who had run away from home, or was homeless, or was a child. The December 2012 case, which was part of this dataset, stood out precisely for how unusual it was.

In such cases, the consistent testimony of the complainant played the most important role. Judges were usually willing to convict in the absence of medical evidence, and in one case, a judge convicted a man of raping a mentally challenged minor girl even though she was unable to depose in court apart from nodding.

Even while activists often use the low conviction rate in rape cases (27 per cent for India in 2018) to make the point that the police and judicial system are stacked against victims of rape, the judges I interviewed were equally insistent that the conviction rate be highlighted because it shows how poor the quality of evidence coming before them is. In fact, in interviews with them, it was immediately evident just how heavily the acquittal rate statistic—and its coverage in the media—weighed on their minds. Some opened up case files to show me the failures of the prosecution to produce usable evidence or present a coherent chronology. 'The acquittal rate clearly shows that most of the cases coming before us are not rape cases as you might imagine them like the [December 2012] Nirbhaya case,' one judge told me, 'but the public thinks we are taking the side of the accused.'

As a result of the sheer number of such cases, in off-the-record conversations with me at least, both cops and judges said they tend to be sceptical of cases in which the complainant and the accused were romantically involved. When asked about cases in which a couple is romantically involved but the boy might sexually assault his partner, one judge shrugged it off: 'If he beats her or attacks her there may be a case, but this never happens.' Intensely conscious of media scrutiny of their rulings, judges, however, were quick to add that their reading of 'reality' never biased them against outcomes. Yet, it is clear that this nexus of problematic FIRs and stenography by the media is wreaking damage on not just the public's understanding of crime and safety, but also on judicial willingness to believe complainants.

It isn't just that India's crime statistics end up showing a misleading picture, or even that the young couples at the heart of these tragedies are put through untold misery. It's also a major problem for the future of how criminal trials are decided in India.

Meow Meow and the Mumbai Police

The competing forces of patriarchy and rebellion make sexual crime statistics in India particularly problematic. But a closer look at most types of crime—even if this scrutiny emerges by chance—reveals that similar forces are at play behind the scenes of most FIRs.

Sometime in 2013, the Mumbai police decided it had to do something about Meow Meow. Mephedrone, known on the street as Meow Meow, was cheap and widely available, and the police were having a hard time keeping up. Possession of the drug had not been made illegal under the stringent Narcotic Drugs and Psychotropic Substances (NDPS) Act, despite the Mumbai police making multiple representations to various Central agencies for the substance to be banned.

So, in 2013 then city police commissioner Rakesh Maria directed his force to start arresting pedlars of mephedrone under the next-best option: Section 328 of the IPC, 'causing hurt using a poisonous substance'. Quite apart from the Mumbai police's inability to correctly collect, label and present evidence—as borne out by the observations of district court judges in every single case—the basic problem was clearly the application of the wrong law. 'You need to show intention to cause hurt. How hard is that to understand and how many times did I need to tell the police that? No effect,' one judge who had seen dozens of such cases said.

The Mumbai police knew this. 'See, the hands of the police were tied. So they had to use whatever tool was available,' Shivdeep Lande, deputy inspector general of police from the anti-narcotics cell of the Mumbai police, who arrived in Mumbai with the nickname 'Bihar's Chulbul Pandey' for his upright conduct and penchant for tight-fitted short-sleeved shirts in his previous posting, told me in an interview. An assistant commissioner of police was more explicit: 'We wanted to throw them in and create some fear. It didn't really matter that they were getting acquitted; anyway courts always find fault with our evidence.'

For a conviction under IPC 328, a court needs to see proof of intention to cause hurt, and the law is typically invoked in cases of food poisoning or the knowing adulteration of food. Because of the consensual nature of most drug transactions, the intention to cause hurt is by definition absent. 'Section 328 was bound to fail because the section requires the prosecution to prove that a drug was administered to a person with the intent to cause hurt to the person,' Neha Singhal, senior resident fellow at the Vidhi Centre for Legal Policy, told me.

And fail it did—most comprehensively. Between June 2015 and November 2016, Mumbai's sessions courts pronounced judgments in at least hundred such cases. Not a single one ended in a conviction.[11] All the charge sheets from that time followed essentially the same script. The complainant's brother, son or friend had become increasingly ill. On enquiry, the complainant found that the victim had been forced to consume a drug by the accused. The police swooped in to arrest the accused, who was found with a white powder on him. This powder was later 'discovered' to be mephedrone.

Except, none of this ever stood up in court. In no more than three cases were the police even able to prove possession of the drug. Time and time again, the basic evidence to show that the drug was found on the accused was not produced, and in dozens of cases, the judge accepted that the panchas (eyewitness to the recovery) were 'habitual panchas' set up by the police. And then there was the matter of proving intention to cause hurt, which the police made virtually no attempt to do, in the cases I investigated. The result: an acquittal rate of 100 per cent.

In all, nearly 150 young people spent more than a year in jail on charges that the police knew early on were bad in law, but persisted with nonetheless. Yet, no one—not senior police officials, prosecutors or annoyed judges—stopped what was going on. Ultimately, the inclusion of mephedrone in the NDPS in February 2015 brought this to an end.

Of the seven acquitted men who spoke to me, two admitted to petty peddling and drug use, but disputed all the stated facts of the police case. The five others said they had nothing to do with drugs. Bhajan Lal (name changed) was a vegetable vendor near Dadar, the busy heart of central Mumbai. 'I had a dispute with a local cop, that is all. I make enough selling vegetables and I have no time for drugs. They picked me up, showed my arrest in some other part of the city and kept me in for a year,' he said. IPC 328 is a non-bailable offence; the accused in the cases I saw spent between one year and twenty months in custody. An analysis of their names shows that 119 of the 148 acquitted were Muslim.

For anyone looking at crime statistics of the time, as I was for what began as unrelated research on sexual assault FIRs in Mumbai, it would have seemed as if the city was awash with incidents of poisoning, mostly committed by Muslims, and the courts were failing victims. What would have remained hidden between the lines is that forming any assessment of India from police reports or from media reports of them is an exercise in futility—or worse, in deception.

When More Crime Is a Good Thing

Not every journalist in the country can investigate every crime statistic for six months before she publishes it, and a reading public cannot be expected to be doing their research before forming views on the statistics they're reading. But understanding the universe that produces these statistics is essential, and the only way to derive greater use out of them.

Indian crime statistics begin from a point of significant under-reporting, and not just for sexual crime. The country's officially recorded crime rates are lower than the global average, substantially lower than developed countries, and even low by middle-income country standards.[12] In 2019, the highest crime rates in India were in the two most developed states—Delhi and Kerala. The rates of recorded crime in most other Indian cities and states, quite frankly, defy belief. Uttar Pradesh with over 200 million people recorded just over 10,000 cases of 'grievous hurt' in 2014, while London with under 9 million people recorded over 70,000 cases of 'assault with injury offences', according to its police statistics for 2014-15.

Countries like the United Kingdom use a parallel official system of crime reporting—crime victimisation surveys based on household-level surveys, not requiring the crime to be registered with the police. While India does not yet have such a national survey, other data provides some clues. A large survey on crime in Rajasthan found that most crime victims never report their experienced crime to the police. Only 29 per cent of crime victims surveyed stated that they had visited a police station to report the crime. The biggest deterrent to reporting a crime was the victim's perception that the crime wasn't important enough (28 per cent). The next most significant deterrent was the belief that the police could not help (20 per cent) or did not want to help (17 per cent). Among those who attempted to report crimes, 17 per cent were not able to register them. In an experiment conducted by the surveyors, where they sent decoys to report crimes, the police were willing to register FIRs only 54 per cent of the time.[13] In a 2015 survey in Mumbai and Delhi, 13 per cent of households surveyed in Delhi and 15 per cent in Mumbai experienced at least one of the seven crimes under study, with theft being the most common. But only half of these were reported to the police, and only half of those registered as FIRs.[14]

Some crimes suffer greater under-reporting than others. In the Rajasthan survey, self-reported crime rates were substantially higher than police-recorded rates for property crimes in particular: survey theft rates were over 800 per cent higher than registered rates, and robbery rates were over 1,100 per cent times higher than in police records. The differential decreased for violent crimes: rape or molestation surveyed rates were 43 per cent higher than the rates reported to the police, and assault was only 11 per cent higher in the survey. Motorcycle thefts, where a police complaint becomes essential for insurance claims, were most likely to be recorded by the police.[15] (Fig. 1.2)

It isn't just some crimes that are more likely to be reported than others; some places are also more likely to report crimes than others, with reasons that have relatively little to do with the crime itself. Inter-state comparisons are particularly important in the way the media reports crime. Globally, countries with wide income disparities are four times more likely to be afflicted by violent crime than more equitable societies, and high levels of crime are both a major cause and a result of poverty and underdevelopment, says the United

Figure 1.2: Property crimes are least likely to make it to police records

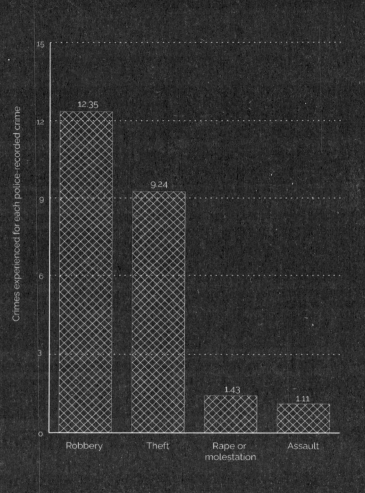

Crimes experienced for each police-recorded crime

Robbery	12.35
Theft	9.24
Rape or molestation	1.43
Assault	1.11

Source: Abhijit Banerjee, Raghabendra Chattopadhyay, Esther Duflo, Daniel Keniston, Nina Singh, 'Improving Police Performance in Rajasthan, India: Experimental Evidence on Incentives, Managerial Autonomy, and Training,' *American Economic Journal: Economic Policy*, vol. 13, no 1 (2021)

Nations Office on Drugs and Crime. However, this observed association between income disparity and crime applies only to states in which full registration is the norm, and that is almost certainly not the case for most Indian states. Yet, the vast majority of academic work on crime in India attempts to correlate socio-economic variables like levels of urbanisation, poverty and inequality with the rate of reported crime, unmindful of the factors that affect the reporting of crime.

This is likely less of a problem for crimes like burglary or theft, where the incentives to report the crime are high, and the incentives to not record them low. A comparison of crimes reported in a household survey and recorded by the police for the same states shows that while there is significant under-reporting, states with higher rates of reported burglary, theft and hurt also have high recorded rates of these crimes.[16] But for other types of crimes, there are indications both from interviews with police officials and from some data, that the states with higher reported crime might actually be the ones doing a better job of ensuring full reporting, rather than being the ones that are the most unsafe, particularly for some types of crimes. People often use Kerala's high rates of reported crime, particularly against women, to criticise the state, former state police chief Jacob Punnoose pointed out recently. 'But what this shows is that with more female police recruitment, more women felt confident to approach the police. We should celebrate this,' he said. Not all crime is under-reported equally, Punnoose cautioned. 'I would not say that I will celebrate an increase in the numbers of all crimes—auto theft or murder, for example. But if the state police is able to significantly increase the registration of crimes in which grievous physical injury does not take place, I will congratulate that police commissioner.'[17]

Comparing the rates of sexual crime reported in household surveys with police records for the same year shows that Delhi had consistently higher reporting and lower incidence of actual violence than other states, while Bihar had low rates of reporting and high actual incidence. Among larger states, both actual violence and the extent of under-reporting were higher in northern states with poor gender indicators than in southern states with better gender indicators.[18] (Fig. 1.3) Not that you would know this from the media reporting. 'Uttar Pradesh safer for women than many big states: NCRB report,' read the headline in the *Times of India*, India's most widely read English newspaper, the day the 2019 NCRB statistics were released.[19]

Moreover, when it comes to sexual crime, the largest part of the violence India is missing is the violence it is yet to criminalise. A comparison of police statistics for 2019-20 with relevant data from a large national health survey conducted the same year suggested that over 95 per cent of the sexual violence women experienced was within marriage, unsurprising for a country where the median age at marriage for women is just over eighteen.[20] Yet, in the slew of legal reforms India undertook in the years after the December 2012 sexual assault, it failed to criminalise marital rape: India's rape laws contain a 'marriage exception'.

The police establishment knows this, and also knows of the perverse incentives it creates for the police of a state to suppress numbers. 'The unreliability of crime statistics in India is well known . . . Whenever a genuine effort was made to register all crime . . . the figures showed such fantastic jumps as were impossible with any normal increase in one year,' the National Police Commission said, as far back as 1979.[21]

Figure 1.3: States that report the most crimes against women aren't the ones we should be most worried about

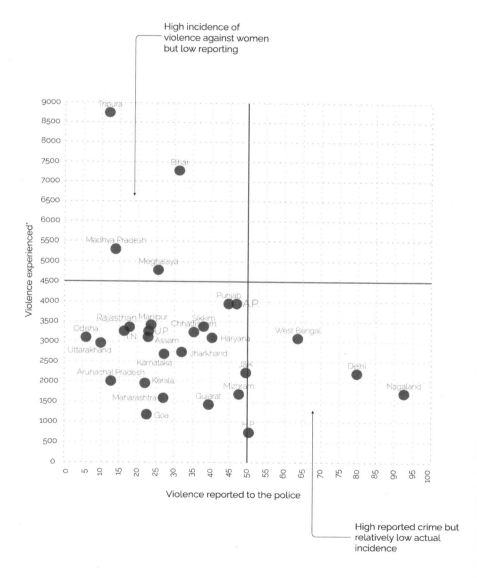

Note: All numbers for 2005
'As told to NFHS household surveyors
Source: Aashish Gupta, 'Reporting and incidence of violence against women in India', Rice Institute Working Paper, 2014 (based on NFHS and NCRB)

Some conscious strategies can improve the rates of reporting. When female political representation rises, crimes against women rise in officially recorded statistics, through better reporting.[22] The opening of all-women police stations increased reported crime against women by 22 per cent.[23]

Police Statistics as a Piece of the Puzzle

India needs more and better qualitative research into crime than currently exists; unusually high numbers, sudden declines, high conviction or acquittal rates, all need more nuanced investigation before being declared in the media as crime waves or the failure of the police or judiciary. Along with these improvements in the analysis of police statistics, India's legal data system needs an even greater overhaul—cases are designated by their own unique classifications and abbreviations in every high court jurisdiction in a state, making comparisons virtually impossible, although a number of public-spirited tech-driven attempts at reform are now underway.

Registration of crime is the culmination of multiple realities: the existence of a grievance, the empowerment of an individual to report it, the decisions behind the police choosing to register it and mechanisms for accountability. With the last three components so sorely lacking in most of India, it might at the very least be time to stop treating crime statistics as spectator sport.

There is much of value that we can derive from India's official crime statistics, even if they are not telling us the stories they are supposed to. These could be the stories of states that do better at empowering even the powerless to feel that their lives matter and injustices against them are worthy of the state's time. They could be stories of incremental change, of police officers whose hard work may show up in terms of more rather than less reported crime. Statistics could tell us about the battles women are waging for their autonomy and agency, even if they come disguised as crime statistics. On their own, India's crime statistics might be problematic, but combined with a deeper understanding of the country itself, they offer an insight into the churning within. They need triangulation with other data, including indicators of levels of development, female empowerment and state capacity, as well as independent household surveys. For citizens to get a true picture of crime and safety in their district or city, we will have to take that next step—providing them a framework with which to understand crime statistics. Perhaps then they can use this data to create real democratic pressure for the right to live their lives without fear.

II

WHAT INDIA THINKS, FEELS AND BELIEVES

At its core, India is conservative—even fundamentalist. If there is going to be change, it will take work.

Democracy and Authoritarianism

Who are Indians really? What makes us tick? What do we truly believe in? Among the most popular narratives about India is this one: despite poverty and apparent conservatism, Indians are at their core liberal and secular in their values, and it is political parties who appeal to their base instincts and trap them into narrow identities.

Yet, for decades now, data has been telling us a markedly different story about the deepest—and darkest—thoughts of Indians.

The vast majority of opinion polling in India is centred around elections. The best estimates of Indian attitudes and beliefs too usually emerge from surveys done before and after elections. The National Election Studies conducted by the respected Lokniti programme at the Delhi-based Centre for the Study of Developing Societies has provided the most detailed time-series data on Indian attitudes and thought for over fifty years now. More recently, a few other surveys have emerged from transparent and well-regarded polling agencies: the India Human Development Survey (IHDS) (conducted in 2004-05 and 2011-12, and ongoing in 2021), the Lok Survey conducted between 2013 and 2016 by the Lok Foundation, University of Oxford and the Centre for the Monitoring of the Indian Economy (CMIE), and opinion polls conducted by international agencies including the US-based Pew Research Center and the World Values Surveys.

What this limited data shows is that for some time now, Indians have held fairly conservative views about how the country should be governed in broad terms. The World Values Survey, a conglomerate of various country-level polling agencies, has surveyed sample populations around the world on their views on various social values for nearly forty years. In the latest round (2010–2014), the Indian sample demonstrated a lower commitment to democratic principles than most other major countries. India, along with Pakistan and Russia, featured below the global average on the importance accorded to democracy. Indian respondents had an even lower regard than Pakistani respondents for civil rights that protect people's liberty against oppression as being an essential part of a democracy. Indian respondents expressed greater support for a 'strong leader' and for army rule than most other countries and the global average. The share of Indians who thought that a strong leader was 'very good' for the country was higher than in any other country—even Russia.[1] (Fig. 2.1)

Figure 2.1: How Indian views of democracy have changed over time

India placed lower emphasis on democracy than most other countries

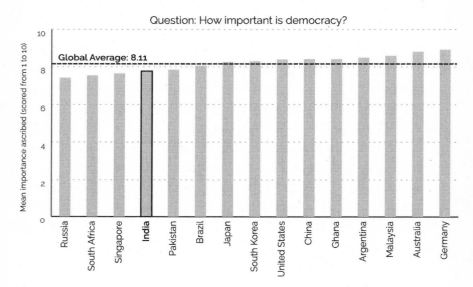

India placed even lower than Pakistan on the belief that civil rights were an essential feature of a democracy

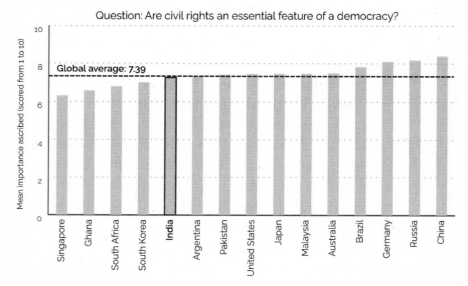

Source: R. Inglehart et al. (eds), World Values Survey: Round Six - Country-Pooled Datafile. Madrid, Spain & Vienna, Austria: JD Systems Institute & WVSA Secretariat, 2018.

What's worse, India may be getting even less democratic

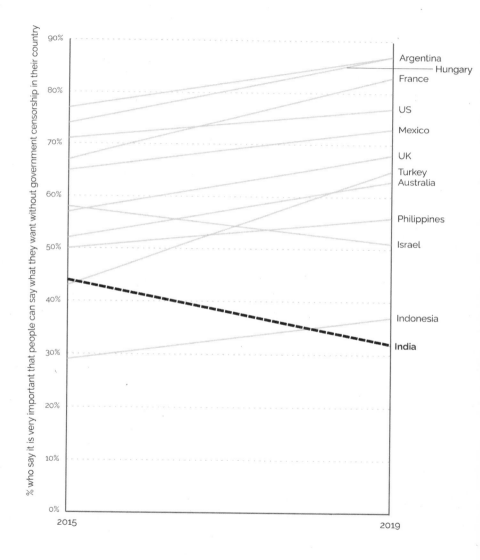

% who say it is very important that people can say what they want without government censorship in their country

- Argentina
- Hungary
- France
- US
- Mexico
- UK
- Turkey
- Australia
- Philippines
- Israel
- Indonesia
- **India**

2015 — 2019

Source: 'Democratic Rights Popular Globally but
Commitment to Them Not Always Strong', Pew
Research Center, February 2020

'Elections are just a waste of time. We should have a strong leader, a saintly and noble man who we can trust, and then he and the army can run the country in the right direction,' Mahesh Shrihari, a thirty-three-year-old accountant based in Bengaluru in southern India, told me. Shrihari's grandfather was a Gandhian who had spent time in jail during the struggle for Independence. His father, Ramalingam, had been a lifelong Congress supporter, until he discovered the anti-corruption crusader Anna Hazare who captured middle-class India's imagination in 2013. Ramalingam then lost all interest in electoral politics. Shrihari, however, is a dedicated supporter of Prime Minister Narendra Modi and has only ever voted for him—'I'll discuss anything with you,' he told me, 'religion, spirituality, science, feminism. I am up for a good debate. But I will not hear a word against Modi from anyone. That is the end of the conversation for me because I know the person is not worth wasting time on.'

India ranks poorly on relative commitment to democratic principles on other international opinion polls. In a 2015 Pew Research Center global survey, the importance that the sample of Indians gave to freedom of expression was lower than all the surveyed countries but Indonesia; by 2019, the share of Indians who said that it was very important that people could say what they want without government censorship was the lowest in the world, lower even than Indonesia, and lower than in 2015. India joined Tunisia and Lebanon at the bottom of the list of countries that believed that it was important for the media to be able to report and people to be able to talk on the internet without censorship.[2]

In 2019, India was below the median of countries that believed it was very important for human rights organisations to operate freely in their country without State interference, as compared to European nations, which valued this highly.[3]

'NGOs [non government organisations, or charities] are out to defame the country. They take money from foreign countries and from the Church and they instigate poor tribal people against the government,' Manu Koda, a twenty-four-year-old from Raipur in eastern India's Chhattisgarh, told me. Koda, who now lives in Kolkata, studied in a missionary-run school that functions as a charity in Raipur, and when the country went under the COVID-19 pandemic lockdown in March 2020, a local NGO arranged for dry rations for his mother and grandparents back home, he told me. But those were the only good ones, he insisted. His friends in college who were affiliated with the militant Hindu right-wing Vishwa Hindu Parishad, and a well-known Hindi nightly news anchor, had convinced him of the evil of NGOs. He was now part of a Facebook group that called itself Fans of [News Anchor]. Koda regularly saw pictures of NGO signboards posted there, with lurid tales of kidnapping and sex abuse in the captions. He did not need more evidence.

The country was also below the median in its commitment to the free operation of Opposition parties. India was at the bottom of thirty-four countries surveyed in the share of respondents who believed that a fair judiciary that treated everyone equally was important. Only four countries had a lower share of respondents who said that it was very important that honest elections were held regularly with a choice of at least two political parties.[4]

Yet, Indians remain believers in their government. In a 2019 Pew survey, a median of 64 per cent across the nations surveyed believed that political elites were out of touch, disagreeing with the statement, 'Most elected officials care what people like me think'. This opinion was particularly widespread in Europe where a median of 69 per cent expressed this view. Seventy-one per cent shared this opinion in the US. In contrast, just 31 per cent in India felt this way. Indians were also particularly likely to agree the State is run for the benefit of everyone. Most Indian respondents believed that voting gave people like them some say about how the government runs things. Indians in 2019 were among the most satisfied in the world with how democracy in their country was working.[5]

But alongside this belief in the State comes a muscular majoritarian notion of what the State should regulate.

A study of four Indian states—Gujarat, Haryana, Karnataka and Odisha—found that two-thirds of respondents felt that the State should punish those who do not say 'Bharat Mata ki Jai', a nationalistic slogan that Muslims say militates against their religious beliefs, in public functions, and those who do not stand for the national anthem. As levels of education rose among respondents to the survey, so did support for restrictions on free speech; close to half the respondents with a college education or more supported restrictions on freedom of expression.[6]

Three-fourths of respondents expressed what the survey described as a majoritarian form of nationalism. Only about 6 per cent subscribed to a strongly liberal nationalism and a further 17 per cent took a weak liberal nationalist position. The highest proportion of respondents with this majoritarian nationalist position were those with a graduate or postgraduate education. These positions included the belief that the State should punish those who do not 'respect' the cow, considered sacred by some Hindus, or eat beef. About two-thirds of respondents supported the view that the State should punish those who engage in religious conversion.[7]

Hindus in particular tended to see their religious identity and Indian national identity as closely intertwined: nearly two-thirds of Hindus (64 per cent) said it is very important to be Hindu to be 'truly' Indian.[8]

Religious Lines in the Sand

Indians may not always accept that they hold conservative positions on religion. One beloved narrative about India is that while political parties might trade in the business of communal polarisation for votes, the average Indian is actually a liberal person who looks forward to his colleague's invitation for a home-cooked Eid feast and brings celebratory sweets to the office for Diwali, as the stereotype from innumerable Indian advertisements indicates. The truth is more complicated. Not every Indian might want their religion imposed on the whole country, but that doesn't mean they want to be friends with people from other religions, let alone accept them as part of their community or family.

In a thirty-four-country Pew survey, India was above the median in its support for people to have the right to practise their religion freely.[9] On the whole, Indians would appear to see religious tolerance as a central part of who they are as a nation. Across all major religious groups, most people said it was very important to respect all religions to be 'truly Indian' and that respecting other religions was a very important part of what it meant to be a member of their own religious community.[10] Newspaper headlines quickly seized on this finding to reiterate the beloved position that Indians were on the whole tolerant of all religions.

But more specific questions that do not allow for broad hand-waving about tolerant beliefs uncover deep religious illiberalism and, indeed, outright hostility.

A majority of Hindus in India see themselves as very different from their Muslim compatriots (66 per cent), and most Muslims feel the same way, saying they are very different from Hindus (64 per cent).[11] Over a third of Hindu respondents in a 2019 national survey considered Muslims to be unpatriotic (although the Muslim respondents did not feel that way about themselves).[12] In a four-state survey, 40 per cent of Hindus and 43 per cent of Sikhs considered Muslims to be mostly violent, while Muslims did not consider people from any religion to be mostly violent.

Indians generally stick to their own religious group when it comes to their friends. Hindus overwhelmingly said that most or all their close friends were also Hindu. Even among Sikhs and Jains, who each form small minorities, a large majority said their friends come mainly or entirely from their small religious community.[13]

The housing segregation that Muslims in particular experience is borne out by the data. Jains and Hindus were the most likely to not be willing to accept a neighbour from another community—particularly Muslims. Thirty-six per cent of Hindus were not willing to accept a Muslim neighbour, while the distaste for Hindu neighbours was much lower at 16 per cent among Muslims.[14] In a 2015 experiment, decoy prospective tenants with upper-caste Hindu, Dalit and Muslim surnames answered rental listings in and around Delhi. Despite being identical in every other way, all upper-caste decoys were met with a positive response—the landlord expressed a willingness to give the accommodation on rent.

On the other hand, 59 per cent of prospective Dalit tenants received a positive response, 23 per cent received a positive response but with differential terms and conditions (including higher asking prices), while 18 per cent were rejected. In the case of Muslim decoys, only one of every three received a positive response, another 36 per cent got a positive response with conditions and a full 30 per cent were rejected outright.[15]

Sana Iqbal grew up in Delhi's Jamia Nagar, an area she describes as a Muslim ghetto. Having studied in the United Kingdom and worked in Mumbai, where she met her husband, Iqbal was certain that she wanted to live in a more mixed area when the couple moved to Delhi in 2018. 'We weren't bothered about neighbours. We just wanted to live in an area where you can buy Southeast Asian ingredients and get a drink—the usual yuppie stuff,' the documentary film-maker said self-deprecatingly. After seven weeks of unsuccessful house-hunting and over fifteen discussions that fell apart after their names were revealed, their broker suggested that they change their names, and the couple gave up and returned to the familiar embrace of Jamia Nagar. 'To my mind, this is ghettoisation—being forced to live with your own community because no one else will have you,' she said.

When people from other religions are largely unacceptable as neighbours, crossing the boundary into accepting them as family is an intolerable thought for most. In a large national survey, 85 per cent of people said that marriage between two people of different religions was not acceptable. Young people in their late teens and early twenties were even more likely than older people to say that inter-religious marriage was unacceptable, and neither income nor education made people more likely to accept inter-religious marriage.[16] A majority among both Muslims and Hindus supported action against religious conversion.

Preventing inter-religious marriages animates far more Indians than is commonly believed. Across a range of religious groups, large majorities said that it is very important to stop people in their community from marrying into other religious groups. Roughly two-thirds of Hindus in India wanted to prevent inter-religious marriages of Hindu women (67 per cent) or Hindu men (65 per cent). Even larger shares of Muslims felt similarly: 80 per cent said it is very important to stop Muslim women from marrying outside their religion, and 76 per cent said it is very important to stop Muslim men from doing so.[17]

Younger people do not have much more progressive beliefs; a 2017 survey on the attitudes of young people found that six out of ten respondents supported banning movies which hurt religious sentiments, even more so among Muslim youth, 70 per cent of Hindu youth were opposed to allowing anyone to eat beef, and one-third of young people opposed inter-caste marriage.[18] (Fig. 2.2)

Muslims in India do not demonstrate more tolerance to people from other religious groups than Hindus; the difference lies in the patronage and State backing that muscular Hindu majoritarianism now receives.

Muslim youth were much more likely than others to report having experienced religion-based discrimination. About one in every seven or 13 per cent of them said they had been discriminated against based on their Muslim identity. Muslim youth living in smaller cities were most likely to have been victims of religious bias—27 per cent reported having faced discriminatory treatment for being Muslim. This is double of what all Muslim youth reported.[19]

Figure 2.2: Younger people do not necessarily hold more liberal views

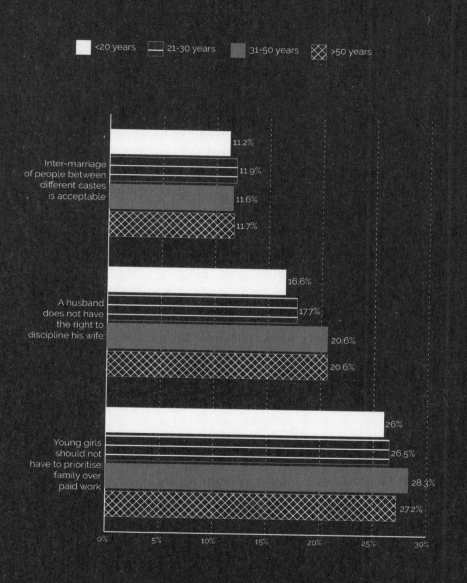

Legend: ■ <20 years ▭ 21-30 years ▨ 31-50 years ▨ >50 years

Inter-marriage of people between different castes is acceptable
- 11.2%
- 11.9%
- 11.6%
- 11.7%

A husband does not have the right to discipline his wife
- 16.6%
- 17.7%
- 20.6%
- 20.6%

Young girls should not have to prioritise family over paid work
- 26%
- 26.5%
- 28.3%
- 27.2%

Axis: 0% 5% 10% 15% 20% 25% 30%

Source: Lok Foundation-Oxford University survey by the Centre for the Monitoring of the Indian Economy, 2015, 2017

Shoaib Akhtar (twenty-five) grew up in an affluent family in Aligarh in Uttar Pradesh, the son of a university professor and captain of his school's cricket team. 'Up until college, I can honestly say that I personally experienced very little discrimination. It was more something I read of in the papers than experienced,' he said. All that changed when Shoaib completed a business degree and was sent to Bharuch, a town of 150,000 people in the western state of Gujarat, an outpost of the petrochemicals company he had landed his first job with. 'I think the idea of a young Muslim man who was better educated than them, wore more expensive clothes and had the latest phone rankled them even more,' he said of his now former colleagues. In the beginning there was a slight distance, reminders that the office was vegetarian, and some pointed talk in Gujarati about Modi when Shoaib was around. Things escalated quickly to him being reprimanded for speaking to a female colleague ('About accounts! She was the accountant!') and being told that he couldn't wear a skullcap during the holy month of Ramzan. One morning, Shoaib opened his office email to find a graphic death threat from an unknown email address. Two weeks later, he was out. 'It wasn't the end—it was just the beginning of my realisation of what being Muslim in India is like now,' he said from Toronto, Canada, where he migrated in 2019. 'I still can't post a tweet about an Indian batsman playing a loose shot without someone calling me a [cuss word for Muslims]. At least they aren't my colleagues and neighbours now.'

There is some evidence that India has become more muscularly majoritarian. A survey of young Indians found that more than half of those surveyed (53 per cent) felt that people had become less tolerant of the views of others and one-fourth of the youth (23 per cent) said that they had hesitated to express their opinion on a political issue. Youth from religious minorities like Muslims and Sikhs, who were more likely to bear the brunt of this intolerance, were likelier to agree that people had become less tolerant.[20]

Caste Matters

Despite what many Indians, particularly the English-speaking urban elite, would like to tell themselves, caste remains central to modern Indian association and conflict. A majority of people across caste groups—but most of all among 'upper' castes—say that their caste plays an important role in how they see themselves.[21]

In the four-state survey mentioned earlier, people from India's historically privileged upper castes were most likely to say that the relative lack of educational and income attainments of those from SC or Dalit and ST or Adivasi groups was a 'lack of effort', while backward groups—OBCs, who find themselves placed in between the 'upper' and 'lower' castes on the traditional hierarchy, Dalits and Adivasis—saw it as a result of unfair treatment. At the same time, a majority of those from the upper and dominant castes believed that they themselves needed state assistance.[22]

Youth among all castes and communities broadly supported the existing affirmative action 'quotas' for SCs, STs and OBCs—barring Hindu upper castes. However, the economic background of a young person belonging to a beneficiary group seemed to matter in how they viewed the issue of reservations for their community. Youth belonging to economically well-off sections within SCs, STs and OBCs were found to be slightly more opposed to reservations for their community than those who were less well-off within these communities.[23]

One survey tried to measure social bias by asking people from different communities who they would not like to have as a neighbour. Overall, 27 per cent of the sample population directly admitted that they were against having a neighbour from a different religious or caste community. Upper-caste respondents were more likely to say they did not want to live near OBCs than any other group. Among those who perceived themselves as middle class, 39 per cent indicated social bias against a religious or caste community, over twice the share of those who self-identified as non-middle class. 'A modernising India may trigger the erosion of certain traditional hierarchies while, at the same time, opening the way for new cleavages based around social and economic contestation,' the authors noted.[24]

In a broad national survey, 34 per cent of rural respondents reported having been discriminated against based on their caste during the preceding year alone, as against 29 per cent of urban residents. The experience of discrimination was more common among Dalits. In Odisha, Jharkhand, Uttarakhand and Tamil Nadu, Dalits reported having experienced discrimination the most often.[25] Among younger people, 9 per cent of Indian youth reported having experienced caste-based discrimination in the five years preceding the survey. The experience of caste-based discrimination was most common among young Dalits at 15 per cent, followed by young Adivasis (11 per cent) and young Muslims (10 per cent).[26]

Even now, outright untouchability is rife. In a large national survey in 2011-12, 30 per cent of rural households reported practising untouchability, while in urban areas, the corresponding figure was lower at 20 per cent. The practice of untouchability was most common among Brahmins (the priestly caste group that historically formed the apex of the hierarchy), with 52 per cent of them accepting that they followed this practice, followed by OBCs. Among religious groups, people belonging to the minority Jain religion practise the most untouchability followed by Hindus and Sikhs. Households that had greater networks outside their own communities were less likely to practise untouchability. Households with better-educated adults were less likely to practise untouchability, but higher income levels were associated with more untouchability. The practice was more prevalent among households in the central, northern and hill regions, and less common in the south, east and west.[27]

Smaller, more focused surveys uncover even higher levels of untouchability: more than half of non-Dalit Hindu respondents in Rajasthan and Uttar Pradesh lived in households where someone practised untouchability, a survey focused on discrimination found. In the big cities studied—Delhi and Mumbai—the reported prevalence of practising untouchability was lower, but still very high at 39 per cent and 21 per cent respectively.[28]

'When people say that untouchability is over, what they mean is that the most crude form of untouchability—like not being allowed to wear a saree blouse, as my grandmother experienced, or having to take off your slippers when crossing in front of a caste Hindu's house, as my father experienced—is less common now,' Santhosh Ramaswamy, a young data analyst from the Madiga caste, an SC group of Andhra Pradesh, who now works in Visakhapatnam, told me. Ramaswamy experiences not just caste discrimination, but untouchability as well, he explained. 'When the Madiga boys were all put together in the same hostel block [in university], the one with the worst leaks and farthest from the academic block, that was untouchability. When my colleagues even now paste a sign on the office microwave that says "no non-veg", that's untouchability too. When my ex-girlfriend's father told her that an inter-caste marriage was okay, but no SCs or Muslims, that was untouchability too,' he said.

Three-quarters of urban respondents said that they would not accept an inter-caste marriage for any of their children. Education and income group made next to no difference to attitudes to inter-caste marriage. Over 80 per cent replied to another variation of the idea—'Is inter-marriage acceptable when the two people are of different castes?'—with a clear 'no'. An overwhelming majority of 83 per cent also said that marriage between people who spoke different languages (who would also tend to be from different castes) was unacceptable.[29]

An identical proportion (59 per cent) of Dalits and upper castes said that stopping inter-caste marriages is very important. A majority of Hindus, Muslims, Sikhs and Jains consider stopping inter-caste marriage of both men and women a high priority. By comparison, fewer Buddhists and Christians say it is very important to stop such marriages, although for a majority in both groups, stopping people from marrying outside their caste is at least 'somewhat' important.[30]

Even among people in their twenties, over 70 per cent said that they would not accept an inter-caste marriage for any of their future children.[31] Over time, views on inter-group marriage might give the appearance of getting more 'liberal', but younger people are not walking the talk. While far more young people professed an acceptance of inter-caste marriage in a youth survey in 2016 (55 per cent) than in a similar one in 2007 (31 per cent), the share of married young respondents who said their spouse was not from their caste was just 4 per cent.[32]

Views on Gender Norms and Sexuality

On questions surrounding the rights of women, too, India would seem to be above the median in its support for equal rights for women when asked a broad question.[33] But when queried about the specifics of interpersonal relationships, particularly within marriages, it becomes clear that Indians largely believe that women should be subservient to their husbands.

These attitudes begin even before the birth of a child and are further forged through adolescence and adulthood. One-third of respondents said that for their families, having more boys than girls was preferred.[34] Few Indian men and women experience mixed gender interactions outside of their families. Just one in five men and an even lower share of women reported having a close friend of the opposite sex.[35]

Unsurprisingly then, a majority of both men and women agreed that a husband has the right to 'discipline' his wife.[36] Even among young people, a majority said that they concurred with the statement that wives should always listen to their husbands. Two-fifths of the youth were also in agreement with the proposition that it is not right for women to do paid work outside the house after marriage. A fairly high proportion of young women respondents held such conservative views; about one in every three young women was of the opinion that women should not work after marriage and over two out of every five favoured the idea of an obedient wife.[37]

In a recent national survey, this divergence between generic statements about women's equality and substantive actions that could achieve parity was elegantly demonstrated. Most respondents said that they supported gender equality—but believed that women should prioritise home over outside work. Support was higher for women's freedom to choose their life partner and marriage, but dropped off when it came to issues of equal education for men and women and equal wage for equal work.[38] Over 60 per cent in a different survey said that it was good for the family if women were able to earn and contribute to the household. Yet, 38 per cent felt that a mother working outside the home had a negative impact on the well-being of children and 43 per cent felt that young women should prioritise marriage and family commitments over paid work.[39]

While women did support greater equality with men, the difference in levels of support for women's rights was not very significant between men and women. Better-educated women and those in urban areas expressed higher support for gender equality norms.[40]

Yet, men were slightly more likely to believe that they suffered discrimination on the basis of gender than women (28 per cent as against 26 per cent).[41]

On his first day of undergraduate studies, Santanu Patnaik rode his new motorbike not to his own college, but to the college that he had missed getting into because of what he believed was a cruel roll of the dice. The college was a moderately well-known one in Bhubaneshwar, the biggest city in the eastern state of Odisha, and popular among students who wanted to pursue banking and accountancy. On the waitlist, Patnaik and a female student whom he did not know had the same marks. Yet, she had made it to the final list and not he, and over the wait for his next choice college to begin classes, he became convinced that she had been selected because of her gender. He had looked her up on Facebook and waited near the college gate to spot her until a security guard sent him on his way. 'I just wanted to ask her—did I commit a crime by being born a boy?' he asked me querulously. By the end of his first year in college, Patnaik was the administrator of a Facebook page called 'Save Mens Injustice' and had sworn never to marry. I asked him about his family, he told me that his younger sister had recently been married off at the age of seventeen. Didn't the fact that she was never given the opportunity to go to college change his mind about the direction of gender bias? I asked. 'She gets to enjoy her husband's money without having to study to earn,' he countered. There was no winning.

On the question of what people should be 'allowed' to do in their personal lives, most Indians, including young people, hold what would be described as conservative views. Two-thirds (67 per cent) of young people did not approve of live-in relationships as of 2017 and over half (53 per cent) were opposed to dating before marriage, with only about one in every seven approving of it. Two in every five (40 per cent) were opposed to the celebration of Valentine's Day[42]— the public celebration of the day has become a flashpoint in some states, with militant Hindu groups calling it an affront to 'traditional' Indian mores.

Until 2018, consensual same-sex relationships in India were criminalised by a colonial law that successive governments chose to keep on the books. It took a long-drawn out legal challenge, including India's Supreme Court reviewing its own previous ruling that supported the law, for same-sex relationships to finally be legalised. Support for same-sex couples among Indians polled prior to the 2018 decriminalisation was low. The share of those who thought that homosexuality was 'always justifiable', to use the awkward phrasing of the original question in the World Values Survey, was just 3.5 per cent, and the majority of Indians were against it. Fewer people thought that cheating on taxes or avoiding a ticket on public transport was 'never justifiable' than those that thought homosexuality was 'never justifiable'.[43]

But, as with the rest of the world, young Indians could be getting more liberal on what people should be able to do in their personal lives.

Between 1990 and 2014, the share of Indian respondents who believed that 'homosexuality is never justifiable' fell from 89 per cent to 24 per cent, from an overwhelming majority to a clear minority.[44] By 2014, 30 per cent of Indian respondents were broadly supportive of homosexuality (the rest ranged from somewhat opposed to completely opposed), which placed India towards the liberal top of the distribution of sixty countries.[45] Another indirect estimate of views on homosexuality came from asking the question: 'Could you mention a group that you would not like as neighbours?' In 1991, 91 per cent mentioned homosexual persons; in 2014, fewer than half (42 per cent) did. Instead, by 2014, unmarried couples and people from a different religion or part of the country were less desirable as neighbours than those who were homosexual.[46] The 2018 decriminalisation may have pushed the needle further: in another global study, the share of Indians who believed that homosexuality should be accepted by society more than doubled between 2014 and 2019.[47]

While only a minority of young people approve of same-sex relationships (roughly the same levels as their approval or disapproval of live-in relationships), this could change. Younger people across the world tend to be more accepting of homosexuality than older people, and acceptance of gay marriage has sharply accelerated in the Western world. In India, too, there is a broad move towards more liberal values. Young people are more accepting of inter-religious marriage, affirmative action and pre-marital dating than they were ten years ago.[48]

'Our parents wasted so much time on casteism and religious intolerance. When I speak to my mother on the phone, she asks me if I fast on Tuesday and if I am sure none of the girls in my hostel are bringing non-veg food in. I tell her I don't have the time to play these games and I hang up the phone,' twenty-two-year-old Naina Gadhvi tells me one evening, in 2021. Her parents are in Bharuch in the western state of Gujarat, but Naina is studying in Mumbai. When the list pasted on her college board showed that she was going to share a room with a Brahmin girl from the northern state of Uttar Pradesh, Gadhvi absorbed her mother's anxieties and fretted about how the new girl would treat an OBC roommate. It never came up.

Gadhvi now has bigger things to think about, like the fact that she has realised that she is gay, and her partner is from a different caste. 'Not all the girls have left their parents' prejudices behind. There is a lot of anti-Muslim talk that still goes on,' she says. With her hostel-mate and partner Priyanka Parmar who is also from Gujarat, Naina has started a 'study circle' in her hostel. 'We call it a study circle so that the warden will not mind. But we discuss issues around caste, sexual orientation and religion,' she says, playing an audio recording for me of a recent meeting of the group where they talked of the role of caste in food.

Change Is Possible, but Not Inevitable

This is not a 'liberal' country, nor do most Indians likely see liberalism as a virtue. Under 17 per cent of respondents in a nationally representative survey described themselves as 'modern'—this included just 16 per cent of the youngest respondents. A majority of all respondents, young or old, rural or urban, uneducated or graduates, described themselves as 'traditional'.[49]

There was once perhaps an assumption that education and urbanisation would automatically drive change towards more liberal values in India. But it no longer seems as if these transformations are inevitable. The education level or wealth of respondents had little impact on the likelihood of experiencing social bias according to a recent survey. Moreover, there was little difference between the experiences of rural and urban respondents; 28 per cent and 27 per cent of rural and urban respondents, respectively, indicated that they had faced social bias. These findings suggest that urbanisation and improved access to education may not automatically reduce social bias.[50]

Greater exposure to more tolerant and egalitarian messages could play a role: in one experiment, a group of business school students in Delhi were shown either a TV program on caste injustices or an unrelated cartoon program. The group that watched the show on caste demonstrated significantly lower implicit bias and expressed higher preference for reservations in the private sector. These effects persisted even three months later.[51] In another experiment cross-caste cricket tournament in rural Uttar Pradesh, mixed caste teams led to improved cross-caste friendships and team selection, meaning that collaboration improved casteist attitudes. However when caste groups were opponents at cricket, they did not develop any such affinity, suggesting that adversarial contact did not improve casteist attitudes.[52]

Such interventions could move the needle slightly. But for lasting change, the hard work of rewiring values will come from politics and the creation of social norms.

Greater opportunity, including that enforced through legislation, improves outcomes for marginalised groups and broader societal attitudes. Affirmative action in education and jobs raises achievement levels and incomes for the groups that are being supported. The election of a Dalit politician changes attitudes in society towards all Dalits. The presence of women in positions of power drives up the reporting of crime.

For broader attitudes to change, more work needs to be done to build wider acceptance for different social norms, and for casteist, patriarchal and Islamophobic behaviour to be seen as socially unacceptable. Far fewer people admit to racist beliefs in the US than those who admit to casteist attitudes in India. Decades of civil rights movements and advocacy have created an atmosphere in the US where racial prejudice has by no means disappeared, but to publicly admit to racist attitudes is no longer acceptable. In India, in contrast, this momentum has not yet built; near-majorities of people in two polled states felt comfortable advocating for laws against inter-caste marriage[53] eighty-five years after B.R. Ambedkar said, 'The real remedy for breaking Caste is inter-marriage. Nothing else will serve as the solvent of Caste.'[54]

On a reporting trip to Madhya Pradesh in central India,

I visited the house of Deviram Oike, an Adivasi farmer who had died waiting to sell his wheat in a seven-day line at the government procurement centre. His son, Kashiram, told me the story over a cup of tea as we sat by his small farm outside his tiny house in the state's Raisen district. When I was leaving, the grieving son refilled my water bottle and handed me a bunch of sweet potatoes he had just pulled out from the farm, dusting off the mud. As soon as we got into the car to head back to the city, the local journalist who I had given a ride to so that he could report the same story for his Hindi newspaper asked our driver to stop at the nearest tea shop—he was desperate for a cup of tea, he said. So he wasn't fasting, as he had told Kashiram? I asked. No, he said—he was Brahmin, and couldn't eat or drink from Kashiram's house.

Before I returned to my hotel, the journalist asked me to stop by his house. His daughter was a few months away from starting college and he wanted her to meet me, a working woman travelling alone, so that she too would be inspired to stand on her own feet. At their house, I declined a cup of tea and told them I'd already had one but told the young girl about her father refusing to have tea at Kashiram's. She rounded on him: 'I hope you said you were fasting! They won't change their ways,' she said to me in exasperation, waving her hand in the rough direction of her parents, 'but I am at least trying to teach them how to talk.'

III

HOW INDIA (REALLY) VOTES

Flawed opinion polling and a selective misreading of poll results have created the myth of the model voter, one unshackled by identity and devoted to development. It's just not true.

By 9 a.m. on 8 November 2015, as viewers began to tune into the results of the election in the eastern state of Bihar, it would have seemed as if not one state, but two or three entirely different universes were being discussed by the talking heads on television. On many of the news channels, the declaration was that a novel coalition built to counter the Bharatiya Janata Party (BJP) had won, and it was a victory of 'oppositional' or 'opportunistic' politics. On one English channel, the news anchor had called it early; the BJP had won because the voter wanted more than bijli, sadak, paani—electricity, roads and water, or the most basic of necessities—and now wanted vikaas too, the intangible promise of development that Prime Minister Narendra Modi had successfully used as an election mantra the previous year, the anchor said. Over the next hour, as results from subsequent rounds of counting came in, it became clear that a newly cobbled together alliance of former rivals had won and the early call was wrong. The same arguments were neatly pointed the other way to explain why the Opposition had won. On one Hindi channel, the day's discussion began pegged to a poll the channel had commissioned, which showed the BJP was headed for a big win. As the results came in, the pollster announced why he had got it wrong: a 'coding error' had interchanged the columns for the winner and the loser, they neatly claimed.

The Bihar 2015 car crash was only one particularly visible and un-self-aware demonstration of the extent to which the analysis of Indian voters and elections is based on either incorrect data or a selective misreading of limited data, a veneer of empiricism that allows analysts to dust off their preferred tropes about Indian voters. The data that we do have on Indian elections is wide-ranging and acquired with difficulty, but potentially nuanced. It could help explain how one of the world's most complex democracies functions and clarify the relationship of the citizen with her state. It could help politicians better understand the people they are sworn to serve and empower the voter.

To reduce every election to a vote against caste, a vote for development, a vote against corruption, an aspirational vote, a vote against dynasty, or an anti-incumbency vote is a mistake. Figuring out what we can accurately say about how India votes, then, is essential to understanding Indian democracy.

Who Votes?

The first step would be to understand who is voting. Two out of three registered voters voted in the last national elections. Given that developing countries tend to have a lower voter turnout than developed countries,[1,2] voter turnout in India has been reasonably high, and in 2019, was at its highest-ever level. For context, the United States recorded its highest-ever turnout in November 2020, and that was an estimated 66.7 per cent, roughly the same as in India.[3]

These high numbers are relatively new to India. But the increase in voter turnout is almost exclusively a female story, with the gap between male and female voter turnout narrowing steadily and finally closing in 2019. In India's most recent parliamentary election, female-voter turnout was higher than male turnout for the first time in history. What makes this story that much more dramatic is that it isn't a statistical quirk—something very real has changed. This increase in female turnout isn't just an effect of the Election Commission's (EC's) attempts to get more unregistered women on the electoral rolls; between 1999 and 2019, men and women were added to India's electoral rolls at the same pace. Yet, over the last twenty years, the number of female voters has grown by over 75 per cent, while the number of male voters has grown by just over 50 per cent. Women, quite simply, are turning out to vote in unprecedented numbers. (Fig. 3.1)

Shipra Singh, a twenty-one-year-old who lives in Alwar, Rajasthan, voted for the first time in 2019, but was also the first woman in her family to vote. 'They used to do voter awareness camps in my college, so we all went together to get registered,' she said. Her mother, aunts and grandmother are registered to vote but did not vote in 2019. 'They wear a ghoonghat so they feel shy to go out. I told them last time—all the women in front of me in the line were also in ghoonghat—no one will make you lift it!'

For such an essential component of the democratic process,

Figure 3.1: The increase in voter turnout in India is almost exclusively a female story

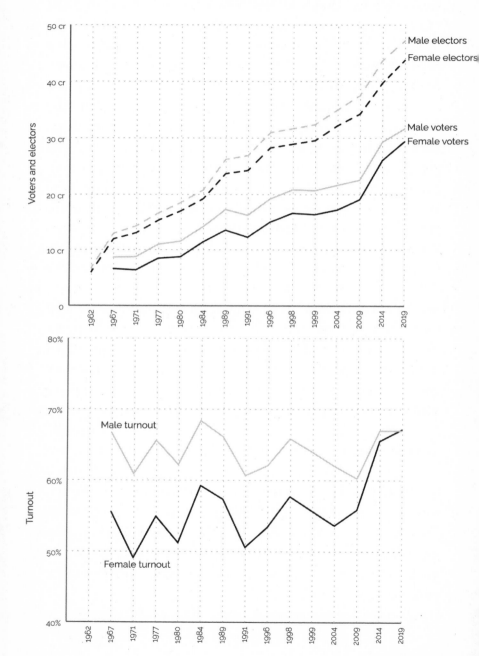

Source: Election Comission of India

we know surprisingly little about who votes. Some research indicates that the poor and less educated are more likely to vote than the rich. But on the other hand, states with higher literacy rates have higher turnouts and the presence of a larger urban population depresses turnouts.[4] Despite the standard media narrative that an elevated turnout indicates a 'wave' against an incumbent, there is no empirical relationship between turnouts and outcomes. These seemingly contradictory pieces of evidence reinforce the need to avoid easy narratives, particularly because national- and state-level turnouts can hide smaller but significant changes: in the 1990s, for instance, overall turnout remained the same, but the political scientist Yogendra Yadav argued that the participation of marginalised groups had increased substantially—what he called the 'second democratic upsurge'.

We remain some distance from fully understanding who votes in each election. However, who does not vote also tells a story. Polling day news coverage often laments the 'apathy' of urban voters, particularly in the richer parts of big cities, concurring that for the poor, elections are a matter of life and death, while the rich are insulated against their outcomes. Research indicates that the voting motivations of the poor and rich are significantly different—the poor say they turn out to vote because it is their right, while the non-poor report they vote because they expect material benefits from the State or because it is their duty.[5] But the narrative of rich South Mumbai and Delhi residents who head for the beach or hills on election weekend is more likely an urban legend that arises from a misunderstanding of just how big and diverse constituencies—both parliamentary and assembly—are. Even the most affluent-seeming constituencies in the big cities of

India contain pockets of great poverty. Hyderabad had the lowest voter turnout (after three constituencies in Jammu and Kashmir) in India in the 2019 Lok Sabha elections, but nearly one in three people in the constituency is under the poverty line. Meanwhile, Kannur in Kerala had one of the highest voter turnouts, but had a poverty rate that was over ten percentage points lower than that of Hyderabad.[6] Affluence does not directly correlate with apathy, and in any case, apathy may not be the explanation. Assumptions about the apathy of big city voters, too, rest on similarly shaky methods of estimating urban turnout and do not hold up uniformly.[7]

What's far more likely to explain missing voters is simply this—Indians are often on the move and the electoral process is not nimble. Being out of town on polling day has systematically been the single biggest reason why those who do not vote miss out, post-election surveys show. In Banda district in Uttar Pradesh, India's biggest state, turnout in polling stations with high migration (with 25 per cent or more out-migrants) was three percentage points lower than the district average. Migrants will tell you as much, that work comes in the way of voting. On a breezy evening in October 2020, twenty-eight-year-old Bishnu Prakash was immersed in a video—on the phone screen, Bihar's Chief Minister Nitish Kumar declared that this was his last election. 'If I could have, I would have voted for him. He's saying it is his last election!' the Madhubani native said animatedly, 2,250 km away in Chennai. 'In normal times, I would have tried to go home for the election and stay there for Chhatth Puja [Bihar's most popular festival],' said Prakash. 'But now I will not be able to afford a trip home until next Chhatth, I think.'

Prakash works for a contractor who installs flooring in

homes in Chennai. When post-COVID travel restrictions were lifted in May 2020, he returned home and waited out the monsoon with his family. But money was tight, especially with the looming prospect of illnesses and hospitalisations. Prakash returned to Chennai in August 2020 and was lucky, he says, to find work again. A politically active man, he was pragmatic too. 'Elections aren't going to send my children to private school!' he said.

Even for those whose lives undergo more modest changes, one immediate impact can be that they disappear from electoral lists. In a survey of a sample of Delhi's voter lists, 11 per cent of the addresses could not be found on the ground, while 21 per cent of the people had moved to a different place than the one listed. When a sample of citizens was surveyed, meanwhile, nearly half could not find their names on the voter list for their areas.[8]

Not everyone can vote, but missing voters are more likely those forced to miss out, rather than those choosing to.

Elections Are about Ideas

To try to answer what Indian voters are thinking when they press the button on the Electronic Voting Machine has become a choice between listening to two sets of people, both flawed in their own ways—journalists and pollsters. That hours and pages worth of news are filled in the days before elections by journalists reporting on who voters say they are going to vote for is testament to the fact that some still believe that a journalist can get the 'pulse' of a state or constituency by talking to her chosen cross-section of voters. The outright bias and politics of access at worst, and the sheer human subjectivity at best, that are on display in election reporting could make a strong case for the entire genre to be ignored altogether. Ah, but, the argument always goes, polls get it wrong too.

The election polling that is made available to the Indian public through agencies falls broadly into three categories—at the head is the respected Lokniti programme at the Centre for the Study of Developing Societies (CSDS), a venerable New Delhi institution known for its academic approach and transparency (although with limited public access). Then there are two respected international polling agencies—Pew and Gallup—which occasionally produce some insights on Indian voters but do not forecast results and are constrained by small sample sizes. The next category is the largest—commercial polling agencies commissioned by media houses to poll voters on their voting decisions. This includes pollsters like CVoter, Hansa Research, Nielsen, Jan Ki Baat, Axis My India and Today's Chanakya. Of these, CVoter is the most upfront about its methodology, and open to sharing raw data. The rest operate at varying degrees of dubiousness and opacity. Today's Chanakya enjoyed a string of 'successes', but when it got its 2015 Bihar election result completely wrong, it attributed its incorrect prediction to a coding error that interchanged the columns of the winner and the loser. Axis My India has had a good track record of accurate forecasts in the last two years and partly attributes its success to the fact that it samples voters in every constituency, rather than in a sample of constituencies like other pollsters. While this is too expensive a proposition for others, Axis counts among its clients political parties whose pockets are deep, making the raw data hard to come by and the cross-subsidising model ethically problematic.

Over the last decade, pollsters and journalists have together framed a neat narrative around Indian elections: caste, religious identity and individual leaders do not govern the decisions of Indian voters; they typically vote for 'development', a better economy and jobs. These 'truths', established through a basic reading of the answers that sampled voters give pollsters, have been repeated long enough to take on the appearance of fact. But at the core of these misunderstandings—and they are misunderstandings—lie the two key reasons why there is such a distorted picture about so much of India, and not politics alone: problematic data and selective reading of that data.

The problem with these surveys is not (for the most part) that they are proxies for political parties, or swayed by their funders, or pushing a narrative for a political party. The problem is that they are limited in imagination, do not typically allow for analysis across variables, and have become formulaic and purely predictive. As a result, the first level of analysis that they throw up is deeply problematic.

Taken at face value, surveys would appear to show that 'development' matters most to voters; that is certainly what CSDS and CVoter's post-election surveys show. But forming an opinion based on these responses alone is naive at best. What's more likely is that while voters do care about the material improvement of their lives, they use a much more complex decision matrix to arrive at decisions, one that the current structure of news reporting and opinion polling cannot capture. Most parties do promise development, but despite the common refrain that 'they're all the same', the key political antagonists in India are ideologically distinct, particularly on religion, and voters know clearly where to align themselves.

These issues of ideology and identity are so varied by

region that they further complicate news analysis and 'outside' analysts always run the risk of seriously misunderstanding how deeply they are held—issues of language and self-respect in Tamil Nadu or fears of mainland cultural imposition in Nagaland, for instance. These, moreover, are hard to capture through surveys—a voter in Tamil Nadu is unlikely to say that respect for her language governs her voting decision, but her distaste for the two national parties could include within its universe the fact that they don't seem to 'get' Tamil pride.

Before even starting on this path, however, one must accept that Indians care about ideas; ideas, in fact, are what elections in India are fought over, and dismissing them by saying that elections are fought over money, identity or 'development' alone is to miss the point entirely.

Indian Voters Are Polarised but Practical

Indian parties and voters are strongly and consistently ideological:[9] BJP voters systematically support core Hindu nationalist issues like a ban on cow slaughter and oppose religious conversion, while Congress voters systematically oppose them. The one exception among Congress voters—its upper-caste voters. This trend has not changed with time; to argue then that voters do not care about religious hot-button issues would be disingenuous, given that their positions on these issues are strong and consistent over time, and firmly aligned with one party or the other. (Fig. 3.2)

Since the first term of the Modi government, while older, core 'Hindutva' issues, including the banning of cow slaughter and religious conversion, forcefully integrating Kashmir into the mainland through the abrogation of Article 370 that granted it some legislative autonomy, building a temple to

Figure 3.2: BJP and Congress voters differ systematically from each other

Each number is the average number of standard deviations from the mean, on an index measuring voter support derived from various rounds of Lokniti's National Election Studies. A positive number indicates support for the issues and negative indicates opposition. Larger the value, larger the support or opposition

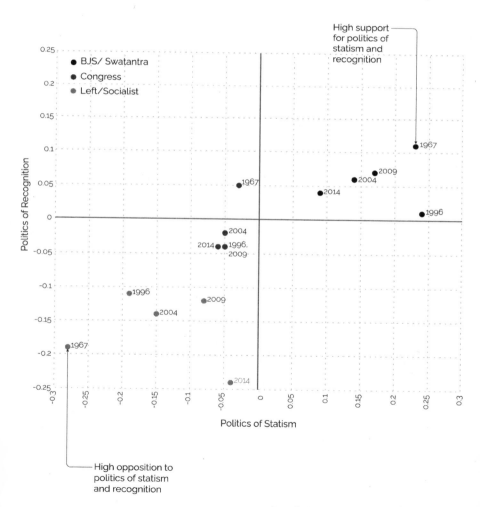

Source: Pradeep Chhibber and Rahul Verma, *Ideology & Identity: The Changing Party Systems of India*, 2018 (based on Lokniti-CSDS National Election Studies, various years)

Lord Ram in Ayodhya over the ruins of a demolished mosque, have been revived, the party has also come up with newer Hindutva 2.0 issues. One among these is the Citizenship Amendment Act (CAA) that grants citizenship to non-Muslim illegal immigrants and asylum-seekers only, which became a flashpoint for protests when it was passed alongside attempts to build a new national register of citizens, widely seen as a way of forcing Indian Muslims into second-class citizen status.

The narrative around the February 2020 Delhi state elections, held against the backdrop of the protests against the CAA, depending on which side you spoke to, was that this was an election pitting 'development versus communalism' or 'handouts versus nationalism'. Hidden among the weeds of the opinion polling around that election, however, was an elegant demonstration of the futility of a single diagnosis of what voters are truly voting for.

When the crusading former bureaucrat Arvind Kejriwal-led Aam Aadmi Party (AAP) won the Delhi election, on the face of it, it would have appeared that yes, Delhi voters truly were voting for 'development'. The exit polls suggested that for Delhi, the real issue was development and not the CAA or similar 'Hindu/Muslim issues'. Certainly, that is what voters appear to have told surveyors. In the Axis My India exit poll for the India Today Group, over a third of voters said that 'development' was the top issue, while fewer than 10 per cent cited 'national security'. In the CVoter exit poll, three times as many voters said that they were voting for 'development' as those who said the top issue on their mind was the CAA.

But looking deeper at who Hindu and Muslim voters voted for, and why, is important. The BJP, which lost the election, actually held on to over half of its base. It got over half of the upper-caste Hindu vote in 2020 and its vote-share was higher than it was in 2015. But the AAP got the lion's share of the Muslim vote—significant in a state with 13 per cent Muslims. Hindu voters in Delhi were more likely to support than oppose the Act, while Muslims were more likely to oppose it.[10] Why did Muslims not vote for the Congress, then, which backed the anti-CAA protests more strongly than the AAP, which largely sidestepped the protests? 'When asked about the reason for voting in favour of the AAP, the Muslim voters said it was on account of its winnability against the BJP. In other words, the Muslim voters of Delhi voted for the AAP because they felt it was better poised to defeat the BJP in comparison to the Congress,' the Axis pollsters said.[11] For Muslim voters, then, keeping the BJP out was strategically most important and a party that did not outright support the CAA was palatable, while for Hindu voters, the development agenda of a party with a relatively neutral position on the CAA could drive voting decisions.

Just as the citizenship issue became important to Muslims, its ideological signalling was of value to some Hindu voters too, even when the law was actually against their own material interests. In the eastern state of Assam, for instance, where illegal immigration from neighbouring Muslim-majority Bangladesh and its intersection with religion is a particularly charged issue, and where a similar exercise to force residents to prove their citizenship caused untold suffering to lakhs through 2019, a 104-year-old Hindu man died in December 2020, unable until the very end to produce documents to prove he was not a foreigner. Nevertheless, he remained a true believer in Modi and a supporter of the government's targeting of 'outsiders', despite having been turned in his final days, on paper, into an outsider.[12]

Religion is not the only axis on which Indian voters are distinctly committed and polarised. The political scientists Pradeep Chhibber and Rahul Verma document that particularly until the 1990s, there was a distinct economic right-wing that stood against reservations for the backward caste groups and wanted less state intervention in the economy. The BJP's voters were consistently to the right, both on social issues and economic ones, while the Left's voters occupied the opposing quarter. Since the 1990s, however, this axis has become less salient to India's voters, with economic distinctions between political parties diminishing and religious distinctions sharpening.[13]

These are sophisticated decision matrices, yet the Indian voter is rarely considered sophisticated. Instead, voters are characterised as making decisions purely on the basis of who offers them more money. The handing out of cash to electors the day before elections is now a norm in Tamil Nadu; as the political scientist Milan Vaishnav has documented, political parties do not see cash as a pathway to victory, but they do see giving cash as necessary to be taken seriously, now that the norm has been set. Yet, in the 2021 elections, multiple journalists and political analysts said that the election could be decided the day before, when cash began to go out, as if votes were there to be sold to the highest bidder.

S. Valli and P. Vasanthi are neighbours in Burma Colony, a low-income housing settlement along the massive Old Mahabalipuram Road around which Chennai's software parks and the housing that services them have been established. Three days before the 2021 Tamil Nadu assembly election, the two women sat on their doorsteps, fanning themselves in the April heat and commiserating over their kids learning nothing in 'mobile-phone school'. Both had received money, each from the party that she traditionally votes for. Vasanthi was going to continue to vote for the AIADMK, in memory of the late J. Jayalalithaa, because 'she was a woman in a man's world, and I know how hard that can be'. In academic terms, one might call it a feminist vote. Valli was going to vote for the DMK because she counted on them to stand up to the BJP, who she described as 'not for people like us'—it was a Hindi-speaking party of upper castes in her view. In 'sophisticated' terms, you could call it a vote for federalism, for social justice. Or you could choose to see them as two women who handed over their sacred votes for money.

Vote-banks Are Real

When we choose to see poorer, or less-educated voters, or those from particular social groups as people who vote in herds like sheep, they are snidely labelled as 'vote-banks'.

Muslims in India largely give the same answers in opinion polls as Hindus do, answers that can mask the complex thinking that governs vote choice; in fifteen years of surveys from Uttar Pradesh, the self-reported biggest priorities of Muslims were no different from the state average.[14]

But 'development' alone can never be a sufficient answer for the Muslim voter, with political disenfranchisement, social and financial boycotts, and physical insecurity being very real threats. When a Muslim politician is elected in India, the odds are that her constituency is overwhelmingly Muslim. Despite lazy characterisations of a range of constituencies as 'Muslim-dominated', there are only fifteen constituencies that actually have a population that is more than 50 per cent Muslim. Thirteen of them elected Muslim MPs in the 2019

Lok Sabha election. But in the rest of the country, the odds of getting elected decline sharply for a Muslim hopeful; if a constituency had fewer than 20 per cent Muslims, the odds of a Muslim winning went down to under one in a hundred in 2019.[15] Three constituencies that have always sent Muslim MPs to Parliament, because they have between 95–100 per cent Muslim population, are in the erstwhile state of Jammu and Kashmir. The impact of the 2022 delimitation in the 'reorganised' union territories is yet to be seen.

The political ghettoisation of Muslims has only got worse since the BJP came to power; the party had no Muslim MPs in 2014 or 2019, and in Bihar's 2020 elections, no Muslim MLA made it to the treasury benches despite the state having a Muslim population of 17 per cent. In the 2017 Uttar Pradesh assembly election, the BJP did not give a single ticket to the community in a state where one of every five people was Muslim. The most egregious case is in Prime Minister Narendra Modi's home state of Gujarat, where the party has systematically shut out Muslims, who form 9 per cent of the population. The last time the BJP fielded a Muslim candidate in the state's elections was in 1998 (and he lost). 'What they want is not ghettoisation, they want Muslim politicians to feel like there is no space for them and just leave the democratic space entirely,' Asaduddin Owaisi, Hyderabad's MP, had once told me when I tallied these numbers. The electorate is religiously polarised too: 58 per cent of respondents in a four-state survey said that they would prefer to approach a political leader of their own religion for work-related matters, the proportion being substantially higher among Hindus.[16]

Some amount of strategic ideological voting is an important approach, then, for Muslims, even if at a broad individual level, rather than at a systematic, coordinated pan-community level. In states like Rajasthan, Gujarat and Madhya Pradesh where electoral contests are straight fights between the Congress and BJP, Muslims overwhelmingly vote for the Congress. But in states like Assam, Kerala or West Bengal where there is a third option, the Congress vote-share among Muslims declines.[17]

Since 2014, when the BJP swept to power with Modi at the helm, voters have become increasingly polarised on religious lines, with the 2019 election in purely empirical terms the most communally polarised election in India's history—the gap between the beliefs and political support of Hindu and Muslim voters was wider than it had ever been.[18] In February 2020, turnout was highest in Delhi's high-Muslim constituencies, indicating perhaps a greater degree of politicisation and mobilisation. Just as Hindu voters', particularly upper-caste voters', assertion that they are voting for development does not mean that they do not strongly believe in Hindutva issues and hence the BJP, Muslim voters saying that they want development does not mean that they will not vote for the party best poised to keep the BJP out. '[Aam Aadmi Party leader Arvind] Kejriwal has always seemed like a closet Hindutvawadi to me. But right then we needed protection. Think of it like paying hafta [protection money] to a cop,' Anas Alvi, who runs a small shop in Delhi's Jamia Nagar area, told me.

These are the sorts of calculations that lead commentators to describe Muslims as a 'vote-bank', or a bloc of loyal voters. But if there is a truly loyal vote-bank in India, it is the BJP's upper-caste Hindu vote-bank. The BJP is no longer a party that derives most of its support from upper castes; it is now a broad-based Hindu party, preferred over the Congress by Other Backward Classes (OBC) and Scheduled Caste (SC) voters by a significant margin. But the commitment of upper-caste voters to the BJP is near-universal, and vis-a-vis the Congress, is higher than it has ever been. The BJP has consistently polled better among upper castes than the Congress does with Muslims—a more mathematically sound description of a vote-bank than the usual charge.[19]

The Dalit Vote—Power and Powerlessness

The upper-caste vote may have remained steadfast, but what has changed is how other communities, who were not traditionally seen as BJP supporters, vote. In the 2014 election, the BJP won its highest ever vote-share among Dalits, India's most marginalised caste group with the most adverse development indicators—the first time in an election that more Dalits voted for the BJP than they did for the Congress. The other, larger shift since the late 1990s has been the middle-caste groups' support, which the party, now led by Modi, himself an OBC, has steadily built.

Some of this expanded support was won through shrewd calculations and effective campaigning. In Uttar Pradesh, the Jatav community—a sub-category of the SCs—remained steadfastly aligned with the Bahujan Samaj Party and its Jatav leader Mayawati, the state's most important Dalit politician. So, in building towards its massive 2017 victory in the state's election, the BJP cultivated and targeted non-Jatav SC groups, including Valmikis and Pasis, who felt relatively disempowered, party strategists said. The then incumbent Samajwadi Party had nurtured a Yadav (a dominant OBC caste) vote-bank, so the BJP similarly teased out and nurtured

EBCs—a sub-group of Extremely Backward Classes within the OBC umbrella who felt ignored by the Samajwadi Party. These fault lines were based on real differences in progress, but additionally assiduously exploited by the BJP. This 'nurturing', however, is not without a sharp edge. There is some evidence of what political workers and analysts take as understood in India—communal violence benefits the BJP electorally. Two pieces of recent research have suggested that riots raise the vote-share of the BJP in the subsequent election.[20] The BJP and its Hindutva hardline ecosystem's relentless propaganda, fear-mongering and outright violence against Muslims could produce some of these unusual caste coalitions as well. That, ultimately, is what polarisation is, banding together Hindu caste groups who may not all have traditionally voted for the BJP against the Muslims of that area in an 'us vs them' scenario.

Yet, this would gloss over one important consideration for Indian voters—that representation matters. For the most part, voters are not voting for someone who looks like them; the median Indian MP is older, more likely to be an upper-caste Hindu male and far richer than the median Indian.[21] But Modi is India's first full-term prime minister from a backward caste, and a man who rose from humble origins. 'In our fathers' generation, we would have not even been the chaprasis (peons) in Parliament. When Modi touched his forehead to the steps of Parliament on his first day, it felt like we were being given entry into a temple,' Shyamlal Yadav, a small farmer in UP's Basti district told me. In state elections, Yadav had voted for the Samajwadi Party, also associated with OBC castes. In the 2014 national election, he wore his vote for Modi with special pride.

The salience of caste is often missed by analysts, who would like to believe that 'development trumps caste now', as headlines around the 2014 election declared. Survey data too would seem to support this—Indian voters systematically rate 'development' as their top priority at the time of voting. But approaching the caste question obliquely provides greater nuance; over 45 per cent of voters said in a pre-2014 election survey that it was important to them that a candidate of their own caste wins elections in their constituency.[22] Sixty per cent of respondents in a four-state survey said that they would prefer to approach a leader from their own caste for work-related matters.[23]

How to ensure the political representation of Dalits was one of the key issues in debates around the framing of independent India's Constitution. Since 1961, India has had constituencies reserved for SC and ST politicians to contest from as a form of affirmative action. After the last redrawing of constituency lines, there are eighty-four seats reserved for SC politicians and forty-seven seats for STs. Despite the remaining 412 seats being technically open to candidates of all castes, both the BJP and the Congress have systematically given fewer and fewer tickets to SCs and STs in these 'general' seats, thereby ghettoising them into reserved seats only. In 2014, just one Dalit MP won from a non-reserved constituency. In 2019, the ghettoisation was complete; Dalit MPs won from SC-reserved constituencies only, the boundaries to socio-political mobility drawn tight.

Nor is there much discussion in the political space about this ghettoisation: in 2014, Nirmala Sitharaman, then the BJP's national spokesperson and now India's finance minister, dismissed such concerns in an interview to me: 'What we look for is a person who enjoys good standing in the community and the goodwill of all of the people. It would not be right for us to nominate an SC candidate just to be seen as being inclusive.'[24]

The outcome of the election in a reserved seat is often used as shorthand for 'how Dalits' voted. So, for instance, the BJP winning forty-six of eighty-four SC-reserved seats in 2019 was described in the media as 'Dalits preferring the BJP'. However, even though reserved seats are meant to have a concentration of the population they are reserved for, this is especially not the case for SC constituencies, because, unlike India's STs, who are concentrated in forested or hilly regions for historical and anthropological reasons, Dalits are much more geographically spread out. As a result, SCs are a *minority* in all SC-reserved seats. This, in turn, has a real impact on the ability of SC politicians to deliver development gains to SC voters.[25]

At the moment, there is little constituency-level demographic and electoral surveying; as a result there is no publicly available data from the 2019 (or other recent) elections on how the upper castes who live in reserved constituencies voted, even though they were numerically more likely to have determined the outcome. What exist are some clues.

Even though Dalit voters who live in reserved constituencies are more likely to vote than those who live in 'general' constituencies, the overall voter turnout is usually lower in reserved constituencies than in general constituencies.[26] One plausible explanation for this could be that upper castes are less motivated to vote for SC candidates. In 2019, Chitradurga (Karnataka) MP A. Narayanaswamy made news when residents of a village inhabited by the Golla OBC community refused to allow him to enter their hamlet because, as a Dalit man, his presence would 'pollute' and 'bring misfortune' to them.[27,28]

Ravikumar, a Dalit MP from Villupuram, Tamil Nadu, from the VCK party, said he too has faced similar experiences. Upper-caste settlements refused to allow him in when he was campaigning, and once there was stone-pelting during a campaign, injuring a party-worker. As an MP, he hasn't yet experienced such casteism, he said. 'But officials respond to Dalit MPs with distinct indifference,' he added.[29]

Another explanation for the lower turnout in reserved constituencies is that SC politicians have weaker networks and mobilisation capacity. As they have become better integrated in political parties, the gap in turnout has narrowed; in 2019, the turnout in SC constituencies was higher than in general constituencies.[30] Narayanaswamy, the MP who was turned away, was a BJP MP, and while he tried to reason with the priests who blocked his entry, he did not press charges—even the OBC hamlet had voted for him in 2019, he said.

There appears to be some hope for change over time even if the motivating factor is less a genuine reform of the mindset and more the awe of power. Since the early 1990s, a share of village council posts are reserved for Dalits on a rotating basis, creating far more regular exposure to Dalit politicians at the local level. In UP, those who lived in a village that had been reserved for a longer time had a more positive view of SC politicians.[31] Dalit politicians still face discrimination and bias (including untouchability of the sort experienced by Narayanaswamy), but their status, education, power and money provide them with some defences.[32] In Rajasthan, the election of an SC village head did not change the dominant caste members' stereotypes about Dalits, but it did change what they thought were acceptable and legal ways to interact with Dalits.[33]

Women Voters as a Sum of Their Parts

Women voters, too, have historically been used to seeing their MP not look like themselves. But the 2019 elections appeared to be marked by a new acknowledgement of the importance of female representation in positions of power. At least one state election had already shown that this made political sense: in the 2016 Tamil Nadu assembly election, the AIADMK's winning margin was made up almost exclusively of women.[34]

During the campaign for the general elections, Naveen Patnaik, leader of the Biju Janata Dal in Odisha, announced that he would give 33 per cent of party tickets to women. Mamata Banerjee's Trinamool Congress, which has historically fielded a higher share of women candidates than most other major parties, followed suit by declaring that 41 per cent of its candidates were women. The current Indian Parliament has the highest number of women in history, though India still ranks abysmally low in terms of female representation in Parliament—148th of 190 countries.

Some political leaders have a clear advantage in the eyes of women voters. Regional political parties led by women—the Mehbooba Mufti-led People's Democratic Party in the erstwhile Jammu and Kashmir, the Mayawati-led BSP, the AIADMK in Tamil Nadu which was led by the late Jayalalithaa, and the Mamata Banerjee-led Trinamool Congress—all did better among female voters than among male voters in 2019. Among male leaders, Nitish Kumar of the Janata Dal (United) in Bihar, Shivraj Singh Chouhan of the BJP in Madhya

Pradesh, K. Chandrashekar Rao of the Telangana Rashtra Samithi in Telangana, and Naveen Patnaik of the Biju Janata Dal, all enjoyed an advantage among female voters, survey data indicates.

At a national level, the BJP has historically had trouble appealing to women voters, and even with its gains in 2014, preference for the party among women remained four percentage points lower than among men. On the other hand, despite losing support across the board, the Congress remained more popular among women than it was among men in 2014.[35] Post-election 2019 surveys clearly indicated that the BJP made gains among women, but key pollsters disagreed about the extent of its gains, and here lies one of the most worrying problems with relying on polls to form broad theories about Indian voters. The Axis My India exit poll, whose vote-share and seat projections were close in accuracy to the final result, found that the BJP has reversed its historical female disadvantage; the party had found greater support among women than among men in 2019, the survey said. Another reputed polling agency, CVoter, concurred. Lokniti-CSDS was the lone dissenter; the organisation said that its post-poll survey indicated that the BJP's female disadvantage remained unchanged, and in subsequent academic publications, it is this data that has been cited.

When polling agencies differ so much from each other in their estimates of how women vote, is there anything useful that can yet be said on the subject?

If the BJP did make big gains in its appeal to women, the reasons can at present only be hypothesised about. Women in India have not historically expressed substantially different views on what they are voting for than men. There have only been marginal differences in what men and women have said about the issues that would most influence their voting choices—women appeared to care a little more than men about inflation and a little less about corruption.[36]

One beloved theory about voters, particularly women voters, is that 'schemes matter'. Some commentators claim that the 'Ujjwala' scheme aimed at enabling families that use solid fuels for cooking to switch over to gas earned the BJP the gratitude of women. Others have suggested that the BJP's focus on sanitation struck a particular chord with women, who bear the brunt of the hygiene and safety concerns of open defecation. Indeed, the Ujjwala Yojana was the top answer when voters were asked to name one policy or programme of the Modi government that they liked the most. Among women beneficiaries of the scheme, more women voted for the BJP compared to those who did not benefit from it (41 per cent and 33 per cent, respectively). Among women beneficiaries of the Jan Dhan Yojana, a scheme to improve banking penetration, 42 per cent opted for the BJP compared to 34 per cent of non-beneficiaries.

On the whole, however, there isn't yet direct evidence that women voters had any of these schemes in mind while voting for the BJP; after all, voters typically tend to give state governments more credit for flagship Union government welfare schemes. In West Bengal, for instance, welfare schemes might have worked in the eyes of female voters, but these were schemes run by and credited to the state government rather than the Central government.[37]

Moreover, women are not a homogenous bloc; multiple identities intersect in the decision matrix of a voter. A young Dalit girl in Agra, a first-time voter, was motivated both by a desire for women's safety and her yearning for self-respect and opportunities for marginalised people like herself.[38] A Muslim woman in Godhra was proud that a man from her state was prime minister and wasn't familiar with the term 'Hindutva'.[39] A farmer in Telangana believed she must vote for the party her village head chose.[40]

How the Youth Both Care and Do Not

Young voters' motivations add a further layer to these complex decisions, and yet again, there are revealed preferences—those preferences that are not stated. Not only did 2014 have a historic share of young people of voting age, they also showed up to vote in historic numbers; youth turnout exceeded the general turnout for the first time.[41] States that had a higher share of first-time voters in 2014 also saw the biggest increases in the BJP's vote-share.[42] What is also historic about the last decade is that first-time voters were the greatest supporters of the BJP; twice as many eighteen–twenty-two year olds voted for the BJP as did for the Congress in both 2014 and 2019. This was a significant shift—in previous elections, young people had not expressed any clear preference for the BJP. In 2014 and 2019, the older the voter, the more likely she would be to support the Congress and the Left.

Once again, it isn't apparent that young voters have particularly different decision structures from older voters. Younger voters are only slightly more disapproving of dynastic politicians, but are less disapproving of criminal politicians than older voters. They are as likely as older voters to want their local candidate to be from their own caste.[43]

Young people may say that they have no interest in politics. However, most have fairly strong conservative views on hot-button political issues—six out of ten people aged between fifteen and twenty-four supported banning movies which could hurt religious sentiments, nearly half believed that the consumption of beef should not be allowed, and half wanted to retain capital punishment. In particular, Hindu youth strongly opposed the consumption of beef, as did BJP- and AAP-supporting young people (while Left-supporting young people felt that people should eat what they like).[44] Similarly, when asked after the 2014 elections what the first priority of the new government should be, one of the issues slightly more important to first-time voters (under the age of twenty) than to older voters was 'protecting the interests of the Hindu community'.[45]

More young people are voting than ever before, and they are more likely to support the BJP. But distilling this to an 'aspirational' young vote beyond the issue of 'identity', for economic growth alone, would once again be a fundamental misreading of India.

Missing Reality, Manufacturing Reality

Why aren't journalists and pollsters able to capture the multiple motivations of voters? In part, it is because they are asking the wrong questions and are too quick to use one answer as *the* answer. But part of the issue also is that people's beliefs colour what they think of as their reality.

First, there are information asymmetries. Indians might not always believe that government programmes have benefited them to the extent that they credit a state or national government. Despite a majority across states saying that they use government schools and hospitals and a large majority saying that they use the PDS, 45 per cent said immediately following the 2014 election that no government programme had benefited their family in the last year, or they did not know if any had.[46]

Sometimes, the blame or credit for a scheme is laid at the wrong door. Following the 2014 elections, 20 per cent of people said that they had benefited from the UPA's Mahatma Gandhi National Employment Guarantee Scheme, but over two out of three credited the local or state government for it. Over 20 per cent benefited from the National Rural Health Mission, but over half of them credited the state government for it.[47] Modi's relentless personal messaging around schemes is, however, trying to fix this problem in his favour: in 2014, compared to earlier elections, voters were more likely to give credit to the Union government for welfare schemes, as opposed to state governments or local politicians.[48]

Post-election analyses abound with assertions that the presence or absence of 'development' makes all the difference. One argument is that an individual's perception of economic progress is associated with a more favourable opinion of politicians: in one survey, among those who believed that their households were in a better economic condition than in the past, 56 per cent had an unfavourable opinion of the government; among those whose view of their own economic condition did not change, 58 per cent had an unfavourable opinion of the government; and among those who felt they were doing badly, 65 per cent had an unfavourable opinion of the government.[49]

On the whole, however, evidence for such claims remains weak. Globally, the evidence on whether voters reward better government service provision is mixed. In South Africa, a comprehensive study of post-apartheid service provision showed that voters did not systematically reward the African National Congress in constituencies where basic services reached or improved.[50] In Uganda, a government scheme to provide grants for skilled enterprises successfully raised employment and incomes, resulting in voters being able to free themselves from patronage systems. But this also made them more involved in Opposition mobilisation, research suggests.[51]

Perhaps the problem is with the very notion that voter motivations can be objectively quantified and measured, something that recent evidence contradicts.

Before the 2014 election, a majority of urban respondents said that economic growth would be the biggest issue influencing their voting choice. That should have meant that if the economy was doing well, the government in charge would be re-elected. Yet, after an election in which the incumbent was dislodged, more than half said that their financial situation was better than it was five years before.[52]

This disjunction can be seen in other instances too. In the weeks and months after Modi's sudden announcement of the demonetisation of high value currency notes in 2016, the distress caused to the working poor as they stood in lines to turn in their money, and as the circulation of cash came to a grinding halt, was evident across the country. Yet, in opinion polls, the move continued to be supported, including by those whom it affected the most; the belief in Modi as a man committed to doing good remained strong.[53]

In the months immediately before the 2019 election, there was talk that the Indian government's air strikes on what it claimed were terrorist targets in Balakot, Pakistan, had led to a surge in nationalistic support for the BJP. But opinion polling data of the time shows that the 'Balakot bump' that the air strikes gave to the issue of national security in the minds of voters appeared to have faded before the election, meaning that the key concerns before voters were once again from the usual bouquet of economic problems, with unemployment leading the lot. (Fig. 3.3) Despite evidence of rural distress, historically high unemployment, as well as slowing macro-economic indicators in 2018, voters consistently reported the economy as being in good shape. BJP voters were even more likely to rate the economy well, and it isn't just the rich who vote for the BJP any more.

An eventual BJP voter telling a journalist or pollster that unemployment mattered to her was largely meaningless then—it did 'matter', but her ideological commitment to the BJP was strong enough to colour her reality of under whom it had worsened. The Balakot 'bump' may have flattened, but the goodwill it created among a large section of voters might have adhered to Modi.

What appears most likely is that voters' feelings about the BJP and Modi, and the Congress and its leader Rahul Gandhi—sentiments that are less transactional than 'who will get me a job?'—did not really change between 2014 and 2019, and so, significantly, neither did the result.

This isn't to say that these sentiments have evolved organically. Indians are more exposed to the media than before, have significant trust in it, and those with greater media exposure, particularly in Hindi, which is spoken widely in north India, prefer the BJP. It outdid the Congress at every level of media exposure, though a small constituency, those who got their news from the internet, were particularly likely to prefer the BJP. Moreover, as the election proceeded, support

Figure 3.3: All voters claim they want development

What was the most important issue for you at the time of voting?

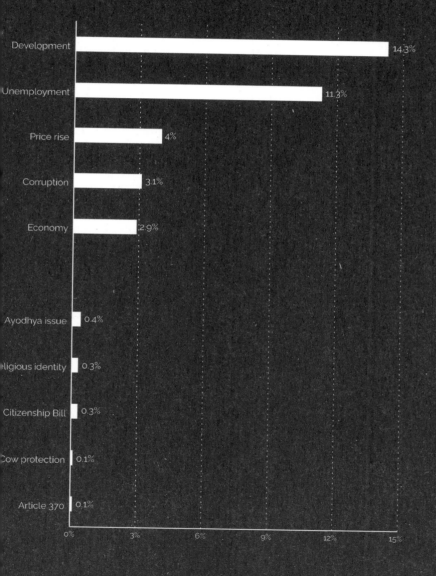

Issue	Percentage
Development	14.3%
Unemployment	11.3%
Price rise	4%
Corruption	3.1%
Economy	2.9%
Ayodhya issue	0.4%
Religious identity	0.3%
Citizenship Bill	0.3%
Cow protection	0.1%
Article 370	0.1%

Source: Lokniti-CSDS post-poll survey, 2019

for the BJP and Modi grew at all levels of media exposure. Those with high media exposure also tend to be richer, more urban, upper caste and younger—the quintessential BJP voter. The Congress, meanwhile, always does better than the BJP among voters with low media exposure.[54]

With such a real impact on voting, the content of this media becomes important. At the height of the 2014 election campaign, between 1 March and 11 May, Modi got more airtime during the 8–10 p.m. slot on a sample of Hindi and English news channels than the next nine top leaders put together. In all, Modi was discussed for over a third of the time.[55] The coverage of the BJP also exceeded that of the Congress by over ten percentage points. This was an unprecedented gap. In 2009, the difference was not more than a percentage point or two. It is unclear whether the coverage of Modi and the BJP in 2014 was positive or negative, since the study of viewership did not carry out a sentiment analysis. But there is plenty of anecdotal evidence to suggest the coverage of the BJP and of Modi in particular has not only been extensive ever since, but often, particularly on TV, fawning.[56]

This might not be something viewers and voters even mind. A 2017 global opinion poll found Indians were the most accepting of political bias in their media of all the countries surveyed. Many more Indians said that it was sometimes acceptable for a news organisation to favour one political party than those who said it was never acceptable—the only country where the scale tipped this way.[57]

Notions of fairness and bias in Indian elections are often romanticised. One of the ideas most dearly held by many in India's commentariat is that the Election Commission (EC) is what keeps the country's elections honest. The EC, the argument goes, is one of the country's few remaining independent institutions, insulated from the pressures of politics, power and money. Whether decisions taken by the EC have favoured one party over the other is hard to prove empirically. But the one time that processes around elections could be tested empirically, what became evident is that the EC does not function in a relatively unbiased way because it is 'above' politics; on the contrary, what keeps it relatively 'neutral' is precisely multi-party electoral politics.

In 2002, India began the process of redrawing electoral constituencies based on the Census of 2001. The aim of the exercise was to equalise the population across electoral constituencies within each state, and to re-assess which constituencies be reserved for SCs and STs. The delimitation, as it was called, would hold good until at least 2031. The exercise was carried out by an 'independent' three-member Delimitation Commission, comprised of a former Supreme Court judge, the chief election commissioner of India and the state election commissioner of the state concerned. Five MLAs and five MPs from the state were selected as 'associate members' to advise the Delimitation Commission in each state, although they had no voting power on the final decisions of the commission.

Research in Rajasthan and Andhra Pradesh has shown that MLAs and MPs who were members of the ruling party at the state and national level respectively were not insulated from inconvenient redistricting. Ministers, too, were unable to avoid inconvenient delimitation. However, there was one exception: the five MPs and five MLAs across political lines from each state who were on the advisory committee to the delimitation commission in that state.

Constituencies where the incumbent was a member of the advisory committee were significantly less likely to be reserved either for SCs or STs, after controlling for the population percentage of such groups, researchers found. Membership of the advisory committee was also associated with a 'significantly lower degree of demographic change, a higher proportion of original voters remaining in the electoral constituency of the politician in question'.[58]

N. Gopalaswami was the chief election commissioner at the time and ex-officio member of the three-member Delimitation Commission. 'Overall, we were remarkably successful in applying the rules in an unbiased manner,' he told me. 'But of course we can't be 100 per cent certain. Maybe in some cases, we did marginally accommodate people who made representations that weren't too out of the way,' he admitted.

What likely kept the process relatively non-partisan was not the *absence* of politicians, but the *presence* of multiple politicians representing multiple groups and parties.

How India (Probably) Votes

A more honest assessment of Indian voting is probably this: Indian voters care about ideas, they are more ideologically committed than ever before, they care about people who embody some of these ideas. There is no doubt that they want material improvements in their lives, but the ideological signalling—whether overt or implied—by the leaders and parties they vote for and the ones they hope to defeat matters and is something they factor in. These ideas they might arrive at through their life experiences and through targeted messaging. And they're not telling surveyors all of this—they might not even know it themselves.

Five years after the disastrous 2015 Bihar election call, the state went to the polls in February 2020. This time, the exit polls almost unanimously called it for the anti-BJP Opposition. The incumbent government had failed to deliver on development, the same set of talking heads declared, and aspirational Biharis wanted change. The lessons of 2015 had been clean forgotten. As it happened, the election's result was a clear mandate in favour of the BJP.

The day after the 2015 Bihar election call, Prannoy Roy, one of India's best known election analysts and the co-founder of the news channel that got it so wrong that morning, put out a heartfelt mea culpa. A global agency that NDTV had relied on to feed them the results as they came in had got inaccurate early results, he said, apologising sincerely to his viewers. This time around, Axis My India's Pradeep Gupta suggested that women had been difficult to poll and had swung the election.

But opinion polls don't just produce electoral predictions: the same sample that produced the erroneous results is also the one that produces 'research' about what voters voted for. While a bad call can be apologised for and retracted, the narrative that the faulty data was based on can outlast the wrong call.

Make no mistake—this is not an easy electorate to survey and draw conclusions from. India's politics are unique in myriad ways; the social heterogeneity of voters, the high turnover of incumbents, the frequent changes in alliances, all add up to a pollster's nightmare. However, and partly for that very reason, information on who votes and why is invaluable. As political parties increasingly turn to data to understand their electorates, ensuring that voter motivations are not misrepresented and the big ideas that voters care about are communicated to leadership becomes an important project of democracy. So how can we do a better job of capturing the Indian voter's decision-making process?

One, opinion polling that is not transparent about its methodology and sampling deserves to be excluded from the public record, else the assumptions that stem from this data live on, unchallenged. Problematic opinion polling helps strengthen a growing narrative that all electoral polling is 'fake' or 'paid'. It is only by separating the wheat from the chaff that we can build public trust in credible polling.

Opinion polling that is transparent needs to be held to better standards as well; if a pre-election poll or an exit survey significantly deviates from the final vote-share outcome, there's a good chance that it got its sampling wrong. Instead of allowing these surveyors to merely recalibrate their findings about voter motivations to the final numbers (the current accepted practice), there's good reason to consider discarding, or at the very least caveating, such surveys.

Two, there needs to be much more high-frequency, easily accessible opinion polling. Greater public scrutiny of opinion polling can only happen if the data is made public, which, in the case of a number of pollsters, is not currently the mode of operation. For this to change, the mode of funding of opinion polls—currently paid for either by media organisations or political parties—will need to be reimagined. In the US, for instance, Pew is a non-profit organisation supported by charitable funds.

Three, surveyors, journalists and analysts need to get more creative about the questions that they ask, knowing as we do now, that voters do not state their motivations upfront. Ahead of the 2014 general elections, a group of researchers conducted a survey where they tried out an experiment: first, they asked voters directly whether they would be willing to support a candidate who could deliver benefits but faced serious criminal cases—26 per cent of respondents said yes. But, since this sort of question is subject to a social desirability bias, they also asked the question indirectly through a list experiment. They randomly assigned all respondents to one of two equal-sized groups: a control group and a treatment group. The control group received a list of three types of candidates (a candidate who was wealthy, a candidate who was poor, and a candidate who did social service but was not affiliated with any party) and were asked how many trouble them. The treatment group was provided the same three options but also a fourth option, a candidate who delivered benefits but faced serious criminal cases. Since the respondents were being asked how many—and not which—types troubled them, any difference in the average responses between the treatment and control groups would be due to the inclusion of the fourth option. They found that unlike the first time around, when only 26 per cent said that they were untroubled by a candidate facing criminal charges, the indirect question elicited this response from 48 per cent of respondents. This meant that the direct question got an answer that was an underestimate by twenty-two percentage points. Thus, questions that seek to better understand the voter's world view might be more effective than those that ask her to simply choose what she is voting for from a list of options, a strategy that almost demands virtue signalling. Random response techniques, endorsement experiments and survey experiments are other methods that surveyors can employ to reduce biases associated with the misrepresentation of data, the researchers suggested.[59]

Four, there could and should be more triangulation

of information between what seasoned reporters see on the ground and what the data says, instead of the current atmosphere of mutual distaste and suspicion.

Finally, we might not be able to get analysts, whose job it is to spin quick and pithy narratives on-air, to be more circumspect, but there's no reason to allow these narratives to dominate our understanding of how India really votes. Perhaps their narratives confirm our own biases and play to our own desire to understand the voter as an 'aspirational' creature. The more complicated truth is harder to fashion into six-word headlines, and is messier, a bit more unexpected and a bit less saccharine—much like Indian democracy.

But this is a worthy endeavour. Indian voters are inspiring in their idealism. Indian politicians are moving in the odds they have overcome and the changes that their pioneering paths have produced in broader society. The way a voter is able to engage with the world of ideas, with real tangible benefit and change, with self-respect, with an entitlement to be heard is transformational—few other interactions with the Indian state offer her that true egalitarianism, that power. It could be that even the best data is never able to capture this. But we needn't let our notions about the universe of democracy be defined by the much smaller world of numbers.

IV

EAT, PRAY, ENJOY, LOVE, MARRY— HOW INDIA LIVES LIFE

In many ways, young Indians live their lives much like their grandparents. But rebellion is coming in, at the margins.

When twenty-two-year-old Nitin Kamble* gets on an overnight bus twice a month from Mumbai, where he works, to a village* in Satara district where his family lives, he imagines himself packing two bags: one to take on the trip, and the other filled with all the parts of himself he cannot take along, stowed under the bed in his shared one-room tenement. He cannot tell his family that he eats chicken now and drinks an occasional beer with his friends in the motorbike repair shop where he works—that goes in the second bag. He still wears a religious thread around his wrist and occasionally ducks into a temple—that can go in the first bag. He will have to stay off the phone with his girlfriend Seema, who is of Kannadiga origin and of another caste—that will definitely have to go in the second bag. Bags packed, Nitin heads home to confront the multiple realities of life as it is in modern India.

Data answers some of the biggest questions about India—how Indians make and spend their money, what work they do, how they vote, what kills them. But numbers can also fill in the minutiae of people's lives and draw a picture of what they do when they're just living it. They don't always align with easy binaries—Left/Right, liberal/conservative—and change emerges almost unnoticed, at the margins.

Eat

For one, numbers can tell us what Indians eat. Cereals—rice in the south and wheat in the north—still form the major part of most Indians' diet. Every rural Indian typically consumes 6 kg of rice and 4.2 kg of wheat in a month, and every urban Indian consumes 4.5 kg of rice and 4 kg of wheat.[1] The north-and-south difference is stark—the average rural Bihari consumes over ten times as much wheat in a month as the average rural Tamil person.

India's favourite vegetables are the staples: onion, potato, green chilli and tomato are the most commonly consumed vegetables, followed by leafy greens and brinjal. In the cities, people eat more carrot, lemon, cauliflower, cabbage, tomato, ladies' finger and beans, while in villages, cheap, locally grown potato, onion, gourd or pumpkin and brinjal are more likely to be on the menu. The poorer eastern states of Bihar, West Bengal and Jharkhand eat the most potatoes and rural areas much more so than urban areas; when money is tight, the focus shifts to high-energy starchy tubers and vegetable diversity suffers.

Bananas, apples and mangoes are the most commonly eaten Indian fruit; of the Rs 90 spent per month on fruits and nuts by the average urban Indian, more than half is spent on apples, bananas, coconuts and mangoes. The average Malayali eats the most fruit, consuming ten bananas and five coconuts every month per capita.

The average Indian gets her protein from a range of plant and animal sources. Tur, followed by moong and masur are the most widely consumed dals. In the rural north, mustard oil dominates, while refined oil dominates most of the rest of the country's kitchens.

There is enormous geographic disparity in milk consumption, with people in Punjab and Haryana consuming over twice the national average, and more than double the quantity than people in otherwise rich states like Tamil Nadu, Kerala, Delhi and Goa. Clearly, drinking milk is not a question of affordability alone. A combination of cultural, environmental and economic factors determines what's on the table in most households, and national data cannot do justice to the vast variety of food on Indian tables.

Thirty-eight-year-old Lakhidevi Munda lives with her three children and mother-in-law in Jariya, a tribal village of 400 families, in Khunti district in Jharkhand. In the morning, the two women drink tea without milk. Lunch is eaten in the late morning and is usually watery rice with sun-dried leafy greens—katai saag or leaves of the beng or koinaar plant that were foraged in their season. On the side, Lakhidevi might cook a tuber or a gourd if she has been able to buy one from the weekly market, and the children will eat that with their rice. The kids would like chicken every day, she says, but they only get to eat it when there's a celebration in the village. Dinner is similar, but there's rarely a vegetable, and usually a dal instead. The children haven't had milk since they stopped breastfeeding.

Rinku Malan's day begins at 5 a.m. with starting up the wood-fired stove in her two-room house in Faridabad, a region in Haryana that abuts Delhi. The twenty-nine-year-old has a gas connection but currently finds LPG too expensive to use. She makes a stack of rotis to pack for her painter husband and his whitewasher brother's dabbas. Today, she makes chholiya—black-eyed beans—in a watery onion-based gravy to go with the rotis. Other days, it's potatoes in a tomato-onion gravy, or chana in an onion gravy. On weeks when money is tight, she only packs chopped onions spiced with chilli powder as the side. Before the two men leave for work, she gives them tea with rusk biscuits. At work, the men will usually buy two more cups of tea on their breaks. By the time they return home, dinner will be ready. It will be chapatis or rice with a gravy—whether the gravy has any vegetables in it usually depends on how work has been that week. Once in a while there is chicken, occasionally there is curd.

Divya Raju's day begins at 7 a.m. when she boils milk to add to the tea for herself and her husband, and for her daughter and spaniel to drink. Lunch will be a rice dish with a poriyal and a salad, made before 8 a.m. and packed into three lunch boxes, along with fruit for snacks. Then the three sit down to breakfast—usually toast with jam, or cornflakes and milk, or daliya porridge. Divya's mother will pick her granddaughter up from school at 3 p.m. with a packaged snack for the car ride back—biscuits or chips. Dinner will be relatively quick after Divya returns from her office in Chennai's IT zone, Tidel Park: stir fried noodles, dosas or chapatis with a leftover gravy. Twice a week they order in, either pizzas or Chinese food. The family does not eat meat.

*

Despite its frequent portrayal as a vegetarian country, India is actually no more than one-quarter to one-third vegetarian.[2] These estimates are likely to be overestimates to the extent that some households may be reluctant to report meat-eating to a surveyor, especially those from castes or groups that may feel the pressure to mask meat-eating. The geographic divide in food habits is stark. States in the west and north have relatively higher incidence of vegetarianism, while states in the east and south have relatively lower incidence. In six Northeastern states, less than 2 per cent of the population is vegetarian, and in a further three states—Assam and West Bengal in the east and Kerala in the south—less than 5 per cent of the population is vegetarian. In contrast, over 75 per cent of the population in the northern states of Haryana, Rajasthan and Punjab is vegetarian. (Fig. 4.1)

Apart from the Jain and Sikh religious minorities, other religious groups are majority meat-eaters; more than half of Hindus, and the vast majority of Muslims and Christians are non-vegetarians. Vegetarianism is more strongly associated with being upper caste and upper class in India: 79 per cent of people from the SCs and 82 per cent of those from the STs eat meat, as compared to 68 per cent among OBCs and 65 per cent—the lowest among all caste groups—among the upper castes. Just 15 per cent of the poorest fifth of Indians are vegetarian, compared to 35 per cent of the richest Indians who do not eat meat.[3]

Meat-eating in India has been growing over time.[4] In the early 2000s, over 58 per cent of Indians reported that they ate eggs, fish and meat. Less than ten years later, the proportion had already grown by five percentage points. The meat most commonly eaten in urban India is chicken, while in rural India

Figure 4.1: Vegetarianism is largely confined to a handful of states

Percentage of the population who eat fish, chicken or meat

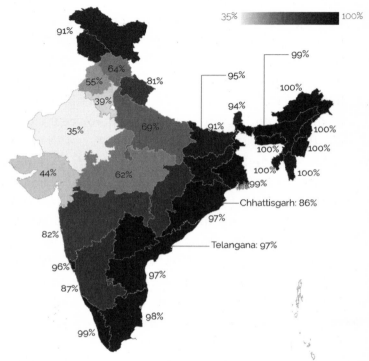

Note: Refers to those who eat one or more of chicken, fish or other meat ofter occasionally or even rarely
Source: National Family Health Survey (NFHS-4), 2015-16: India. International Institute for Population Science (IIPS) and ICF, 2017

Percentage of non-vegetarians among:

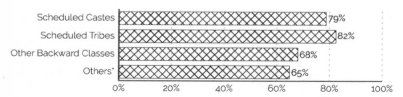

Note: State-wise data is for men and caste-wise data is for women with children
Non-vegetarian includes people who eat fish, chicken or other meats regularly or occasionally
Source: Derek D. Headey and Giordano Palloni, 'Stunting and Wasting Among Indian Preschoolers have Moderate but Significant Associations with the Vegetarian Status of their Mothers', *The Journal of Nutrition*, vol. 150, no. 6 (2020).
Based on NFHS 2015-16

it is fish. Kerala eats the most fish, Jammu and Kashmir the most mutton, and Andhra Pradesh the most chicken.

Yet, the Hindu Right continues to peddle the upper-caste Hindu narrative that India is a vegetarian country—when E. Sreedharan, the 'Metro Man' who contested the 2021 Kerala state elections on a BJP ticket, said in an interview that he didn't 'even eat eggs' and wouldn't like it if others ate meat, he was effectively dismissing the food preferences of 98 per cent of the state.[5]

The Left has some blind spots on dietary data too. For the last five years or so, there has been a push for state governments to include eggs in the mid-day meal scheme. States like Tamil Nadu and Kerala give children eggs a few days a week, and some Left-leaning economists and food security activists have been advocating for other states—particularly in northern and central India—to include eggs in their state-level diet plans. In Madhya Pradesh, this became an overt political fight: in 2019, the Congress-led state government announced it would distribute eggs in anganwadis and schools, and then in 2020 the new BJP government announced that it would not.

At such times, one map made by leftist economists and activists is frequently shared online. It maps states that provide eggs against those that have voted strongly for the BJP, and there is a neat overlap. But this is a profound misunderstanding. The correlation here is not only between being a BJP-ruled state and refusing to provide eggs, it is also between being a state that is more vegetarian and being a BJP-supporting state—those are the maps that overlap neatly. In the egg battleground state of Madhya Pradesh, for instance, over half the women surveyed reported that they never ate eggs, while in Tamil Nadu, which does provide eggs, just 6 per cent of women reported that they never ate eggs. It isn't a question of affordability alone, either. Punjab is one of India's richest states, but just one in three women reported ever eating eggs, and the state government does not provide eggs in the mid-day meal, despite being headed by the Congress. The Left is correct in its assessment that when the choice to eat eggs is not provided, this creeping Brahminism excludes those belonging to religious and caste minorities. But it is dishonest to present vegetarian preferences as purely BJP-imposed either.

It is entirely likely, though, that responses about meat-eating suffer from social acceptability bias. In an ethnographic study of a village in Tamil Nadu, the researcher Christina Sathyamala found that along with cost and availability, the association with lower-caste status drove down the consumption and/or reporting of some flesh foods, beef in particular.[6] In recent years, Hindu right-wing groups have responded with violence to meat-eating, attacking and even killing Muslim men associated with the cattle trade, and on occasion, violently attacking Muslim men who they believed had beef in their possession. In other places, the violence has taken on a faux-legal appearance: in Gurgaon now, meat cannot be sold on Tuesdays, when some Hindus undertake vegetarian fasts, and since 2014, some states have outlawed the consumption of beef.

'Beef is typically called peddakura, which translates to big meat, to avoid spelling out the name of the meat or the animal. Growing up, I was asked to quietly celebrate in my house since I lived in an urban town with upper-caste neighbours. The education my parents received could bring us out of food scarcity but not out of fear due to the humiliation and stigma attached to us. Some relatives, who've moved out of our gudem, have even given up eating beef despite their fondness for it,' the Dalit journalist Jahnavi Uppuleti writes of living in Telangana.[7]

'Growing up, many Sundays involved my mother and grandmother making a big Sunday spread using offal or blood, and my brother and I relished it,' says Arya Varshini, a native of Telangana whose family is Madiga, an SC. 'But once we were a little older, we quickly picked up from our classmates that it was something to be ashamed of. There was no question of taking meat to school. My mother has now turned vegetarian and my grandmother only cooks meat for us when we go back for the holidays. It's only now, living by myself with roommates, that I feel confident of cooking beef again,' says the young IT professional who lives in Chennai. If a surveyor came to her house, says Arya, there is no way her mother or grandmother would admit to eating meat.

*

Data food fights are not uncommon in India.

Through the 1980s and 1990s, many economists in India struggled with the question of what precisely was going on with food intake in India. In an influential 2008 paper published in the *Economic and Political Weekly* journal, Nobel Laureate Angus Deaton and India's leading development economist Jean Dreze pointed out that per capita calorie consumption was falling, even while Indians were getting richer, with reduced physical activity levels being one possible explanation for the decline.[8] The article set off a firestorm of criticism among many Left-leaning economists; the notion that Indians would consume more calories if only they had more money had become so ingrained that challenges to the dominant narrative—perhaps more money did not necessarily mean people ate more nutritious food? Perhaps calories alone could not guarantee better health?—were strongly pushed back against.[9]

In 2011-12, the most recent year for which calorific-intake data is available, the nutritional intake recovered slightly, potentially reversing the trend of the previous few decades. Over time, the share of calorific intake from cereals has dropped. However, protein intake has also fallen on average, although there are significant differences among the rich and the poor on this.

As Indians get richer, they consume more fruits and vegetables, but they also begin to consume far more dairy, fat and sugar than is recommended. Meanwhile, the consumption of pulses does not rise substantially among the richest 5 per cent of people, and the consumption of meat still lags behind the recommended average—even the richest Indians eat less protein than recommended. Instead, the consumption of junk food skyrockets with rising incomes. While roughly 20 per cent of rural Indians and 23 per cent of urban Indians are still undernourished, around 18 per cent are at what the government politely calls the 'over-nourished end'.[10]

Eating 'right' is expensive. Nearly 40 per cent of Indians would not be able to afford what is described as a healthy diet.[11] Consuming the recommended share of fruits and vegetables is particularly expensive and it would take up a third of the total cost of food in South Asia; unsurprisingly, fewer than 80 per cent of rural households report having eaten any fruit at all over the preceding month. Meat is expensive too. Despite making up just 6 per cent of the daily recommended calorific intake, the recommended quantity would amount to nearly 20 per cent of the entire food cost of a healthy diet in South Asia. For India in particular, poultry, eggs and fish, fruits and legumes and nuts would make a healthy diet expensive. The poorest in India already spend upwards of six out of every ten rupees on food, leaving little space to raise their expenditure on food, particularly on expensive fruits, vegetables, legumes, nuts and meats.

Indians have been consuming less paan and tobacco over time (although those who do smoke are more likely to be bidi-smokers than cigarette-smokers), but they're drinking more alcohol. In rural areas, country liquor is India's preferred tipple, while in urban areas, it is foreign or refined liquor or wine.[12] Income starkly affects alcohol consumption; in rural areas, toddy and country liquor consumption rises with class and falls only in the richest 5 per cent, while beer and refined liquor rises with class. For urban areas, country liquor consumption falls as people get richer, while beer and refined liquor consumption rises exponentially.

Pray

This is undoubtedly still a religious country. With 84 per cent of Indians saying that religion is very important in their lives, India is far more religious than Western Europe, Central and Eastern Europe, Israel, Latin America and the United States. Only in sub-Saharan Africa and some regions with large Muslim populations do similar or higher shares of the public say religion is very important to them. Just 3 per cent of Indian adults say religion is 'not too' or 'not at all' important in their lives.[13]

Nearly all Indians say they believe in God (97 per

cent); the main exception is Buddhists, one-third of whom say they do not believe in God. Unlike the experience of Western European countries where belief in God subsided with economic advancement after the Second World War, there has been little change in the small share of atheists in India. Across the country, there is little difference in personal religious observance between urban and rural residents or between those who are college educated versus those who are not. Overwhelming shares among all these groups say that religion is very important in their lives, that they pray regularly, that they believe in God and are raising their children with religion.[14]

Sixty per cent of people say that they pray every day, and half go to a temple, mosque or other house of worship every week. Muslims are more likely to pray daily or visit a mosque daily than Hindus, driven predominantly by Muslim men— over 40 per cent of Muslim women never visit mosques. Across religious groups, women are more likely than men to pray daily, and more likely to pray at home than go to houses of worship. Older people are more likely to pray regularly than younger people, but people of different education levels pray daily at similar rates.[15]

Dalits are less likely to regularly visit temples compared to other caste groups. Middle- and upper-class respondents were slightly more likely to report visiting temples. Education levels do not seem to influence religious practice, the data suggests.

Young people are quite religious too. About 78 per cent of respondents in a youth survey reported praying quite often, 68 per cent said they went to a religious place of worship frequently, 49 per cent reported watching religious shows on television quite often, and 46 per cent often engaged in activities such as singing religious songs, bhajans or taking part in satsangs. Another 46 per cent reported keeping fasts either regularly or sometimes and, finally, 39 per cent said that they read a religious book quite often.[16]

Ashmita Chauhan met her now husband Yogesh at a satsang in Indore, Madhya Pradesh, when she was twenty-three. 'After college, I got a job in a call centre. I felt that all the young people around me had money and were getting Westernised. I started going to the satsang to feel peace and stay true to my values. I'm glad I met someone who feels the same way about our culture,' she says. The fact that he was religious and of the same caste allowed her parents to accept a 'love marriage', she said. For their honeymoon, the couple went to Delhi and on the top of their list of places to visit was the Akshardham temple.

Could the hold of religion loosen over time as it has in much of the rest of the world? It's unclear yet, but there are signs: nearly nine in ten Indian adults say religion was very important to their family when they were growing up (88 per cent), while a slightly lower share say religion is very important to them now (84 per cent). The southern states (Andhra Pradesh, Karnataka, Kerala, Puducherry, Tamil Nadu and Telangana) show the biggest downward trend in the perceived importance of religion over respondents' lifetimes: 76 per cent of Indians who live in the south say religion was very important to their family growing up, compared with 69 per cent who say religion is personally very important to them now.[17]

The practice of religion in India is a fascinating mix of strictly demarcated and hybrid practices. Roughly eight in ten Indian adults have an altar, shrine or religious symbol in their home for worship. A majority of Hindus (72 per cent) and Jains (62 per cent) have a tulsi plant at home. Roughly half of Indian adults say they watch religious programs or TV serials at least weekly (but more watch other TV serials or the news).[18] Around one-fourth of Hindu respondents regularly participated in kathas (religious story-telling and talks) and bhajans (religious songs and hymns performed in a group). Public events like processions and religious gatherings are also important for religious practice in India.[19]

Most Hindus say they have made a religious pilgrimage, but the majority of Muslims say they have not made a pilgrimage. Older adults are more likely than younger people to have made a pilgrimage, and people in northern and central India are most likely to have gone on a pilgrimage. Nearly two-thirds of Hindus say they have received purification by taking a dip in a holy body of water, such as the Ganga.[20] Roughly half of Hindus said in a 2019 survey that they had a picture or an idol of a godman at home. A third said that they were likely to consult a godman if they, or someone in their immediate family, were in distress. Nearly a fifth had a picture at home and were likely to consult a godman—they could be considered as followers of godmen. More than a fourth (28 per cent) of respondents said that they had a great deal of trust in godmen from their own religion. Reverence for godmen seems to be higher in rural areas—20 per cent of rural respondents and 13 per cent of urban respondents were active followers of godmen. Like other religious practices, following godmen transcends class, but the poorest were slightly more likely to be followers (22 per cent). In terms of caste too, the patterns are similar to other religious practices. Dalits are slightly less likely to follow godmen actively. Only 15 per cent Dalits are active followers of godmen as compared to 20 per cent among the upper castes.[21]

A number of practices cross religious lines into the broad sphere of 'cultural beliefs'. Eight per cent of Muslims say they have prayed at a Hindu temple and 6 per cent of Hindus have prayed in a mosque. Sikh gurdwaras and Sufi shrines in particular attract followers of various faiths. Seventeen per cent of Hindus say that they have celebrated Christmas and an even greater share of Muslims have celebrated Diwali.[22]

D. Suguna is a schoolteacher in Madurai, Tamil Nadu. Her daily go-to God is Pillaiyar (known as Ganesh or Ganpati in other parts of the country), whose statue she prays before every morning in a small cubby in her kitchen. At times of great stress, the one she thinks of is Shirdi Sai Baba—her 2005 trip with her schoolteacher friends to visit the temple was one of the highlights of her life. Her husband's family believes in a godman based in Rameswaram who they must visit once a year. Her daughter Vani follows all of her mother's practices, but in her heart, she says, is Jesus. Suguna is not unhappy: 'Vani's wedding will be in a temple only. I know she asks for Jesus's blessings for her college exams. I don't mind—as long as someone makes her pass!'

Enjoy

Caste, class, gender and geographic location determine not just what Indians eat, but also how they spend the hours in a day—how much paid work they can do, how much unpaid work they must do, and how much leisure time they have. The average Indian spends ten minutes each day in 'private prayer', nineteen minutes playing a game or doing a 'pastime activity', sixty-five minutes watching TV, and three minutes reading a book. They get over eight hours of sleep every night.

Women spend 84 per cent of their working hours on unpaid activities, while men spend 80 per cent of their working hours on paid work. Just 6 per cent of men participate in cooking in any manner, and just 8 per cent do any house cleaning.

Upper-caste men and women—who are among India's richest—have the most time for self-care and maintenance activities, including sleep, while SC and ST men and women have the least time among social groups. The rich and upper castes spend the most time on religious practice, have the most time to watch television and use other media, and have the most leisure time. 'Almost 40 per cent of SCs work in wage labour, and much of this is casual labour,' said the economist Sukhadeo Thorat, professor emeritus at the Centre for the Study of Regional Development at Delhi's Jawaharlal Nehru University. 'What this means is that however much time you have, you must work! Of course there is no time for leisure. The upper-caste men who employ SC people as wage labour in their farms and enterprises will naturally have time freed up for leisure.'

Leisure can mean different things to different sets of Indians.

A survey of north Indian teenagers found that riding motorbikes, chatting on the mobile phone, using the internet, listening to popular music and visiting religious places were the most popular leisure activities, but these were deeply gendered; girls were less likely to engage in sports but more likely to be involved in singing religious songs or chants. The use of the internet was substantially different between urban and rural settings.[23]

A 2016 national youth survey found that 50 per cent of the young respondents had never used any social media—75 per cent reported having never used Twitter, 62 per cent had never used YouTube, 54 per cent had never used WhatsApp and 51 per cent had never been on Facebook. Just 8 per cent reported high usage of these platforms. In terms of daily usage, WhatsApp was used the most (30 per cent), followed by Facebook (25 per cent), YouTube (11 per cent) and Twitter (7 per cent). There was a big increase in phone ownership compared to the previous decade, but though 81 per cent of young people owned a mobile phone, fewer than half of them had a smartphone. While 24 per cent had access to a laptop, and the number had gone up three-fold, just a third of them had access to the internet. Overall, the survey found that 64 per cent of the youth had no immediate access to the internet whatsoever.[24]

Leeai Konyak, twenty-four, says that watching K-pop videos on YouTube and Korean dramas downloaded on her phone is her favourite leisure activity. She also sews clothes for herself and participates in activities at her church in Kohima, Nagaland. When her mother, Grace, has free time, she talks on the phone to her sister in Mon or to her niece in Bengaluru. She sews clothes to give to the church, looks up recipes on YouTube and sometimes walks for exercise. Leeai's eighteen-year-old brother Nelson plays soccer, watches movies on his phone and joins his friends at a tea shop in the evenings. At mealtimes, however, phones are not allowed. 'We chat together while cooking or cleaning up after dinner and preparing for the next day—that you could say is our family leisure time,' says Grace.

When forty-two-year-old Bunty Ahirwar is finally done

for the day, all she wants is for the television to drown out the sound of talking. 'We are five people in two rooms, and the neighbourhood is crowded too. All day, I work in people's houses, and when I come home, I have to cook, clean and then see what my children need. If I get any free time, I would like to watch a TV serial,' she says. But by the time Bunty is ready to lie down near the TV in their house along the railway tracks near Jangpura in south Delhi, her husband has usually commandeered the TV remote. 'Some movie is usually on. I fall asleep before I can understand what the plot is,' she says with a laugh. Once in a while, Bunty takes a sick day from work to go visit her sister—'For us women, talking to someone is the best leisure, because all week, no one listens to us.'

India's idea of holidaying too is some way from pure leisure. The average Indian household takes four overnight trips a year. Indians are social creatures, who travel largely to see family and friends (75 per cent). The next biggest category for trips in urban India is religious visits or pilgrimages. For rural India, the category is rather grim—medical visits form the bulk, demonstrating just how inadequate rural health infrastructure is. Travel for leisure is still very unusual, with about 3 per cent of the population partaking in it.

Vasant Patil is a fertiliser supplier in Nasik, Maharashtra. Patil and his wife, Smita, and two teenaged children took four holidays in 2019—twice to Panvel for family weddings, once to Shirdi to ask for blessings before his daughter's class ten exams, and once to his native village, Wadgaon, for the annual festival associated with his ancestral temple. 'When we go for weddings, the children get to eat out and see local sights— that's a holiday for us,' he said. Patil has left Maharashtra only once, when he visited the neighbouring state of Gujarat to attempt a business deal, and has never taken a flight. If money was no impediment where would they want to travel to? Smita would like to go to Tirupati to visit the temple, the children would like to go to Mumbai to the beach, and Patil would like to go to Punjab, where he believes the Bhakra Nangal Dam is.

Love

From watching Indian movies, it would seem as if no issue preoccupies young Indians more than romantic love. While that might well be true, the vast majority of Indians still have arranged marriages. As of January 2018, 93 per cent of married Indians said that theirs was an arranged marriage.[25] Just 3 per cent had a 'love marriage' and another 2 per cent described theirs as a 'love-cum-arranged marriage', which usually indicates that the relationship was set up by the families, and then the couple fell in love and agreed to get married. There has been only very slight change over time—94 per cent of octogenarians had an arranged marriage, and the figure remains over 90 per cent for young couples in their twenties.

Manisha Mondal always thought she would have a love marriage. 'I was used to fighting with my parents. I fought to study commerce instead of arts, I fought to go to a college that was a little far away from home. I thought, okay, love marriage will be the next thing to fight about.' Manisha, an office assistant in Bhilai, laughs as she recollects.

In her first year of college, there was a mixer for boys and girls and Manisha could picture it. She would notice a handsome senior, he would notice her, they would lock eyes, and that would be that. But when a few boys approached her to talk, senior female students took her to the bathroom for a talking to. If she spoke to boys, her reputation would get ruined and her parents would take her out of college—news spreads fast in Bhilai. To keep an eye on her, her older brother would drive past her college a few times a day to make sure he never caught sight of her talking to a boy. College was important to Manisha; she'd rather she got to continue to study and then work than take a chance on love. By her last year in college, her wedding had been fixed to the son of her father's friend from the same community. 'I see my parents. They have never had a fight. So I think it will work for me too,' the twenty-four-year-old said, showing me her crossed fingers over a WhatsApp call.

Richer and better educated people are slightly more likely to have love marriages. Christians and Muslims are slightly more likely to have love marriages than Hindus, but among Hindu caste groups there is little variation. Assam, Kerala, Goa, and Jammu and Kashmir—states with relatively high non-Hindu populations—see more love marriages than other states.

Marrying within your caste remains an important feature of marriage in India. Fewer than 10 per cent of urban Indians said in a 2014 survey that anyone in their family had married outside their caste and not many more outside their sub-caste (jati). Inter-caste marriage is practised slightly more among the poor than among the rich.[26] Another survey, in 2011-12, found that just 5 per cent of urban respondents had had an inter-caste marriage, and that the number had changed little since the previous round seven years prior to it.[27] Inter-religious marriage was even rarer; just 5 per cent of urban respondents in the 2014 survey said that anyone in their family had married someone outside their religion.[28]

What precisely is an inter-caste marriage can be

contentious. The 2011-12 IHDS took the approach that what female respondents interpreted as a 'different caste' is likely to have been subjective, but ultimately closer to the lived reality of an inter-caste marriage. 'Questions on caste are some of the most complex questions Indian surveys can ask. The same person will say "I am Baniya" today and say "I am Modh Banik" tomorrow, and both would be correct,' Sonalde Desai, a demographer who is a professor at NCAER and professor of sociology at the University of Maryland, and led the IHDS, told me. 'So we took a simple approach and asked women whether their natal family belongs to the same caste as their husband's family, allowing us to bypass the complex issue of defining what caste means and get subjective perceptions from our respondents.'

For richer urban Indians, these numbers may seem unlikely, given that younger people often profess their willingness to marry outside their caste. But there is likely a large gap between stated and revealed preferences. In 2015, researchers contacted 1,000 prospective brides through matrimonial websites and found that while half of them expressed an interest in potential partners belonging to caste groups other than their own, nearly all expressed an interest in men of their own caste. The SC man was least likely to be contacted, despite all other variables—educational qualifications, salary and even skin colour—being nearly the same.[29]

While 55 per cent of young people professed an acceptance of inter-caste marriage in 2016, the share of married young respondents who said their spouse was not from their caste was just 4 per cent. Among the 6 per cent of young people who said they had a love marriage, one-third were inter-caste. On the other hand, 97 per cent of arranged marriages were found to be within caste.[30] (Fig. 4.2)

Figure 4.2: Indians get married the way their grandparents did

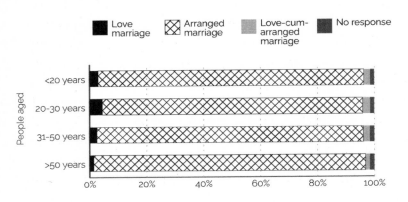

Source: Lok Foundation-Oxford University survey by the Centre for the Monitoring of the Indian Economy. 2017

Percent marrying cousins/relatives

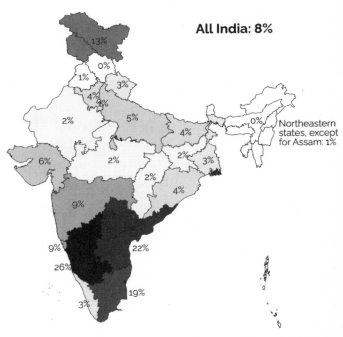

Source: National Council for Applied Economic Research and University of Maryland, 'India Human Development Survey' Round 2, 2011-12

Percentage of married Indian adults whose spouse shares their religion

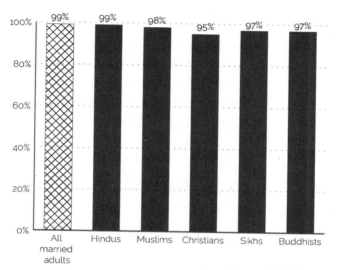

Source: *Religion in India: Tolerance and Segregation*. Pew Research Centre, 29 June 2021

Rates of inter-caste marriage among:

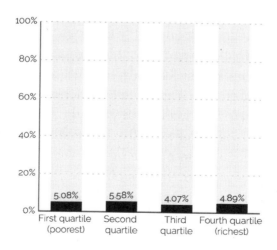

Source: National Council for Applied Economic Research and University of Maryland. 'India Human Development Survey' Round 2. 2011-12

Against this conservative backdrop, any act of personal choice then becomes one of rebellion, and fraught with danger. Until early 2021, India's Special Marriage Act, under which inter-religious marriages can be solemnised, was interpreted to require that the couple publicise their intended wedding thirty days before the date. This offered religious fundamentalists an easy route to browbeat and even physically force inter-religious couples apart. A recent high court ruling in Uttar Pradesh deemed the thirty-day notice unnecessary,[31] but states like Uttar Pradesh, which has added further legal requirements, scrutiny and potential prison sentences for inter-religious marriages, are unlikely to let this pass on the ground.

Shoaib and Monica (they did not want their last names used for fear of being identified) met at a coaching class in Kota, Rajasthan. For five years, the relationship continued, nourished by long late-night phone calls. After Shoaib had finished a year of work and had enough saved up to rent a small house, he told Monica it was time. 'My parents and two brothers took it so calmly that I immediately knew they already suspected this. They told me not to go to work the next day so that they could call relatives over,' Monica said. What followed was pure terror—Monica's relatives landed up the next day and the men sat together plotting Shoaib's murder while the women commiserated with her mother for the foolhardiness of allowing her daughter to study. When everyone had gone home and her family had gone to sleep without giving her dinner, Monica escaped. The couple now lives in Mumbai. 'I got many calls from the police saying I should return or my uncles will come and kill us both. Eventually they stopped. My older sister told me that my mother decided that the family should say I am working in Mumbai, otherwise a scandal would have damaged her marriage prospects,' Monica said. In Mumbai, they were advised to register their marriage under the Special Marriage Act. Too frightened to have their names and photographs displayed in court, the couple decided not to register the marriage at all.

Marriage and sex are synchronous for the most part. There would appear to be little premarital sex in India; just 3 per cent of unmarried women and 11 per cent of unmarried men between the ages of fifteen and twenty-four have had sex, going by what they told surveyors.[32] Part of the explanation could certainly be the stigma of admitting to sexual relationships to an unknown surveyor, but in part it could also be the firm grip of the family—65 per cent of fifteen to thirty-four-year-olds live with their parents and another 31 per cent live with their spouses. The common perception of millennials' lives may be of those who share an apartment or live as paying guests, but just 4 per cent live either with a friend, in a hostel, or alone.[33]

Since marriage is very closely associated with the first experience of sexual intercourse, as people get married later, the age at which Indians first have sex has, counter-intuitively, also been rising rather than falling. Of the seventy-two countries for which there is comparable data, Indian men have their first experience of sexual intercourse the latest, at age 24.3. The median Indian woman, on the other hand, has her first experience of sex at age nineteen.[34]

Marry

Marriage is nearly universal in India. By the age of forty-five–forty-nine, only 1 per cent of women and 2 per cent of men have never been married, but both urban and rural women have been getting married later than before.

Consanguineous marriages, or the practice of marrying a cousin or relative—more prevalent in the south than the north—is becoming less common, but over 20 per cent in Andhra Pradesh and Karnataka still marry relatives.[35] In Tamil Nadu, the word 'maama', meaning maternal uncle, is still sometimes used by women to refer to their husbands.

Since 1978, the legal age at which Indians can get married has been eighteen for women and twenty-one for men. The age for women is in line with global norms, but just one in five countries globally have a different age requirement for men. A quarter of newly married young women got married before the legal age, and more than 10 per cent of women had a child while still a minor. But overall, both men and women have been getting married later and later. Nearly half of married women now in their forties were married by the time they were eighteen, but among women currently in their early twenties, that proportion is down to just 25 per cent. The share of men married before they were twenty-one is even lower now.

Since the 1970s, women were more likely to marry someone older than them than someone of the same age or younger. It is only in the 2000s that this equation flipped. Indian women are now more likely to marry someone around the same age as them, than someone older.[36] The average age gap between husband and wife has changed little over the last decade and remains around five years. However, among newly married women in their twenties, this age gap has shrunk, indicating that the age gap over the next decade might be much narrower.

The government has been contemplating raising the legal marriageable age for women to twenty-one, which would make it one of the highest in the world, with the stated aim of keeping girls in school and delaying childbirth.[37] For both marriage and childbirth, however, the evidence shows that urban women, and those who are richer and better educated get married later. The poorest 40 per cent of women are the ones who are married before the age of eighteen, as are those with no schooling or those with only a basic primary education, and those from the poor states of West Bengal, Bihar and Jharkhand.[38] The presence of women in local government also decreases the likelihood of child marriage[39] and states with greater enforcement capacity are those with fewer child marriages.[40]

As for encouraging girls to stay in school longer, girls do report marriage being one of the reasons for dropping out. However, data shows that, financial constraints and the need to look after domestic work are greater considerations for dropping out.[41]

While advertisements for matchmaking websites would like to make it appear that arranged marriages are no longer as rigidly orchestrated as they once were, the data does not bear this out. Forty-one per cent of women had no say in their marriage and just 18 per cent knew their husbands before marriage—a statistic that has not improved. Women's say in marriage rose with their level of education, with income and with level of urbanisation and the southern states did better.[42]

One analysis of matrimonial advertisements in a newspaper in West Bengal found that physical characteristics clearly still play an important role in the marriage market: height was mentioned in the ad by 96 per cent of the women and 90 per cent of the men. A prospective bride's skin tone and beauty were mentioned by groom-wanted ads in 75 and 70 per cent of the cases, respectively.[43]

Above all other attributes, however, is caste. The matrimonial advertisement study found a high preference for caste relative to other attributes. For example, in the bride-wanted ads, the probability of being contacted was the same for a man from the same caste and no education as that for a man from a different caste with a master's degree. Men were willing to sacrifice three shades of skin tone to marry someone within their caste. A woman from a given caste would be as likely to contact a man from her own caste with a given predicted income level than a man from a different caste who was predicted to earn 50 per cent more.[44]

Less than 20 per cent of women knew their husbands before they got married and 40 per cent said that they had no say in their own marriage. Dowry, or bride price, was still rampant, and families paid an average of Rs 30,000 in cash, in addition to 40 per cent giving large gifts like cars and two-wheelers. The practice of giving large items as dowry was most common among upper-caste Hindus and least prevalent among Muslims. Wedding expenses ranged from nearly Rs 1 lakh in the poorest village to Rs 1.7 lakh in small cities, a big jump over the 2004-05 survey. Kerala and Delhi had the most expensive weddings, as did the most educated who also paid the most dowry.

Within marriage, women's autonomy has only been growing slightly. Sixty per cent of women—including 59 per cent of forward-caste Hindus and 83 per cent of Muslim women—practised some form of 'purdah' or 'ghunghat'; this proportion rose to 96 per cent for states like Rajasthan and 91 per cent in Bihar, and was lowest at 6 per cent in Tamil

Nadu. Over half of all women said it was common for women in their community to be beaten if they went out without permission. Eighty-one per cent of women said that they needed permission to go to a health centre and one-third said that they were not permitted to go to a health centre alone. These numbers had not improved since 2004-05.

Less than 20 per cent of women have their names on their house's papers, just half have their names on a bank account, and just 10 per cent could take primary purchase decisions for the house. A study in Andhra Pradesh, Bihar and Madhya Pradesh found that just one in ten women whose parents owned agricultural land inherited any, nearly ten years after the Hindu Succession Act was amended to give sons and daughters equal inheritance rights. The majority of men interviewed for the study said that they were opposed to their sisters or daughters inheriting land.[45]

*

Back among his family in his village in Satara, Nitin wonders sometimes if he will have the strength to mount the multi-front battle that he would need to enter if he decides to marry his girlfriend or, more painfully for him, whether she will ever tell her family that she is seeing a Dalit boy. Living in Mumbai, some of the most painful parts of his family's existence have been erased, but it never all goes away. It would be so much easier to go on as his older brother or father did, without rocking the boat too much. Some days, when he feels especially tired, Nitin suspects he might just do that.

I talked to Nitin about what the data showed and asked him if this made him feel like an exception. He told me I was wrong, but not because he didn't believe the data or because he thought it was fake. 'That's data about marriage, madam,' he said—not about love. 'I think if your data asked people if they have ever fallen in love with someone from another caste or religion, many will say yes. I see that all around me among my friends. But when it comes to getting married, most of us are not yet ready to leave our families. That's why your data looks like that,' he said. As for the rest? 'There is a lot we will not admit to someone doing a survey. But things are changing. At least for some of us,' he said.

V

HOW MUCH MONEY DO INDIANS MAKE?

Data on spending should have been straightforward. But it's become the most polarising fight in Indian statistics.

Of all the narratives that Indians wrap around themselves—whether for disguise or for comfort—none is as dearly held as this one: I am middle class. Before the annual budget, it's appropriated by the media: what about the hard-working, tax-paying middle class, the newspapers ask; will they get some relief? Periodically, it becomes a Twitter trend: '#imsomiddleclass Good Day biscuits were a treat growing up.' At election time, a sense of collective victimhood binds the self-designated middle class: 'Does anyone care about our vote,' they ask plaintively, 'or is it only the freebie-grabbing poor who are vote-banks?'

The truth is that if you're reading this, you're almost certainly not middle class.

All over the world, people who are actually rich tend to self-identify as middle class. India is no exception. Picture

India divided into four groups, where the bottom twenty percentile of households is classified as poor and the top one percentile as rich. The middle-income group ranges from the 21st percentile to the 80th percentile, and the higher middle income group ranges from the 81st to the 99th percentile. A nationally representative household survey conducted in 2014 found that over half the people who are rich self-identify as middle class. Over 40 per cent of the poor also self-identify as middle class.[1]

'I consider myself middle class,' Tanya Ghaiwala, a twenty-two-year-old from Ahmedabad, Gujarat, told me. Here's her thinking: 'I ride a two-wheeler, while the rich kids used to come to even college in a car. I studied to be a chartered accountant and started a job straight after I qualified. I make Rs 18,000 per month and after petrol and little spending money, I give the rest to my father. I carry a dabba to office. I think that's pretty middle class!' She laughs. Her mother, Rina, agrees: 'I am a retired LIC agent. That's a middle-class job. Our first foreign holiday, to Thailand, was after Tanya qualified. We believe in saving, not spending. We are quite modern but also have values. This is what you call a middle-class family.'

But how much money do Indians really make, and who is poor and who is India's real middle class? It seems like an easy question to answer—the poor are at the bottom of the country's income distribution and the middle class is the class in the middle, surely? But in a country that is still as poor as India, deciding who makes how much and what 'class' that places one in is a vexed question.

First, there is the question of what measure of income should be used. Just 4 per cent of Indians currently pay income tax. Just forty lakh people in the entire country report a taxable salary of more than Rs 10 lakh a year.[2] Surely this means the country is rife with tax evaders and household surveys are more reliable?

India does not officially collect data on income: it has tried and failed in the past, India's former chief statistician T.C.A. Anant told me, and the official statistics machinery hasn't quite cracked it yet. 'I belong to a class of economists who believe that what people report as their "income" is akin to an opinion and not something that is easy to pin down,' Anant said. For one, there is the problem of how those working in agriculture, some of whom get paid in grain and many of whom get their payment only at harvest time, can objectively report their income. Then, there is the question of those who work in the informal sector and have irregular wages. Even within the formal sector, says Anant, the legal definition of income and the way people understand it is very different from the economic view of income as all that which gives a person command over purchasing power. Additionally, data collection that relies on a single calendar year or one agricultural year may not coincide with the income cycle; experts argue that in low-income years, households can sell some assets, consume savings or borrow to tide themselves over, while in high-income years, they tend to save more. In addition, there is likely to be under-disclosure at the upper end of the spectrum.

One major (private) national survey—the IHDS conducted by the National Council for Applied Economic Research and the University of Maryland—collects both income and consumption data. It shows that in urban areas, income exceeds expenditure, as you'd expect; but in rural areas, both mean and median expenditures exceed income. That suggests greater measurement errors in rural areas, or greater variability in incomes from year to year, and could partly explain why the official statistical system isn't yet keen to collect income data.

So the measure that India's official statistics, and many global estimates including those of the World Bank, use to study indices like poverty and class is based on consumption rather than income.

The World Bank uses national household consumption-based estimates from a range of countries—the PovcalNet database—and makes them globally comparable using purchasing power parity (PPP) estimates. Using the same PovcalNet estimates but updating for GDP growth until 2020, the Pew Research Center found that a little under 5 per cent of India lives on less than $2 (at PPP) per day ('the poor'), another 87 per cent live on between $2 and $10 per day ('the lower-middle class'), another 7 per cent live on between $10 and $20 a day ('the middle class'), 2 per cent live on $20–50 per day ('the upper-middle class'), and just three million people or 0.2 per cent of the country live on more than $50 per day ('the rich'). (At 2011 prices, one dollar at PPP worked out to roughly Rs 15.)

India's most recent official statistics on consumption expenditure come from the National Statistical Office (NSO), through a household survey that is designed to be nationally representative and asks people every detail of what they spend their money on. It shows that the average Indian spends a little under Rs 2,500 on average every month. Anyone in urban India who spends more than Rs 8,500 would be in the top 5 per cent of the country.[3] And these figures are from before the 2020-21 pandemic.

The numbers seem so low as to be impossible. But when you look around you and break it down, you realise they're not inaccurate.

Thayyal Nayagi's Family Budget

Thayyal Nayagi is a forty-two-year-old woman who lives in the north Chennai suburb of Kasimedu. She works as a cook and housecleaner in south Chennai. Between all her jobs, she makes Rs 19,000 per month. So if you talked to her, you'd think—how can the richest 5 per cent of urban Indians be living on Rs 8,500 per month when a cook makes Rs 19,000? Well, try sitting down for a longer conversation.

Her oldest son, Tamilselvan, makes Rs 15,000 per month from a mechanic's job at Ashok Leyland; he is a contract worker paid by a firm that the company outsources to, and not a full-time employee with any benefits. Her younger son, Sethupathy, is in college, studying law. Her husband died a year ago, but he was an alcoholic who contributed only to consumption expenditure, and not income. Now her elderly mother, Shantha, lives with her to keep house while she is out all day.

So that's Rs 34,000 that comes into the house each month. But by 2020, Thayya (as her family calls her) had racked up a loan of Rs 1.65 lakh, taken from the owner of the local grocery store. Part of it was from supplies bought on credit by her late husband, part of it went towards funeral expenses for him in 2019, and a part towards an unexpected private hospital medical bill from when her son injured his arm. Thayya pays Rs 2,500 in just interest every month; she hasn't yet touched the principal. This does not count towards consumption expenditure. She is also part of an informal self-help group to whom she must pay Rs 3,000 every month. She will receive a lump sum payout of Rs 80,500 from them in November 2021, which she hopes to use towards paying off the informal loan, but other emergency expenses could come up.

That leaves the household with Rs 28,500 coming in each month. But Tamilselvan is repaying a loan too—for a bike that he bought via hire-purchase when he started work because he needed to cut down on commute time. He repays Rs 5,000 per month and has seven more months to go. Which leaves the household with Rs 23,500 coming in each month. Thayya says she has nothing at all left at the end of the month. That makes it a per capita consumption expenditure of Rs 5,875 per month, which would place Thayya in the 80–90th percentile of urban Indians, among the 20 per cent richest urban Indians.

There are substantial inter-state differences, of course. Spending Rs 2,500 would put you in the top 5 per cent of rural Odisha but among the 30–35th poorest of Kerala residents. Spending Rs 1,850 a month would make you among the 5 per cent poorest urban Tamils, but in urban Bihar, you'd be at around the 45th percentile.[4]

This data forms the bedrock of Indian statistics and policy—and by extension public conversation—around poverty, class, mobility and other vital issues. But using consumption as a measure of class has come in for criticism from some economists (see chapter 6). Others have attempted to directly collect information on income by having respondents list all the various avenues through which they make some money and then coming up with an annual estimate. According to the most recent source of income data that India has from the IHDS, the country's average annual household income was Rs 1.13 lakh as of 2011-12. If India were to be divided into five classes of equal sizes, the poorest quintile (20 per cent) would make between Rs 1,000 and Rs 33,000 annually as a household, and the next 20 per cent would make between Rs 33,001 and Rs 55,640 annually. Families that earn between Rs 55,000 and Rs 88,800 annually would be in the third class and fall in the middle of India's income distribution. The richest 20 per cent would make over Rs 1.5 lakh per year. On a per capita basis, only the top 2 per cent of the country would have a household income of over Rs 8 lakh.[5] (Fig. 5.1)

By other measures too, the majority of the country lives on very little. Just over 3 per cent of rural households have a family member who is a graduate. Over half rely on casual manual labour and fewer than 10 per cent have salaried jobs. In over 90 per cent of rural households, the top earning family member makes less than Rs 10,000 per month. Over half have no land and fewer than 5 per cent own agricultural equipment. Less than 4 per cent have access to agricultural credit of over Rs 50,000. Just 20 per cent own a vehicle and just 10 per cent own a refrigerator.[6]

Snapshots do not always capture just how precarious being non-poor in India really is. When India went into lockdown in March 2020 to contain the spread of the SARS-CoV-2 virus, many were stunned by the number of people who began to stream home. In addition to this being a story of migration, it was also a window into just how precarious the lives of the poor—who form a far larger share of the world around us than many of us might have imagined—really are.

In April 2020, Om Prakash, a twenty-year-old construction worker in Uttar Pradesh's Greater Noida, was one among the lakhs who made up the mass exodus from cities to villages when the country went into lockdown. His journey home to

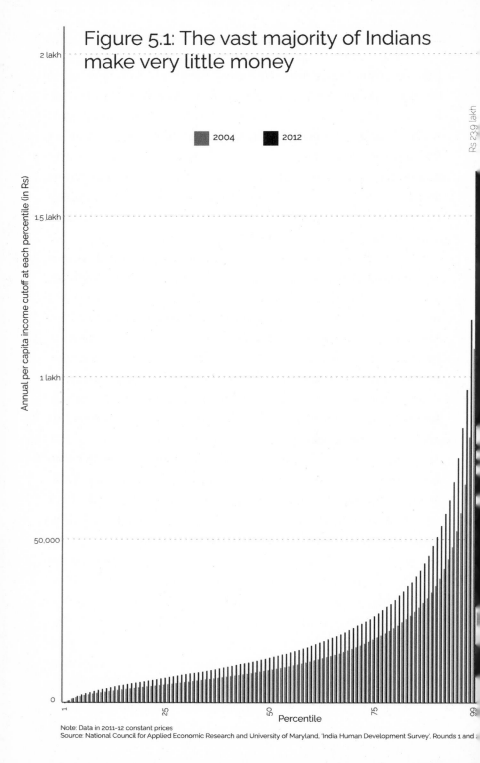

Figure 5.1: The vast majority of Indians make very little money

2 lakh

Annual per capita income cutoff at each percentile (in Rs)

1.5 lakh

■ 2004   ■ 2012

Rs 23.9 lakh

1 lakh

50,000

0

1   25   50   75   99

Percentile

Note: Data in 2011-12 constant prices
Source: National Council for Applied Economic Research and University of Maryland, 'India Human Development Survey'. Rounds 1 and 2

Bihar's Saran district was 1000 km long, and not even a fifth of the way in, he was already completely out of money. Prakash had had to walk 200 km to Agra, where he found a truck driver willing to take him to Lucknow, 350 km ahead. After paying the trucker's charge of Rs 400, he had ten rupees left for the remaining 480 km. There was simply no more money—every day at his job, he had eaten and paid rent from the earnings of the previous day.

Nearly 40 per cent of those who either work in casual labour or salaried jobs get paid at the end of the day;[7] if they can't show up to work, they can't get paid. When the lockdown hit, fewer than one in three households had a stable source of income and was not cash constrained.[8] An estimated 7.5 crore more in India were pushed into poverty once the pandemic hit in 2020, 3.5 crore fell out of lower middle-income status, and another 3.2 crore fell out of middle-income status.[9]

A lot can be explained by what precisely Indians make their money from. Income tax data shows that of the Rs 34 lakh crore individuals reported as income, over Rs 20 lakh crore came from salary income, another Rs 9.3 lakh crore from business income, Rs 67,000 crore from long-term capital gains income, Rs 37,000 crore from property income and Rs 27,000 crore from short-term capital gains. But these numbers can't paint much of a picture. Household-level surveys can do that; they can convey more granular facts about what India makes money from and how much money that is.

A look into the data immediately shows you why it's so hard to estimate people's incomes. More than half of Indian households receive income from multiple sources. In rural areas, one might assume that farmers make their money from farming and labourers from doing labour. But a 'farm household' is rarely just a farm household; more than four out of five farm households also have income from some other source, either wage labour and salaried work (40 per cent) but also from private businesses (17 per cent), particularly among better-off households. Similarly, 'business families' do other things too—71 per cent of households with a private family business also receive other types of income, for instance, from family farms (37 per cent).

Most Indian households, whether rural or urban, receive some farm income. In 2011, 72 per cent of rural households received farm income, but even in urban areas, around 14 per cent of households received farm income, although reliance on agriculture has dropped significantly in urban areas in particular. Yet, farming is relatively less remunerative; agricultural income constitutes only 17 per cent of total income. Even in rural areas, where agricultural income plays a more important role, combined income from cultivation is only 30 per cent of the total.

Salaries are the most lucrative: median incomes from cultivation are about Rs 9,400 and median agricultural wage incomes are Rs 18,000, compared with a median of Rs 49,000 for business and more than Rs 79,200 for salaries. But these salaried jobs are rare. In urban areas over half of the households had someone with a regular salaried income; in rural areas only 18 per cent of the households had a family member with a regular salaried income.[10]

Access to salaried income is one of the primary axes that circumscribes Indian households. Families in which at least one adult has a job with a monthly salary are considerably better off than households that rely solely on farming, petty business or casual daily labour.

Another key axis that divides households into rich and poor is, relatedly, education. Individuals with higher education are more likely to obtain salaried jobs than others, resulting in higher incomes in households with educated adults. The median income of households with at least one college graduate is more than four times the median income of illiterate households.[11]

Education and jobs don't just determine if you are rich or poor; they also determine if you're going to remain rich or poor. Of the 38 per cent of the population that was poor in the 2005 IHDS, 25 per cent had exited poverty by 2011-12, while 13 per cent were still poor. Meanwhile of the 62 per cent of Indians who were not poor in 2005, 53 per cent remained non-poor, but 9 per cent joined the ranks of the poor—their path into poverty is what Sonalde Desai, the sociologist and demographer who leads the IHDS, describes as an 'accident of life', rather than that first 13 per cent, whose poverty Desai describes as an 'accident of birth'.[12]

Caste and Class

Education and jobs don't fall into the laps of a lucky few at random. Nor is this a question of merit. They are the outcome of structural advantages and structural oppression.

Class in India intersects with caste and religion in deep and significant ways, but some of our understanding of the intersections has ossified over time, while some equations have been upended, with far-reaching impacts on modern day conversations and conflicts.

SCs and STs in India earn the least, followed by Muslims and then OBCs. Forward castes are the richest, with a household income nearly one-and-a-half times the Indian average.[13]

In the early 2000s, along with backward castes, Muslims formed a substantial share of the poorest one-fifth of Indians, while forward castes were rare in this group.[14] Even ten years later, Muslims were under-represented among the affluent while forward castes were over-represented.[15] In terms of affluence, Muslims were found to be on par with OBCs but in terms of higher educational attainments, Muslims lagged behind OBCs, and in terms of poverty rates were closer to Dalits.[16]

Moreover, things have been getting worse for Muslims. Since the mid-1950s, inter-generational mobility—the opportunity for a boy to do better in life than his father in this dataset—has improved for SCs and STs. On the other hand, the expected level of educational attainment of a Muslim child has fallen substantially over the last twenty years and inter-generational mobility is now considerably worse among Muslims than among SCs and STs. (Fig. 5.2) Even while the anti-reservation narrative that it is increasingly difficult for higher-caste Hindus to get ahead dominates some of the media and public sphere, higher-caste groups have experienced constant and high upward economic mobility over time.[17] In contrast, SCs and STs were much more likely to see their relative position decline.[18]

Why are these groups so much poorer? Some of this gap can be explained by their lower levels of education and the lack of salaried employment.[19] Marginalised groups, such as Dalits and Adivasis, are disproportionately concentrated in low-skilled occupations in the informal sector of the economy.[20] But studies on labour market discrimination show that over and above the differences in education and skills, there is evidence of discrimination in hiring in the private-sector labour market.[21]

Figure 5.2: Mobility for Muslims has actually been downwards

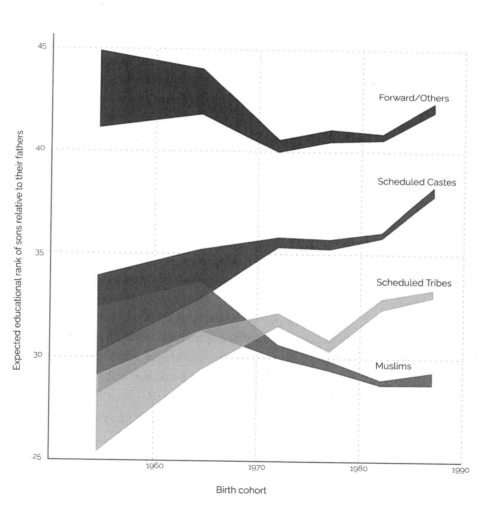

Sam Asher, Paul Novosad, Charlie Rafkin, 'Intergenerational Mobility in India: New Methods and Estimates Across Time, Space, and Communities', 2021

Evidence suggests that quotas can improve outcomes. In 1976, the lists of SC groups were harmonised across states for the first time since Independence, giving fresh SC status to 25 lakh more people. This moment offered a chance to answer the question: had reservation helped? The answer was yes, very much. Those people who had had SC status since Independence had considerably better educational indicators, including years of schooling, literacy and numeracy levels, than those who were of school-going age when they got SC status in 1976.[22] The improved inter-generational mobility of SCs and STs is also hypothesised to largely be a product of affirmative action.[23] Studies have shown that reservation in jobs has led to a gain of at least five percentage points in regular salaried and wage employment for SCs and STs.[24] This has not come at the cost of productivity or efficiency: a study of the Indian Railways, the largest federal employer in the world, shows that reservation for SCs and STs does not reduce efficiency, but in some cases, is seen to improve it.[25]

Yet, the opposition to reservations is strong among upper castes. Facts sometimes don't come in the way of feelings, in this case, the feeling of victimhood. Holding household economic status and education constant, forward castes were about 30 per cent more likely to feel that they were worse off in 2011-12 than in 2004-05, despite this being objectively untrue.

Neha Sharma (name changed) is a third-year medical student at AIIMS. Sharma was born in Lucknow and is convinced that the Dalit students in her cohort have it easy, while 'hum general category ke log have to struggle for a handful of seats. Maybe in the old days people were casteist and these reserved people had a tough life. But now you see, they come back from their hometowns in flights while the general-category students come by trains. They all have lots of land and a car back home. People like me are the ones who have struggled and come up. Really, we are the ones who are poor'.

While Sharma wanted her name changed for this interview, these attitudes are by no means hidden from Dalit and Adivasi students. Her classmate K. Revathi also wanted her name changed, fearing bad blood in her student cohort. 'From our food to our dress to our language, they snigger at everything,' she said. Revathi is the first person from her village in Tamil Nadu to study medicine: 'I have taken one flight in my life—the time I joined college, when a local group collected money for my flight. But there's no point explaining this to Neha*. For her, the problem is not Dalits having money, it's that our place should not be in a plane at all,' she said.

In India, both caste and class circumscribe everything. A child born into a rich household is more likely to be born in a hospital, is more likely to be a boy, is more likely to be a Hindu upper-caste child, is more likely to be attended to by a medical practitioner soon after birth, is less likely to die in his early years, will go to school longer, will grow taller than his poorer peers, will get a more stable and better-paying job, will be less likely to fall ill but more likely to seek treatment, will likely marry a Hindu upper-caste woman, get married and have children later than a poorer person, is more likely to vote BJP, will breathe cleaner air all his life, will make much more money and buy more assets, and will live longer than a poorer person born the same day.

The Great Indian Dream is not one of equal opportunity.

Living a Definition

Slotting people into neat categories is always going to be a vexed issue. Classifying people as poor or lower-middle class can sometimes make things that are actually very fluid take on the false veneer of science or objectivity.

For many, incomes change with the time of year, and shocks—an unexpected hospitalisation or a sudden loss of work, for instance—can easily push people in and out of poverty. Especially if they're close to the poverty line, households may fall into poverty after exposure to shocks; strictly drawn lines don't capture this.

The drawing and redrawing of poverty lines is a hugely fraught issue. Nobel Laureate Angus Deaton, the Scottish-born Princeton economist renowned for his work on consumption, poverty, nutrition and health, described the World Bank's 2015 revision of its poverty line like this: 'You've got a line that no one knows where to put it, PPPs that change, and underlying data that is bad . . . It is sort of a statistical problem from hell.'[26] In 2005, for instance, Deaton has pointed out, India's graduation from the group of fifteen poor countries the World Bank used to fix a poverty line in 2005—because it had now grown to middle-income status—perplexingly increased the number of poor in India.

How on earth did that happen? The World Bank constructs its poverty line by taking the average of the national poverty lines of fifteen of the world's poorest countries and then converting this average into an internationally comparable number. India's poverty line was so low that its graduation out of the group substantially raised the average poverty line—if you've been averaging fifteen poor friends' incomes, then when one of the poorest leaves the group, the group's average income shoots up. Raising the global poverty line increased the number of those officially classified as poor everywhere, including in India.

To make international comparisons, the Bank takes a basket of goods and services and calculates how much it would cost to buy these in various countries. Think of it like a global exchange rate, essentially. In 2015, the World Bank decided to update the prices in this basket to 2011 prices (plus a few other tweaks), since incomes in these countries had risen, and that raised the poverty line—what was $1.25 at 2005 prices became $1.90 at 2011 prices. 'If poverty falls in any country included in the counts, and increases nowhere else, global poverty should fall. The current procedure does not satisfy that basic requirement. Nor does it satisfy the property that global poverty should fall by no more than the fall in poverty in individual countries,' Deaton observes.

Up until 2011, India's approach to drawing up a poverty line was purely food-based; the poverty line as the amount of money needed to buy 2,400 calories in rural India and 2,100 calories in urban India. In 2011, a government committee—the Suresh Tendulkar committee—used a new methodology to draw up a poverty line by calculating the amount of money a person needs to spend to buy a slightly bigger basket of goods and services, including food, education, health, electricity and transport. This the committee worked out to be Rs 27.20 per person per day in rural areas and Rs 33.30 in urban areas. By calculating how many people nationally (according to the most recent NSSO spending survey) could afford to spend that much a day, the Planning Commission would produce estimates of how many people in the rural and urban parts of each state were theoretically under the poverty line.

This is how the line worked on paper. But how the line was then put into practice to estimate who really is poor was even more problematic. The number of poor in each state's rural and urban areas, as worked out in the way described above, were used as caps—the maximum number of poor the state was 'allowed' to have. What this meant was that each state would have to go back to its most recent BPL census, in some cases over ten years out of date, and see how many of those people it could accommodate within the number it had been told were officially poor in its state. The Union government said that these caps were to ensure that the states did not inflate their poverty figures to attract more Union grants. But once a state hit its quota, the most marginalised of its citizens were left out in the cold. This impeded the access of poor people to dozens of schemes meant for BPL persons. Some states bore the burden of subsidised grain for people in excess of the Union's quota. In other states, however, a demonstrably poor person could not get a BPL card if the state had already exhausted its limit.

In February 2010, Dablu from Ejamad village in Manika block in Jharkhand's Latehar district fell while constructing a school in the block headquarters. He broke his spine and was bedridden. He had a wife and two young children, and no adult earning member in the family (his wife spent much of her time tending to his needs). Activists ran from pillar to post to get him an Antyodaya card (which would give the family 35 kg of grain each month for Rs 35), but could not since the state had already met its quota. Dablu finally got a BPL card when a neighbour in his village died, leaving an Antyodaya BPL 'vacancy'.

Sreedevi C.K. lives in Puthenchira village in Kerala's Thrissur district. An anganwadi teacher, she makes Rs 11,000 per month, and her husband, a construction labourer, makes Rs 8,000 per month. As her mother is a 'heart patient', a Kerala State Civil Supplies Department survey found the family eligible for a 'Yellow Ration Card', the Antyodaya Anna Yojana card meant for the poorest of the poor, which entitles them to 35 kgs of free food grains.

Sathi T.K. lives in the same village. Sathi used to work as a food packer at a bakery; she stopped going to work after she fell ill around the start of the lockdown. Her two sons both have jobs—Akshay works in the IT field and Abhiram works at a gold-checking lab. Sathi's husband used to climb trees to cut down coconuts, but ever since a road accident fourteen years ago left him paralysed, he sells lottery tickets. The household makes Rs 20,000 to Rs 22,000 per month. Sathi used to have a 'Blue Ration Card'—the above poverty line (APL) card. After a civil supplies department survey during which she explained her husband's situation, her request for a BPL ration card was granted.

Usha Johnson lives in Shoranur town in the state's Palakkad district. Her children are both in college and her husband works in a watch-repair shop. Despite having a family income of less than Rs 3,000, she has an APL card. With gas costing Rs 850, substantial grocery bills, and educational expenses coming to Rs 4,000 for each child, Johnson's monthly expenses go up to more than Rs 10,000. So the family has taken a loan amounting to Rs 30,000 from Kudumbashree (the state poverty eradication mission of the Government of Kerala) and a loan of Rs 40,000 from Muthoot FinCorp; they pay them off in monthly instalments whenever possible. They haven't been able to pay them regularly since the pandemic started. No money is left over at the end of the month.[27]

The BPL method misidentifies almost half the poor as non-poor; in states like Andhra Pradesh and Punjab, over 75 per cent of the poor are misclassified as non-poor.[28] Two-thirds or more of the poor feel that the official poverty lines are inadequate to meet basic needs.[29]

In 2011, the then UPA government conducted the Socio Economic and Caste Census (SECC) in rural areas. The SECC was not a survey—it was a census of rural India, meaning that every household was covered. The questionnaire was short. It covered the condition of the house, whether the household had someone with a salaried job and whether this was a government job, whether the income of the top earner of the household was more or less than Rs 10,000, and the assets owned by the household.

The census failed in its stated aim of capturing caste data, but what it did do is come up with a more diverse list of deprivations that a household might suffer from than the BPL system could. 'This is a step away from the narrow definition of poverty we have been using, where the line is really what I call a "kutta-billi" line; only cats and dogs can survive on it,' N.C. Saxena, the former bureaucrat who headed the Planning Commission panel that recommended automatic inclusion and exclusion criteria for determining poverty, told me at the time.

The old BPL system had become discredited, and with good reason. The National Food Security Act, 2013 (NFSA), the recast version of the Public Distribution System (PDS), was the first major step towards discarding the BPL system. The NFSA allows states to use SECC data, but relies on exclusion rather than inclusion criteria for deciding who should be considered eligible for the scheme. Households with pucca walls and roofs, government employees, high-earners, tax payers and those with significant asset ownership are automatically excluded. The criteria are quite stringent (a household with a landline phone or a two-wheeler is excluded), but states can come up with their own preferred exclusion criteria.

It would appear that the NFSA's expanded eligibility criteria are working: a survey found that exclusion errors were just around 5 per cent compared to around 50 per cent under the BPL system.[30]

A major government-constituted committee, the Sumit Bose Committee (2017), has now recommended that the SECC data be used to identify beneficiaries for all Centrally sponsored, Central and state government schemes as far as possible. Since then, the government has used SECC data for identification of beneficiary households while implementing its social welfare programmes, including the Pradhan Mantri Jan Arogya Yojana-Ayushman Bharat and the Pradhan Mantri Ujjwala Yojana. It is also being used by several state governments to implement the NFSA.[31]

But 2011 was a decade ago and a lot has changed since. Planning for the next SECC is on,[32] but in the meantime some states like Tamil Nadu have done their own surveys.[33] Ultimately, statistics are by definition static bars, while the forces that push people into poverty are dynamic; they're not mere statistical lines but have a significant impact on the lives of the poor—no definition could, for instance, have anticipated the 2020 pandemic lockdown that fundamentally altered income distribution in the country.

One way to think about poverty measurement is self-reporting. Deaton has argued that given all of the problems with the effort, 'it is worth returning to the idea that people themselves seem to have a very good idea of whether or not they are poor. Indeed, the poverty lines set by politicians and bureaucrats are often informed by community ideas of what is needed to get by, even if they are often subsequently justified by more "scientific" supports . . . [T]here is something to be said for directly asking people around the world how their lives are going, whether they have enough, or whether they are in financial difficulty, and in cases where there are reliable income data, turning those reports into poverty lines.'[34]

The number of poor matters most when it comes to government schemes, but here the solution might lie in ceasing to let it matter at all. Schemes that target the least do the best job at actually reaching the poor, a 2005 World Bank assessment of social protection schemes in India found. India's best chance might be to universalise schemes. Instead of relying on either outdated survey lists or large, expensive, time-consuming surveys to assess the number of people who needed pandemic assistance, for instance, offering universal support might have been the best idea.

Similar issues crop up when we talk of the middle class, but here, it is less a question of life and death, and more a question of economic and political theory. So, who in India is really middle class? If India were divided into five classes of equal sizes in income terms, the middle 20 per cent of Indian households would earn Rs 55,000–Rs 88,800 annually.[35] However, despite being theoretically in the middle in terms of income distribution, a family earning Rs 55,000 would be at or just above the urban poverty line.[36] The true middle of India is still quite poor.

So, the top two classes—or those families earning above Rs 88,800 per year, or Rs 7,400 per month—would come closer to what could be called the middle class. These could be households where the primary breadwinner is, say, a driver of a private car, or a domestic cook—not what most Indians are usually accustomed to picturing when they talk of a middle class. Most of them do not, for instance, pay income tax; on a per capita basis, only the top 2 per cent of the country has a household income of over Rs 8 lakh.[37] Non-agricultural labour is still the most common job for men in families earning between Rs 88,801 and 1.5 lakh per year. For the richest 20 per cent population (above Rs 1.5 lakh per year), however, salaried work becomes the most common occupation.

Another way to think about class is in terms of access to amenities. Just 40 per cent of those in the the top two classes have piped water and only 15 per cent get even three hours of water every day. Just over half have a flush toilet and just half get eighteen hours of electricity in a day.[38] Again, a scenario quite removed from what we imagine middle-class life to be like. (Fig. 5.3)

If being middle class is associated with owning simple consumer goods, middle India is a long way from there as well, even though the purchase of air conditioners, colour TVs, refrigerators, cars, laptops and credit cards doubled between the mid-2000s and the early 2010s—cellphone ownership exploded from 7 per cent of the population in 2004-05 to 82 per cent in 2011-12.[39] Yet, by the early 2010s, just 3 per cent of Indians owned all of five basic consumer goods—a motor vehicle, TV, refrigerator, cooler or AC, and a computer or laptop.

'I think it's more useful to go beyond the income data and look at what we really mean when we talk about a global middle class,' Dr Desai, the sociologist who leads the IHDS

Figure 5.3: The Indian middle class doesn't lead a particularly comfortable life

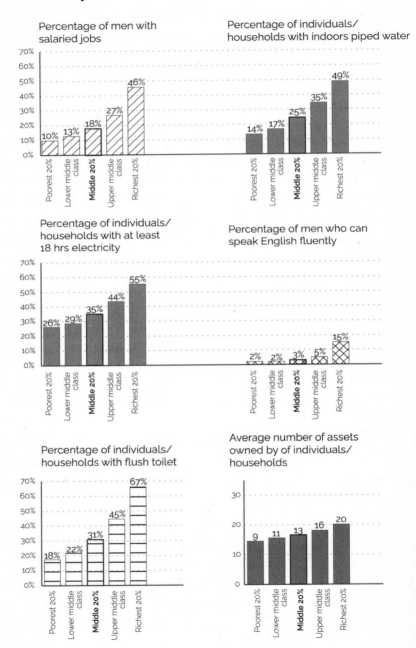

The income classes were Rs 1,000-Rs 33,000, Rs 33,001-Rs 55,640, 55,641-88,800, Rs 88,001-Rs 1,50,000 and above for the riches
Source: National Council for Applied Economic Research and University of Maryland, 'India Human Development Survey' Round 2, 2011-12

surveys, told me. 'This would mean things like a college degree, fluency in English, white-collar jobs among others,' she said. Just 12 per cent of adult men in 2011-12 had a degree or diploma, only 8 per cent could speak fluent English and 14 per cent had some computer skills. Women had fewer skills than men in each of these categories.[40] English is far more an urban than a rural phenomenon; just 3 per cent of rural respondents said that they could speak English, as against 12 per cent of urban respondents. There is a clear class element at work; 41 per cent of the rich could speak English as against less than 2 per cent of the poor. Speaking English is also visibly linked to education—a third of all graduates could speak English. The ability to speak English has strong religious and caste dimensions as well. Over 15 per cent of Christians can speak English, as against 6 per cent of Hindus and 4 per cent of Muslims. An upper-caste person is over three times more likely to speak English than a Dalit (SC) or Adivasi (ST) person. Knowledge of English also has a gendered dimension—a higher proportion of men than women said that they could speak in English—and younger people spoke marginally more English than older people.[41]

The economist Nancy Birdsall suggests[42] that the middle class in developing countries could include people with an income above $10 day, excluding the top 5 per cent of that country. By this definition, India—even urban India alone—has no middle class; everyone at over $10 over day is in the top 5 per cent of the country. This is a combination both of the income inequality in India and the depth of the country's poverty. China had no middle class in 1990, but by 2005 had a small urban middle class (3 per cent of the population). South Africa (7 per cent), Russia (30 per cent) and Brazil (19 per cent) all had sizeable middle classes by 2005. Even if the data was updated with some assumptions, the middle class would be slim—at the most generous estimates, under 9 per cent of Indians make more than $10 per day.[43]

By any measure then, India's upper-middle class is not well-off, and isn't likely to be watching the budget to see if it is getting tax breaks, or to see if duties have been waived on some luxury item. But this isn't to say that the middle class, as much as it might be just two steps away from being poor, doesn't have its own set of deeply held beliefs.

Some economists and political scientists turn to more socio-political or philosophical ways of understanding the middle class. Birdsall says that the middle class is traditionally that segment of society with a degree of economic security that allows it to uphold the rule of law, invest and desire stability. They do not, unlike those defined as 'rich', depend on inheritances or other 'non-productive sources of income'. Over $10 a day is not a lot, but at that level, household members are able to care about and save for the future and to have aspirations for a better life for themselves as well as their children, because they feel reasonably secure economically, she says.

In political science, the middle class is typically seen as a 'product of urbanisation and education, creating a new social group that was neither part of the propertied classes (whether the rural landed elite or the capitalist class) nor labor (whether working on the fields or in factories), but instead occupied a place in the middle. But that was before the advent of mass media and consumerism'. According to political scientists Devesh Kapur, Neelanjan Sircar and Milan Vaishnav, 'India's middle classes are largely first-generation middle-class members, whose families before them were likely poor.' What they share, they argue, is a sense of optimism.[44] Those who self-identify as middle class were more optimistic about the status of their lives today as well as the outlook for the future. When compared to those who believe they are not middle class, larger proportions of the self-identified middle-class respondents believed that their children will have a higher standard of living than they currently enjoy, that their family's social status has improved in a generation, and that India is progressing.[45]

Others link these 'middle-class' sentiments closely with the rise of the BJP. There is now a sharper distinction between voters on economic issues than ever before and more voters leant rightwards on economic issues in 2014 than in previous years.[46] The growth of India's middle class, which believes that subsidies are harmful and wants to see high economic growth, contributed to this, political scientists Pradeep Chhibber and Rahul Verma have argued. What also made people wary of state-led development was the perception that the UPA government was focused on subsidies and support for minorities, as well as allegations of corruption against it. Against this backdrop, Narendra Modi, then BJP's prime ministerial candidate, was able to draw voters opposed to statism with promises of 'no tokenism' and 'no special privileges'.

Where Do Things Stand Now?

Knowing how poor, middle-class and rich Indians are has in some ways become both more and less important than ever before. Less important because as India settles into middle-income status, it should be able to universalise more schemes and then being officially classified as poor will become less salient. More important because increasingly, people will try to convince us that this country is not poor, that we are all middle class, and that there is some sort of evil rich that we can all direct our angst against.

Since 2014, the project of poverty estimation has taken a firm backseat in Indian policy. Officially, there is no new consumption expenditure data since 2011-12, although an unofficial survey was conducted in 2017-18 and then withheld by the government (more on that in chapter 6). But the leaked findings of that survey, obtained by the *Business Standard* reporter Somesh Jha, and viewed by me, could indicate that poverty has grown rapidly or fallen, depending on who you speak to.

Taken at face value, the data shows that poverty rose for the first time in the decades between 2011-12 and 2017-18; 'A rough back-of-the-envelope calculation would suggest that the percentage of people in poverty has increased by at least 10 per cent and will be over 30 per cent now,' JNU economist Himanshu said. This is in sharp contrast to the trend of previous years, including a sharp decline in poverty between 2004-05 and 2011-12. Other data sources point in a similar direction—trends in growth rate of rural wages from the labour bureau have been consistently showing that real wages have stagnated and unemployment rates have risen to the highest ever.[47]

But the economist Surjit Bhalla, a former member of the Prime Minister's Economic Advisory Council under PM Modi, and colleagues use that leaked consumption data, national accounts data, night-lights data and other sources to say that the number of poor people fell from 27 crore people to 8.4

crore people in 2017, meaning that only 7 per cent of the country is still poor.

Estimating poverty might have fallen out of political fashion, but arguing about it remains very much in vogue.

Jean Dreze, the Belgian-born Indian development economist known for his work with Amartya Sen and Angus Deaton, as well as his decades of on-the-ground work in Jharkhand, warns that this neglect of poverty numbers is dangerous. 'The household consumption data was suppressed because it showed a picture of rising poverty. The SECC does not give us the full picture of consumption. And what is happening is that poverty has just stopped being a topic of research and discussion for the government, even while the numbers show it is a huge problem,' he told me on a recent call from Jagdalpur in rural Jharkhand.

Perhaps what the understanding of class in India really needs is two things: more and better data, and less suspicion of the motives of 'the other side'. Not everyone who doesn't buy consumption data is living in an elite bubble. When they look around and see crowded airports and packed restaurants, when they see the number of people who can pay for a 'management quota' seat for their children in college or send them overseas for unpaid internships, they truly feel that this country is getting rich and the money is passing them by, the ladder being pulled away fast. Among right-wing statisticians, the commonly held belief is that divergence from other indicators—GDP per capita, car and auto sales, airline ticket sales—suggests that the rich are not being properly enumerated and the poor are being over-represented in the data. On the Left, the feeling is that right-wing economists, particularly now in the Modi era, are trying to paint a rosier picture of the economy than truly exists.

No one likes to be told that they have fundamentally misunderstood their country and their place in it. The more polarised the conversation, the less chance anyone is actually going to look at the numbers with an open mind. Perhaps it is time to let the number speak for themselves.

VI

HOW INDIA SPENDS ITS MONEY

A generation ago, cereals dominated the weekly spending budget of Indians; that has changed as Indians go out to eat, watch movies, save, fly. But there's also the story of what the data misses and (at least) one gaping hole in official statistics. And then there's the story of how governments try to play with this data.

In January 2019, after spending most of his professional life in Delhi, fifty-five-year-old P.C. Mohanan returned to the village he was born in—Parachottil (as in Parachottil C. Mohanan), 50 km from Kozhikode. Back in the house he grew up in, in a village without electricity, Mohanan reflected on the numbers that he had staked his career on, turning his back on Delhi, and how it played out in the world outside his window.

Mohanan is a statistician who spent thirty years in the Indian Statistical Service, the cadre of government statisticians who man, among other bodies, the NSO, which produces all of the household surveys India depends on for information— from where Indians holiday to how much they spend on food. In 2017, shortly after he retired, he was selected to the National

Statistical Commission (NSC), the apex autonomous agency in charge of the quality, frequency and regulation of the key statistical activities of the Central and state agencies, including oversight of the NSO's functioning. In 2018, he became its acting head. In one short year, he had resigned over political interference in the NSC's functioning. Just months later, the impact of that meddling was exposed by an intrepid young reporter—the government, the reporter found, had suppressed a survey of consumption expenditure that painted it in an unflattering light.[1] Supporters of the government leapt on to the op-ed pages of newspapers. The consumption surveys were rife with problems and missed too much, they could not capture the 'new India', they were useless and needed to go, this camp argued.

On a video call with me in early 2021, each of us locked in as India's second COVID wave began to rage, Mohanan smiled genially as he gestured outside his window. 'Certainly a lot has changed. Look at me—I spend more on the internet and my phone than I spend on food. It is possible that some things like spending on health are not being properly captured. But all of this was known and we were working on fixing it. To suppress it because it shows the government in a poor light—that has never happened before.'

*

The controversy over the 2017-18 household consumption expenditure survey in a way gets to the heart of one key question over statistics in India: how much of the decay is institutional, and how much is new?

Consumption expenditure surveys are part of dozens of household surveys conducted every year by the NSO. The NSO is in a sense the Indian Space Research Organisation, of India's statistical landscape; a Nehruvian edifice that established India as a country that punched far above its weight in the 1950s and 1960s. While the foundation of the statistical system in India was laid down by the British administration, the new government of independent India took quick and decisive steps to establish a statistical architecture that was bold and ambitious. Jawaharlal Nehru appointed P.C. Mahalanobis, whose name is now uttered with pious reverence in statistical schools across the country, as the first statistical adviser to the Cabinet, Government of India. The new government quickly established a Central Statistical Unit (1949), which was later, in 1951, converted into the Central Statistical Organisation (CSO) and the Department of Statistics, which make up what is now the statistics wing of the Ministry of Statistics and Programme Implementation. Earlier, in 1931, Mahalanobis had set up the Indian Statistical Institute (ISI) in Calcutta to carry out research and training, and it gradually became an important part of the statistical system of India. The ISI pioneered research on large-scale sample surveys and quality control for statistics, and was an early leader in computer-assisted statistics. The eyes of the world—the developing world emerging from the shadows of colonial rule in particular—were on India.

With this intellectual foundation, resources and political weight behind it, the National Sample Survey (NSS) came into being in 1950 to collect information through sample surveys on a variety of socio-economic aspects in the country. It was the first household survey of its kind in the developing world.

In the seventy years since then, NSS reports have formed the basis of much of India's social science research, fed into government policy, and formed an important part of the world's understanding of what growth and development in India looks like. There have been controversies earlier—past NSS reports usually run into controversy when they seem to show much higher consumption than anticipated and, since India's poverty estimates until recently were set by the Planning Commission on the basis of this consumption expenditure data, much lower poverty than expected. When the 1987-88 quinquennial (every five years) survey of the NSSO showed that poverty had reduced significantly since 1983-84, there was an outcry, and in response, the Planning Commission set up an expert group to review the methodology for estimating poverty.

The 1999–2000 household consumption survey had a similar issue—the numbers showed much higher consumption than many economists expected to see—but the cause was different. Until 1993-94, consumption information collected by the NSSO was based on a uniform reference period (URP), which measured consumption across a thirty-day recall period, meaning that survey respondents were asked about their consumption in the last thirty days. In 1999–2000, the NSSO switched to a method based on a mixed reference period (MRP). The MRP measures consumption of five low-frequency items (clothing, footwear, durables, education and institutional health expenditure) over the previous year, and all other items over the previous thirty days.

This methodological change coincided with what appeared to be a large increase in consumption expenditure and, hence, a fall in poverty rates. Many economists argued that this apparent reduction in poverty was in reality a result of these methodological changes, which overstated consumption as compared to the old method that had produced the results the 1999–2000 numbers were being compared to.

Debates broke out in op-ed pages and in the pages of the *Economic and Political Weekly*, with Princeton economist Angus Deaton at the forefront of the critique, along with Jean Dreze, Abhijit Sen and Himanshu. Deaton and Dreze argued that poverty had declined, but the change was more modest than the new consumption data purported to show.

'The previous controversy over the recall period was also driven by politics, in that they felt that the consumption expenditure was seeming too low considering that there had been a period of high growth. They were hoping that a shorter recall period would lead to higher consumption expenditure estimates,' Mohanan told me. The response of the government at the time, incidentally a National Democratic Alliance government, was to release the raw data. This contributed to years of arguments about the NSSO surveys, and the government admitted that the methodological change was probably a bad idea, and that the data was not comparable with past years. The Union government, the Planning Commission and the World Bank held workshops with economists, including Sen, to understand the problems they had with the data. The government at the time did not block access to the data or attempt to delegitimise either that or the NSSO survey collection methodology, Mohanan said.

But this time around, something unprecedented happened.

The 2017-18 Consumption Survey Controversy

By January 2019, there were already signs that a problem was on its way. Mohanan quit the NSC and spoke out about how a report on employment had been completed and cleared by the NSC, but was being held back for no apparent reason (see chapter 7). The next month, the report was leaked, and it showed that India's unemployment was at a forty-five-year high. Government functionaries attacked the report and the reporter, Somesh Jha, and attempted to begin an op-ed discussion on the flaws in the NSSO, as well as its inability to capture the 'new economy'. Then, on 31 May 2019, the day after the new Modi government was sworn in, the ministry released the report with exactly those findings reported on earlier by Somesh.

By the middle of 2019, it became clear that the household consumption expenditure survey—historically done every five years and carried out over 2017-18—had been completed and ready since June 2019, but yet again, the government was trying to avoid publishing it.[2] Once more, it was Somesh who came through with the scoop; on 15 November 2019, he published the contents of the report in the newspaper he worked for at the time, *Business Standard*.

*

So what did the 2017-18 consumption expenditure survey show?

On average, Indians spend a little under Rs 2,500 every month, with the average urban Indian spending Rs 3,860 every month—over twice what her rural counterpart does. The poorest 5 per cent of rural Indians spend under Rs 870 per month, and the poorest 5 per cent of urban Indians spend Rs 1,325 per month. The richest 5 per cent of Indians, on the other hand, spend over Rs 5,167 per month on average in rural areas, and over Rs 13,017 in urban areas. Delhi is India's richest state followed by Kerala; people in these states spend over Rs 4,000 per month on average.

With time, the share of food in the total basket of consumption expenditure is falling. The rich have more money to spend on everything, including food, but it forms a smaller share of their total budget. The poorest 5 per cent of Indians spend fifty-eight of every hundred rupees on food, while the richest 5 per cent spend just thirty-seven of every hundred rupees on food. As people get richer, more of their budgets are freed up to spend on education or eating out or travel.

The biggest expense for rural Indians is still as basic as cereals—the rice or wheat that they use for home consumption. While the share of cereals in their total food expenditure has declined as rural Indians have got richer, begun to do less calorie-consuming physical labour, and are able to diversify their diets more to include vegetables, milk and meats, it still forms the largest share—9.4 per cent—of their total expenses.

In urban India on the other hand, the big expense is eating out. In 2011-12, cereals for the first time did not account for the biggest share of the urban Indian's expense basket, and were replaced instead by milk and milk products. Then in 2017-18, the most recent year for which data is available, 'beverages, refreshments, processed food', which includes eating out, for the first time accounted for the largest share of urban Indians' monthly budgets—the average urban Indian now spends Rs 350 every month eating out of her monthly spending budget of Rs 3,860. (Fig. 6.1)

Parents in Dharavi, the massive slum in Mumbai, spent Rs 25–30 every day on packaged snacks for their kids, government officials told a reporter. In the slum's unhygienic conditions, parents often saw packaged foods as clean, unadulterated, healthy options. The promise of nutrition in advertisements swayed some. Glucose biscuits were seen as providing 'taakat'

Figure 6.1: Cereals still occupy the biggest share of the rural family's budget, while for urban residents, it is eating out

Monthly per capita food expenditure

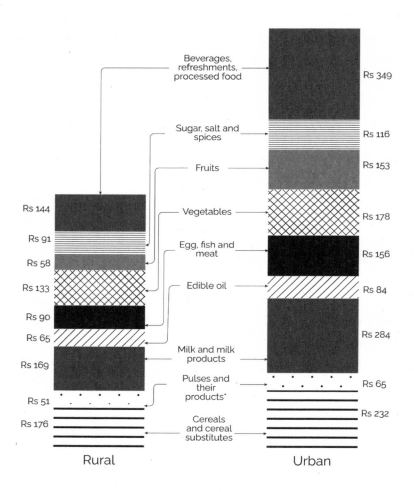

	Rural	Urban
Beverages, refreshments, processed food	Rs 144	Rs 349
Sugar, salt and spices	Rs 91	Rs 116
Fruits	Rs 58	Rs 153
Vegetables	Rs 133	Rs 178
Egg, fish and meat		Rs 156
Edible oil	Rs 90	Rs 84
Milk and milk products	Rs 65	Rs 284
Pulses and their products*	Rs 169	Rs 65
Cereals and cereal substitutes	Rs 51	Rs 232
	Rs 176	

Rural · Urban

*Data as of 2017-18

Urban Indians are able to prioritise education

Monthly per capita non-food expenditure

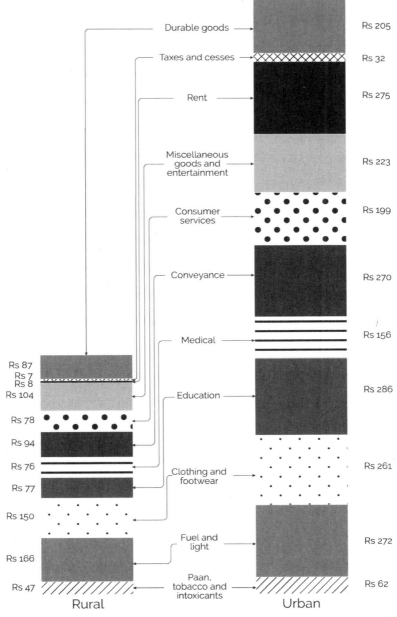

	Rural	Urban
Durable goods	Rs 87	Rs 205
Taxes and cesses	Rs 7	Rs 32
Rent	Rs 8	Rs 275
Miscellaneous goods and entertainment	Rs 104	Rs 223
Consumer services	Rs 78	Rs 199
Conveyance	Rs 94	Rs 270
Medical	Rs 76	Rs 156
Education	Rs 77	Rs 286
Clothing and footwear	Rs 150	Rs 261
Fuel and light	Rs 166	Rs 272
Paan, tobacco and intoxicants	Rs 47	Rs 62

Rural   Urban

Source: 'Key Indicators of Household Consumption Expenditure'. National Sample Survey 75th round, Ministry of Statistics and Programme Implementation, GoI, 2019 (unpublished) to the children while juice packets with pictures of apples were seen as nutritious. Schoolteachers sometimes instructed parents not to send messy food, and ashamed, parents responded by sending packaged snacks as school lunches. Two-year-old Ritu's* first real solid food, according to her mother Prachi, was a plateful of Maggi noodles.[3]

The biggest non-food expenditure for rural Indians is on fuel and light, followed by clothing, while for urban Indians, it is on education, followed by rent.

What do people choose to spend on when money becomes a bit less tight? Spending on milk, for one, rises dramatically—a person in the 20–25 percentile in rural India is able to spend three times as much per month on milk as a person in the poorest 5 per cent of rural Indians. Richer families also spend more on meats and vegetables. Among non-food expenditures, spending on health and education shoots up among the rich. (Fig. 6.2)

That's the snapshot, but the point of the NSO is to give us a sense of how things are changing over time. And that's where the problems come in.

The leaked 2017-18 data showed that real consumption expenditure had declined by 10 per cent per annum in rural areas and increased marginally by 2 per cent per annum in urban areas, with an overall decline of around 4 per cent per annum for the country as a whole. Real consumption expenditure in rural areas declined from Rs 1,587 per person per month in 2014 to Rs 1,524 per person per month in 2017-18. The decline in urban areas was from Rs 2,926 per person per month in 2014 to Rs 2,909 per person per month in 2017-18 (all estimates in 2018 prices). Simply put, Indians were spending less and consuming fewer items.

The last time real consumption expenditure declined

Figure 6.2: Indians are spending a little less on essentials over time

Percentage share in total consumer expenditure, rural

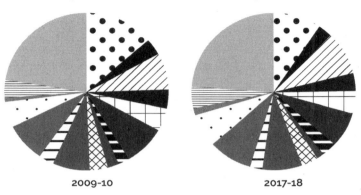

2009-10

2017-18

Misc. goods & services	Durable goods	Footwear · Clothing & bedding
Fuel & light	Paan, tobacco, intoxicants	Processed food Salt & spices
Sugar	Fruits & nuts	Vegetables Egg, fish & meat Edible oil
Milk & products	Gram, pulses & products	Cereals & cereal substitutes

Percentage share in total consumer expenditure, urban

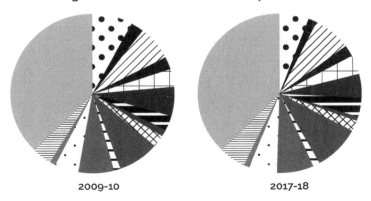

2009-10

2017-18

Source: 'Key Indicators of Household Consumption Expenditure', National Sample Survey
75th round, Ministry of Statistics and Programme Implementation, GoI, 2019 (unpublished)

during a six-year period was between 1960 and 1966, when the country was going through a severe crisis including a major food crisis, the economist Himanshu says. It also declined for a brief period around 1973-74, but not thereafter, he noted. 'The decline is surprising when compared to both earlier episodes, which were periods of economic uncertainty and crisis, because the period between 2011-12 and 2017-18 had reported growth rates at more than 6 per cent per annum.'[4]

*

Somesh's report came out on the morning of 15 November 2019. By evening, the Ministry had put out a statement: it was not going to release the survey results at all.

> The results of the survey were examined and it was noted that there was a significant increase in the divergence in not only the levels in the consumption pattern but also the direction of the change when compared to the other administrative data sources like the actual production of goods and services. Concerns were also raised about the ability/sensitivity of the survey instrument to capture consumption of social services by households especially on health and education. The matter was thus referred to a Committee of experts which noted the discrepancies and came out with several recommendations including a refinement in the survey methodology and improving the data quality aspects on a concurrent basis. The recommendations of the Committee are being examined for implementation in future surveys . . .
>
> . . . In view of the data quality issues, the Ministry has decided not to release the Consumer Expenditure Survey results of 2017-2018. The Ministry is separately examining

the feasibility of conducting the next Consumer Expenditure Survey in 2020-2021 and 2021-22 after incorporating all data quality refinements in the survey process.[5]

These might sound like serious and significant objections to what the 2017-18 survey had found. The problem is that they're not new, and in a sense get to the heart of the two visions of how the country is doing. The discrepancy between survey data and national accounts has been a matter of debate since at least the 1980s. At its heart is this issue: shouldn't the total of Indian consumption based on household surveys equal the nation's total production?

Economists associated with the Indian right-wing certainly think so. Surjit Bhalla told me with a sigh that he has been saying as much for forty years. Dr Bhalla is one of India's best-known conservative economists, who has been arguing in various fora that the NSO's consumption surveys are flawed and miss too much. After Somesh's report hit the news, Dr Bhalla wrote in his column in the *Indian Express*:

> [T]he summary data as published by the national accounts division of the same ministry as the NSO . . . shows that rather than declining, average consumption increased by 37% between the two NSO years. Both cannot be right: a decline of 4% versus an increase of 37%. The figures are so divergent that they cannot be of the same country at the same time.

> Some other consumption indicators are that car sales rose by 31%, two-wheeler sales by 46%, internet usage by 241%, mobile purchases by 44% over the six years, and smartphone usage rose by 786%. Do you still want to believe average per capita consumption declined between 2011-12 and 2017-

18? Keep dreaming, but do recognize that the number of airline passengers went up by 96% over the period when the NSO CES surveys believe average consumption declined.[6]

India's official statistical machinery accepts that there is a divergence. Former chief statistician T.C.A. Anant laid out to me what the NSO's consumption surveys were missing in some detail. For one, he said, in an unequal country, the bulk of consumption of some commodities—the purchase of laptops or diamond jewellery, for instance—is going to take place within a very small segment of the population. This presents statisticians with a serious sampling challenge, compounded by the fact that casualty errors (households that are part of the sample, but from which information cannot be collected) are highest among the richest: they are often not at home, they frequently turn away data collectors and they often under-report. Across the economic spectrum, a lot depends on whether the sample selection is accurate, and India's statistical system acknowledges that there are problems with its urban sample, where the divergence is greatest. Part of the problem is the dynamic nature of Indian urbanisation, to capture which the NSO needs to move to a GIS-mapping system, which is some distance away yet. Finally, household surveys will by definition miss out on all that is consumed outside a household. So a car bought by a private company but given to its director for his personal use will not be declared by him as an asset he owns, yet form part of his consumption. 'This divergence is real, but it is not unique to India. Across the developed and developing world, it ranges from 30 to 70 per cent, and there are methodological and conceptual reasons for this,' Anant told me.

Dr Bhalla believes that the NSO fails at capturing much of Indian consumption, but the bigger problem is that it is getting worse over time. 'Every country has some divergence from national accounts. But in India, the issue is that it's worsening. If we take the 2017-18 data at face value, the NSSO has gone from capturing just 40 per cent of total consumption as measured by national accounts, to just 37 per cent. Consumption surveys will miss a part of consumption. But how can we have this situation, where your consumption data is missing more than half of all consumption [as measured by national accounts]?' he asked me. (Fig. 6.3)

Most leading economists, however, say that while the NSO could be missing some consumption, and does need improvements, national accounts is not the way to go. Perhaps the most comprehensive assessment of why national accounts data should not be privileged over household survey data came from Angus Deaton in 2005. While consumption surveys might understate spending, national accounts-based estimates overstate spending, particularly in a growing economy. Deaton uses the example of cooking oil, particularly vanaspati (cheap hydrogenated vegetable oil). The national accounts estimate the consumption of vanaspati like this: On one side you have the total production of vanaspati in a year plus net exports. You subtract all the vanaspati that is consumed by government or business, which should give you the final number for private consumption of vanaspati. But as the economy grows, people eat out more, so that an increasing fraction of vanaspati is used by caterers, restaurants and street vendors, resulting in the vanaspati used in restaurants being counted twice. When this happens, it inflates the value of national accounts, especially when compared to household surveys. One might assume that

Figure 6.3: The divergence between consumption from the NSS and NAS is a large and growing problem

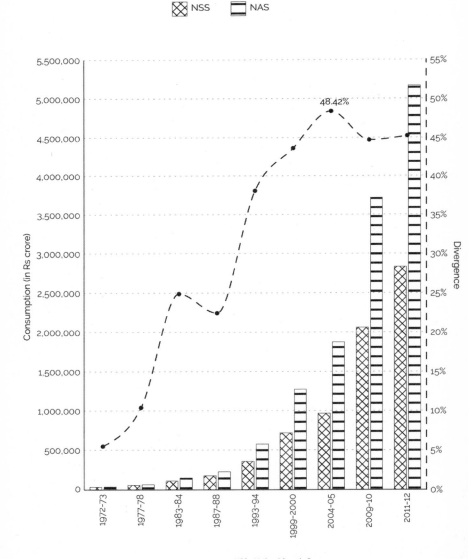

NSS - National Sample Survey
NAS - National Accounts Statistics
Source: A.K. Adhikari et al. *Report of the Committee on Private Final Consumption Expenditure*. GoI. 2015

household surveys do a poorer job of capturing a changing country but in reality, Deaton said, the manner in which national accounts-based estimates are calculated also involves a number of assumptions and old survey information.[7]

'I have used data from India's famous National Sample Surveys to measure poverty,' wrote Deaton in a statement to the Indian media after his Nobel Prize in 2015. 'Perhaps the biggest threat to these measures is that there is an enormous discrepancy between the national accounts statistics (NAS) and the surveys. The surveys "find" less consumption than do the national accounts, whose measures also grow more rapidly. While I am sure that part of the problem lies with the surveys—as more people spend more on a wider variety of things, the total is harder to capture—but there are weaknesses on the NAS side too, and I have been distressed over the years that critics of the surveys have got a lot more attention than critics of the growth measures. Perhaps no one wants to risk a change that will diminish India's spectacular (at least as measured) rate of growth?'[8]

Until recently, there was no real way to test whether the NSSO was getting household consumption right. But since 2004, the National Council for Applied Economic Research has conducted two rounds of the IHDS. In 2011-12, the most recent year for which there is both NSSO and IHDS data, the figures show that the NSSO appears to get consumption data quite right, especially at the lower end. The NSSO estimated the share of people under the poverty line to be 37 per cent in 2004-05 and 22 per cent in 2011-12; IHDS estimates were similar at 38 per cent in 2004-05 and 21 per cent in 2011-12. At the higher ends of the distribution, the NSSO reported slightly lower consumption than the IHDS, but the discrepancies were not significant.

Moreover, other data pointed in the same direction as the unreleased 2017-18 round of the NSSO's household consumption survey was pointing—that there was a crisis in employment and wages, and that this was expected to have an impact on how much money families had to spend. Rural wage data from India's labour bureau has been consistently showing that real wages stagnated between 2013 and 2018, JNU economist Himashu has pointed out. The NSSO's delayed unemployment data, too, showed that the earnings of regular workers declined in both rural and urban areas between 2011-12 and 2017-18. Rural regular wages declined at 0.3 per cent per annum, whereas urban regular wages declined at 1.7 per cent per annum. The fact that unemployment rates rose to the highest ever implied that there were job losses, he adds.[9]

So how do you fix the problems with the NSO?

*

For this, you must first begin with the conviction that the NSO *can* be saved.

When Mohanan and his colleague, the economist J.V. Meenakshi, resigned, the delay in the release of the NSSO employment data was not the only issue. There was also the contentious matter of India's GDP numbers (the core of national account statistics), and how the official statistical system was bypassed by the distinctly political Niti Aayog, which in the Modi era has replaced the Planning Commission.

The GDP is perhaps the most sacred number produced by a country's statistical system. It is supposed to be the summary of all that an economy produces, and in India, the Central Statistical Office is in charge of computing it, using established methodology. In 2015, the NSC approved a big change in how India would calculate its GDP, moving to the use of Gross Value Added (GVA) at basic prices. The GVA, which is GDP minus taxes, was believed to be a better way to measure changes in the aggregate value of goods and services produced in the economy—instead of only measuring how many units of a car or computer were produced, the GVA method would also account for differences in values of low- and high-end products, for example. The method also factored in value addition from activities like marketing, which account for an increasing share of value of companies in the new economy. This method was recommended by the United Nations System of National Accounts in 2008, the government said in support of the move.

But a new formula is only as good as the underlying data it uses. One of the key bones of contention was the database of companies it worked with, which was not made public and had never been used before. Data journalist Pramit Bhattacharya exposed the flaws in a series of news reports that showed that the NSO itself carried out a survey based on the database in 2016 and found that many of the companies were not traceable, or had closed, or operated in a different line of business than what they had reported.[10]

The new methodology also ran into the 'deflator problem', as Bhattacharya calls it. Shifting from the old volume-based approach to the new value-based approach made deflators, which would separate the rise in value from the rise in prices, in each product category newly important. Except, these required very fine price data points that India lacked. This deflator bias has artificially inflated the GDP numbers in the new series, Bhattacharya has argued.[11]

Alongside the changes in methodology, the government

produced a backdated GDP series re-evaluating past GDP growth using the new methodology. Overnight, the backdating of the new series painted growth in the UPA era in an unflattering light. The new GDP series was immediately mired in controversy, painting a far more optimistic picture than other economic indicators suggested, and prompting public criticism from both the then Reserve Bank of India governor Raghuram Rajan and the chief economic adviser to the finance ministry Arvind Subramanian about the change in methodology. All of this caused an enormous scandal. Moreover, the backdated series was released by the NITI Aayog instead of by the Central Statistical Office whose job it is, or by the NSC, which is responsible for data quality.

India's GDP numbers and the NSSO's household consumption numbers lie at the heart of India's official statistics, and if the methodology of acquiring this series data can be called into question, then a thorough investigation is needed. Unfortunately, despite a long history of India trying to both improve its statistical system and insulate it from political pressures, the mechanism that should have been put in place to do this remains toothless, perhaps intentionally.

In January 2000, the government set up the Dr C. Rangarajan Commission to review the official statistical system in the country. The commission's stated position was that official statistics should not only be accurate, but also trusted by the public. So, it suggested that the government establish a permanent and statutory apex body—a national commission on statistics—'to serve as a nodal and empowered body for all core statistical activities of the country, evolve, monitor and enforce statistical priorities and standards and to ensure statistical co-ordination among the different agencies involved'.[12] This body would be independent of the government and answerable to Parliament.

In 2006, the government set up the NSC with Pronab Sen as its first chief. But the NSC lacked legal status and this in part contributed to its powerlessness—NSSO reports could be withheld even after the NSC had cleared them, Mohanan said. Then, in 2019, the government introduced a draft NSC Bill meant to give legal backing to the NSC. But some current and former NSC members told Bhattacharya that they feared the bill did not provide the commission with the kind of authority and autonomy that it would need to restore the credibility of official statistics. Mohanan saw it as a halfway house between where things stand today and where things should be. Sen was less equivocal—in its current form, it would do more harm than good, he said. To have autonomy and to be able to insulate statistics from political pressures, the NSC needed to be able take decisions without ministerial intervention, he said. One unnamed member went even further: the draft bill would not mean much change other than making it mandatory for the government to explain in writing why it did not heed NSC's advice, he told Bhattacharya.[13]

Simultaneously, in 2019, the government approved the merger of the CSO and the NSSO under the ministry of statistics into a single entity, the NSO. Sen criticised the move in an interview: 'There was certain autonomy that NSSO enjoyed. That autonomy is gone. Now, all those decisions will be taken by the ministry, including the decision of whether to release or not to release a report.'[14]

The politicisation of the statistical system and the sidelining of the NSC had only got worse.

For Mohanan, it was time to leave Delhi.

*

Where Does India's Statistical System Go from Here?

When people ask me about official data, the fear of most is that it is 'fake' or 'fudged'—falsified. On a national scale, however, this is highly unlikely, because it would take the kind of coordinated, decentralised falsification that is unrealistic to expect. 'I do not think faking or fudging is a problem, and I have looked at the data very closely,' Pronab Sen, who was also India's chief statistician at one point of time, told me. Dr Sen, who has often been critical of the Modi administration, found himself selected to head a high-level standing committee to review and strengthen India's economic statistics. 'Believe me,' he said, 'I've looked very closely, and from the inside and the outside.' Many others, including Mohanan, echo his views.

It's not falsification that is worrying. It's neglect, discredit and, ultimately, dismissal.

When the government referred the 2017-18 household consumption data to a committee, that committee did not recommend that the 2017-18 report be junked or withheld. It was asked to investigate data quality issues and it made some observations regarding that by checking the internal validity of the data, and based on comparisons with other datasets.[15] Dr Bhalla too, the NSO's indefatigable critic, has urged that the data be released. 'The NSSO must survive, and I don't think this is the end of the road for it. For consumption, they could start by making their form shorter and focus on core consumption instead of hundreds of tiny items like the precise amount of salt consumed,' he told me. Others, like Sonalde Desai, recommend better training of surveyors.

For their part, Leftist supporters of India's storied statistical establishment need to take these data quality issues on board. The NSO says that it is working towards reducing the gap by minimising recall errors and improving its urban sampling system. The last official examination of the growing divergence between household survey-based consumption and national accounts was in 2015, and that committee made a number of useful recommendations. The first was to make the NSO consumption survey shorter so that the respondent was not fatigued by having to answer hundreds of questions, and more focused—NSO surveys on health, for instance, capture higher spending than the broad household consumption survey does. These simple changes have not been implemented yet (although similar improvements to the national accounts estimates suggested by the same committee are also yet to be implemented).[16]

The divergence from national accounts is not nothing, but Leftist economists have not for the most part taken these criticisms of the NSO on board.

Increasingly, Modi, his administration and supporters are feeding a narrative that household survey data is unreliable, paints India in an unfairly unflattering light, and should be junked. When the NSSO's employment statistics painted an unflattering picture of the economy, Modi pointed instead at the number of restaurants being opened, the number of vehicles being sold, and employee savings data. When the household consumption survey made it appear that Modi was overselling his growth and reform story, his supporters point to national accounts and flight ticket sales. When the NSSO's household drinking water and sanitation data indicated that the rapid improvements that Modi had been touting were doubtful on the ground, he turned instead to administrative data on toilets built and taps installed.

The Swachh Bharat Mission, which aims to eliminate open defecation, was Modi's first major scheme in 2014. By the end of 2020, the mission's dashboard claimed that over 99 per cent rural households had access to an exclusive toilet and most villages had been declared open defecation free. In urban India, over 100 per cent of the target of building toilets had been achieved, a massive turnaround from 2011, when the Census had shown that over half of all households had no toilet.

Doubts were first raised about the dashboard data when an NSSO report in 2018 found that nearly 30 per cent of rural households did not have access to a toilet, a higher figure than the portal claimed. The two sources measured different metrics, but the wide gap indicated that many Indians were still having to defecate in the open, contrary to Modi's claims. An unusual caveat preceded these findings: 'It may be noted that there may be respondent bias in the reporting of access to latrine as question on benefits received by the households from government schemes was asked prior to the question on access of households to latrine.' Explaining in an op-ed later, chief statistician of India Pravin Srivastava claimed that respondents could be lying to surveyors despite having toilets, so that they could claim benefits from the government. The report's delayed publication, in November 2019, did not help. According to Mohanan (who had resigned from the commission months before the report came), the delay was 'probably as the contents were not positive for the government'.

Here lies the danger with relying on administrative data: targets are ticked off, often on the basis of reports by village heads, without speaking to the intended beneficiaries. The Swachh Bharat Mission dashboard only records households that have constructed individual toilets on paper. The NSO surveyors, on the other hand, went to people's houses and stood at their doors asking them whether members of the household had access to a toilet, who else used it, what type of toilet it was, and whether the respondents were actually using that toilet.

This could have been another of those intractable fights between administrative data and household survey data. But what helped was more data. The fifth round of the National Family Health Survey (NFHS) was released in December 2020. While the NFHS focuses on health, it also asked whether members of the household had exclusive access to 'improved sanitation', which included a range of types of toilets. The NFHS largely confirmed the NSO's trends and found that in five states, over one-third of the rural population still lack exclusive access to 'improved' sanitation for their households. In Bihar, for instance, this figure was less than half, while in rural Gujarat, nearly 37 per cent residents did not have access to an improved facility. Kerala was the only state whether the situation on the ground was aligned with administrative data.

*

Better household survey data is vital to tell the story that administrative data would otherwise miss. 'Administrative data is controlled by governments. Household survey data is vital for India—there are ways to make it better,' the economist Jean Dreze told me. Increasingly, economists who are stuck without updated government data are turning to private data sources like the Centre for Monitoring Indian Economy's large, paid-access database, but Dreze argued that the push must be for better national data. 'Which country in the world uses private data for consumption? These questions have to be answered from within the national statistical system,' he said. In India in particular, private surveys always run the risk of not being representative enough. Dreze and his collaborators have shown that CMIE's household survey captures a richer, more urban, younger and more male population than a truly nationally representative sample would.

Despite their characterisation as surveys that depress numbers and make people look poorer than they actually are, household surveys can, when done well and with proper oversight, give a far more nuanced picture of India than administrative data ever will. While campaigning in Pathanamthitta for the 2021 assembly elections in Kerala, Modi claimed in a speech:

> Access to drinking water is a problem in Kerala. Only 25 per cent of Kerala households had tap water supply before we started the Jal Jeevan Mission. Since it began, almost 20 per cent households all over India got access to tap water connections. I'm sad to share that in Kerala, the number is only 4.5 per cent. The reason for this slow progress is the poor attitude of the state government! I want to tell the state government in Kerala—please, take all credit, but don't make people suffer!

This would have struck many as surprising—why was a developed state doing so badly on drinking water? The answer lay on page sixty-five of NSS Report Number 584, 2018. Yes, just 14 per cent of Kerala households had piped water coming right to their house and an additional 4 per cent had piped water coming to the yard. But run your finger down the table rows and you'll see that the majority of the state was not getting their water from hand pumps (as 88 per cent of households in Bihar were) or from public taps (as 35 per cent of households in Tamil Nadu were). They were getting it from their own private wells (71 per cent of households in Kerala).[17]

It was Mohanan who directed my eye there. Listening to the speech from his house in Kerala, he exclaimed out loud. 'Tap water use is very low in Kerala because everyone has a well! I have a well, its water is so sweet, I will not use tap water even if it comes to my house!'

In newly independent India, Mahalanobis spent a lot of time in Nehru's cabinet advocating for surveys because they were so new then; random sampling came into being only in the 1920s, and there was no NSS-type survey anywhere until Mahalanobis led one himself. Seventy years later, India finds itself in need of a Mahalanobis to advocate for surveys once again. Their power has been forcefully demonstrated, but this time around, those in power are choosing not to listen.[18]

Household surveys, despite their flaws, can tell us greater truths than any administrative data can—if they can survive this latest onslaught.

VII

HOW INDIA WORKS

There is a jobs crisis. But it is as much about the data as it is about the economy.

On 7 February 2019, Prime Minister Narendra Modi, just a month away from launching his re-election campaign, stood before Parliament to talk about jobs. It was not an easy moment; only a week earlier, Somesh Jha, a young journalist at the *Business Standard* newspaper, had leaked a bombshell report that the government had been suppressing. India's unemployment rates had hit a record high, he found, amidst an overall slowing of the economy and Modi's disastrous 2016 demonetisation experiment. In the days after Jha's report broke, some government functionaries and supporters had been dispatched to trash the report, saying that it failed to capture the reality of how India works. Now Modi stood up.

What he was going to say, he said, was very important. He directly addressed the people watching him on their television sets—he didn't want them misled by what they had been hearing, he said.[1] Until now, employment had been estimated by capturing jobs in seven–eight sectors only, he said, but the world had changed. Moreover, 85–90 per cent of jobs were in the unorganised sector, he asserted. Reeling off numbers about the number of commercial vehicles sold in the year before, Modi asked rhetorically: 'Have all of these vehicles been parked? Have they been kept for display? Won't there be someone driving them? Won't they need servicing?' BJP MPs thumped their desks and laughed in response. Then he listed the number of hotels that had opened up. Were they empty, he asked, mocking again, did no one work there? App-based taxi aggregators had sprung up, he went on. Were they driverless cars? Millions of young people had taken government loans to start new enterprises, but they are not captured by job data, he said. Loud cheers greeted him from the treasury benches.

The speech captured, even if inadvertently, much of the universe of discussions around employment in India. How well does the data really capture the lived reality of working Indians and are things getting better?

*

India's employment and unemployment data comes from the NSSO, the redoubtable government agency that has been conducting large-scale sample surveys since 1950 to a degree of excellence certified by the world's leading data agencies. The NSSO's once-in-five-years employment reports are household surveys, where enumerators visit a sample of respondents, statistically sampled to be representative of the country, and seek details of their participation in the workforce. Since 2017-18, India has moved to more frequent surveying—the Periodic

Labour Force Survey (PLFS), which is conducted quarterly and aggregated annually—but the universe of questions and the answers they seek is much the same.

Here's what the most recent NSSO employment survey asks. It looks at three pre-specified reference periods: the last 365 days for 'usual status', the last seven days for 'weekly status', and the previous day for 'daily status'. A trained field enumerator then asks every adult in the household what their activity status for most of the time period has been—were they employed, unemployed or not seeking work?

Thirty-seven-year-old Sushant Singh works on his father's farm in Bhatinda, Punjab for most of the year. So his 'usual status' is as a family worker in cultivation. While he does farm work, he has little time for other work, and few job opportunities are available for him in the area nearby. So Singh would report being employed in agricultural cultivation as his usual principal activity. But in the summer he drives a taxi in Chandigarh. Would the survey miss this? No, it also asks respondents about another economic activity that they might have done for thirty or more days during the previous year; Singh would be recorded as someone who was employed in driving a leased private vehicle as his subsidiary economic activity.

The surveyor asks every adult in the household a battery of questions: first, to think back to the last seven days. What work did the person do yesterday? For how many hours? How much money did that make the person? How many additional hours in a day would she be available for work, if she had more work? What about the day before? And so on until the surveyor has details for the week just gone by. She assigns a special code to the nature of work as described by the person, from a list of hundreds of different job roles and occupations across a whole gamut of industries she has been given, a list developed and updated regularly by both national and international officials and labour experts. This is the 'current weekly status' method and should capture some of the work of people in the gig economy who might have multiple concurrent or non-concurrent jobs. Later, the surveyor goes back to urban areas for a revisit and asks the questions again, so that fast-moving changes like urbanisation and migration do not mean that some jobs are missed out.

So this immediately gets to the heart of Modi's contentions—the NSSO does in fact capture informal employment and the gig economy.

*

Here's what we know. Official unemployment in India is extremely low, at just a little over 5 per cent. This is because in a middle-income country, everyone looking for employment takes up some form of work, a practice that places India in the bottom third of countries in terms of unemployment rates. But this small figure hides worrying big numbers in a few different ways. The first is that it recently grew, and the government tried to hide it. The suppressed official data—the 2017-18 PLFS—showed that as the economy slowed, unemployment in India rose to an all-time high. The number itself was still low at 6 per cent, but this low number was a forty-five-year high.

Second, low aggregates hide the disproportionately high unemployment rates among some groups. Unemployment rises substantially among the most educated and among rural male youth. In 2011, Andhra Pradesh, Telangana and Kerala had India's highest graduate unemployment rates, at over 25 per cent.[2] To compare, at its highest in 2010, the official unemployment rate for Americans with a bachelor's degree rose to 5.1 per cent. For well-educated women in particular, jobs are simply not there. While the overall unemployment rates are lower than men, women who have more than secondary education face staggering unemployment—17.1 per cent, nearly twice the rate for similarly educated men. The figure is higher still for educated urban women.

*

In India, for women in particular, a second indicator becomes important—the labour force participation rate. This is the proportion of working-age people who report being in the labour force, whether employed, unemployed or looking for work. Those of working age who aren't working or seeking paid work, whether it is because they're studying, or, as we'll see, for other, more complex reasons, are not considered a part of the workforce.

The labour force participation rate for men in India is relatively high—over three out of every four men over the age of fifteen in India are in the workforce, placing India sixtieth out of 280 countries globally in terms of male labour force participation. (The age of fifteen is the cut-off used for global comparisons by the International Labour Organisation.) Among those men who are not in the workforce, the biggest reason to not be working or looking for work is that they're studying.

Things become concerning, however, when it comes to women. Just nine countries around the world, including Syria and Iraq, have a smaller proportion of working women than India, and if Bihar were a separate country, it would have the lowest share of working women in the world.[3] Men's labour force participation rate has always been higher than that for women. But while men's participation remained constant in the period between 1993-94 and 2017-18, the labour force participation rate for women declined. India's female labour force participation rate has been falling steadily over time, and fell to a historic low of 23.3 per cent in 2017-18, meaning that over three out of four women over the age of fifteen in India are neither working nor seeking work. The entire decline is driven by rural women, whose participation has dropped from roughly 32 per cent to 18 per cent over the same period. (Fig. 7.1)

This matters not only for the country in economic terms, but also for the aspirations of women—dropping out of the workforce might not be a choice. In a large survey of teenage girls,[4] nearly 75 per cent of the respondents said that they wanted to work after they finished studying. However, the 2018-19 PLFS found that just half of women were either working or looking for work, with domestic work, including child-rearing, consuming the time of women.[5]

Why this decline in female workforce participation rates has taken place is a matter of debate and explanations tend to depend substantially on the economist or commentator's political leaning. People on the right tend to diagnose the fall as a consequence of one of two things: bad data or good news. For the most part, the bad data argument is of a piece with generic criticisms of the NSSO and isn't substantive. It's possible that better trained enumerators would do a better job of understanding just how much economically productive

Figure 7.1: India is among the ten countries with the lowest female labour force participation rates* (LFPR) globally

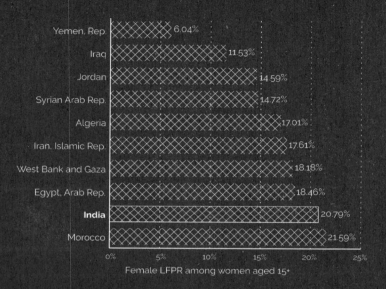

Country	Female LFPR
Yemen, Rep.	6.04%
Iraq	11.53%
Jordan	14.59%
Syrian Arab Rep.	14.72%
Algeria	17.01%
Iran, Islamic Rep.	17.61%
West Bank and Gaza	18.18%
Egypt, Arab Rep.	18.46%
India	20.79%
Morocco	21.59%

Female LFPR among women aged 15+

*ILO modelled estimate for 2019
Source: World Bank World Development Indicators, 2021

. . . And it's getting worse over time

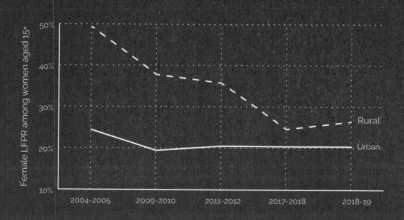

Female LFPR among women aged 15+

Rural
Urban

2004-2005   2009-2010   2011-2012   2017-2018   2018-19

Source: National Sample Survey reports (various years)

work women do, as some experts like the NCAER's Sonalde Desai have been arguing, but it isn't clear that explains the decline.

As for the good news argument—fewer women are working, the argument goes, because more of them are studying, or because their households are getting richer. But young women out of the workforce are not most likely to be studying, but instead most likely to be attending to household chores. Moreover, the decline in labour force participation is substantial among older women too, who are outside the studying age; while some of the fall in women's workforce participation is explained by better rates of higher-education enrolment, the data also points to a fall in working rates for older women. The participation rate for women aged fifteen–twenty-nine fell by eight percentage points between 2011-12 and 2017-18 to 16.4 per cent, but fell by at least seven percentage points for the thirty–fifty age group as well. The decline was highest among women aged thirty-five–thirty-nine years (the labour force participation rate for this age bracket fell nine percentage points to 33.5 per cent). Among women in the prime working ages of thirty–fifty, more than two in three women are not in the workforce, with the majority of them reporting that they are 'attending to domestic duties only'.[6] What's more, between 2011-12 and 2017-18, workforce participation fell even as incomes were declining, so getting richer wasn't the explanation either.

Sher Verick, a labour economist with the ILO and its former head in India, believes that the answer could lie at the intersection of economic and social factors—social norms restrict the educational and employment opportunities for women to more gender-conforming fields, and those happen to be slow-growing sectors of the economy, he thinks.

About half of all adults in six locations that a group of economists studied in 2016 felt that married women whose husbands made a good living should not work outside the home.[7] A sample survey of Delhi households in 2006 found that the decision to work outside the house was usually a household decision and that marriage significantly altered the likelihood of a woman working—both in terms of women joining and leaving the workforce. While the birth of a child is usually associated with women dropping out of the workforce in the West, in India, marriage is one of the most important factors, the researchers said.[8] Since marriage is near-universal in India, this means that the norms of the marital household can decide the pathway into and out of the labour force for women.

When the 2011 Census data came out, it showed that Seelampur, a large impoverished district in Delhi's north-east had the lowest proportion of women in paid work (5 per cent). For a week in 2013, I took the metro across the city and walked around one of its large slums, talking to women who were at home about why they weren't at paid work, and returning over the next few days to talk to the sisters and neighbours who were at work.

Fiza Bi, a lady in her forties, sat bouncing her two-year-old granddaughter on her knee. Her husband had not allowed her to work, but after a fight during which he abused her and threw her out of their one-room tenement, she found herself saddled with two children and the need for rent money to pay for a new roof over their heads. 'So I asked some women who I knew worked in a factory to take me along, and I got a job cutting threads off jeans. It took me half an hour to walk there, and I got paid Rs 4,000 every month for a six-day week.' She could make rent, feed her family and have a little left over for anything the children needed. Then her husband re-entered her life, visiting her once a week and paying the rent. But he had one rule: she had to quit her job. So Fiza rejoined the ranks of Seelampur women who aren't looking for paid work. 'My husband gives me a few hundred from his salary of Rs 9,000,' she said. 'It's not enough, but there's nothing I can do.'

The notion that being able to work outside the home was dependent on husbands was ingrained in the minds of the younger women of Seelampur too. Renu Jaikishen had seen it in her own home. Sisters Renu and Sunita, aged nineteen and twenty-one respectively, also worked in a garment-finishing unit near their home at the edge of Seelampur. When Sunita got married, she had to quit her job. By the next year, she had a child and was back in her parents' home after marital disputes. She watched her sister getting ready for work, pinning her folded dupatta in place, with something approaching envy. 'I'll try going back to work when the baby is older and I can leave him with my parents,' she said. Listening, Renu was taking it all in. 'Until I get married I can work. After that it will depend on him,' Renu said of her own future.

These norms create a social environment where domestic chores and childcare become the sole responsibility of women, leaving them without the option of taking up paid work.[9] Further, they relegate women to slow-growing areas of the economy like agriculture, teaching and crafts, research has found.[10]

Then there is the universe of women who exist between the two extremes of being in and out of the workforce, as the feminist economist Ashwini Deshpande has noted. These might be women who do unpaid economic work in family businesses, or who do small labour-intensive jobs for only part of the day, or those who work occasionally. Women in this last category, Deshpande notes, are most likely to fall through the cracks of the statistical system.[11]

Finally, there is the issue of availability of work and the demand for women's labour. Deshpande is among the economists who in recent years have suggested that this could explain a significant part of why women are not in the paid workforce.[12]

*

What of those Indians in the labour force—what is their work life like? A common trope about India's workforce is that hiring and firing is impossibly difficult on account of antiquated labour laws. The truth is that India's workers are among the world's most insecure and need more, not fewer protections. The most recent official data[13] shows that over half of all those in the workforce are self-employed, another quarter work as casual labour and the remaining are wage workers or salaried workers. The bulk of India's workforce is engaged in the 'informal' sector, meaning that they have little in terms of job protection, benefits and social security. Seven out of ten workers in the non-farm sector are in informal employment, seven out of ten salaried workers in jobs with no written contract and over half in jobs that give them no paid leave or social security benefits.

Here's another reason that low unemployment numbers become meaningless: the quality of the majority of Indian jobs is so poor that it is evident that a lack of viable options is what is keeping many working men and women 'employed' in these jobs.

Indians are among the most overworked workers. Gambia, Mongolia, Maldives and Qatar (where a quarter of the population is Indian) are the only countries where the average worker works longer than an Indian peer.[14] With a forty-eight-hour working week, India ranks fifth among all countries in the time spent working. Within India, it is the better-paid workers in cities who tend to work longer than their rural counterparts. Men work longer hours than women in both rural and urban areas, and for both men and women, the hours of work are longer in urban areas. The average working Indian woman works a longer week than her developing country counterparts—44.4 hours per week (in the April–June 2018 period), as against the developing country average of 35–36 hours, as per ILO estimates. (Fig. 7.2)

In 2019, India conducted its first time-use survey in two decades. The definition of hours worked the country uses includes time spent on actual work, on travel between work locations, and on short bathroom or tea breaks. The time spent commuting to work and on longer meal breaks, however, is not included. Since the data is derived from household surveys, it includes both formal and informal employment of all types. The survey found similar trends. Men spent over four times as much time in their day on paid work as women, and urban men spent over an hour more than their rural counterparts on paid work each day.

Most Indian workers rarely get a day off. Those who work for themselves work virtually every day. Even salaried employees work more than six days a week on average. The majority of Indian workers try to live close to work, and in the case of many women, home and the workplace are the

Figure 7.2: Indian workers put in among the longest hours of any country's workers

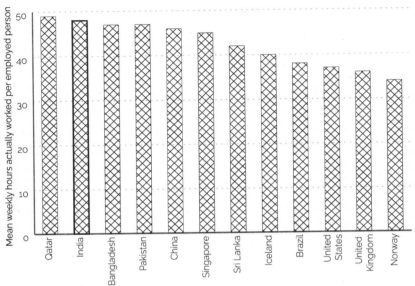

Source: International Labour Organisation Statistics on Working Time (accessed on Feb 2021)

The average Indian worker works virtually evey day of the week

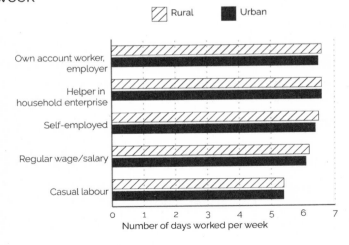

Note: Data is for Jan—March 2019
Source: Period Labour Force Survey (2018-19), National Sample Survey Office

same space. For both men and women across India, walking is the most common commute to work. For women, after walking, the bus is the most common mode of transport. This is in contrast to men for whom, after walking, cycling and riding a scooter or bike to work are the most common. This difference could reflect both the lower rates of asset ownership among women and lack of finances for them to pay for their commute. But it could also reflect the fact that women simply travel much shorter distances to work. Forty-five per cent of women do not even travel for work, meaning that they work out of their own houses. As a result, India has one of the world's most lopsided ratios of male versus female commuting.[15]

Women travelling shorter distances to work—or the gender commuting gap—is a global phenomenon. A big reason for this is that women, rather than men, are more likely to be the primary caregivers for children. This can then have an impact on wages; if women take work closer to home because of caring responsibilities, they may be less likely to find a job well matched to their skills or with a high-paying employer.[16] In India, gender expectations of women working outside their homes and affordability of transport mean that women are restricted to jobs closer to their homes. Women in Delhi slums spend more time travelling on slower modes of transport to access work since faster modes are more expensive.[17] Similarly, women in Mumbai find the bus pass prohibitively expensive and say that cheap bus travel would enable them to better access the local trains which, in turn, could connect them to better-paying jobs in the south and centre of the city.[18]

Despite their long hours, Indian workers are also

not making much money. India had the lowest statutory minimum wage of any country in the Asia Pacific region, except for Bangladesh, as of 2019. India's minimum wages are among the lowest in the world, except for some sub-Saharan African nations.[19] Though actual wage levels can differ from the statutory minimum wages across countries, the two tend to be closely linked, especially for blue-collar workers.

It is true that some employment is not adequately understood yet by the NSSO, but the problem isn't exactly that the government is missing people in the gig economy. A bigger issue is that official classifications can make low-paying, insecure jobs seem like robust employment. Among the codes in the National Classification of Occupations that India follows is this one—Code 121: Directors and Chief Executives. By official data, this is the most common occupation for urban men and the third most common occupation for urban women (after domestic cleaners and garment workers).[20] Sounds high-skilled and well-paying? Not so much, labour economists find; it might just be a fancy-sounding way of describing people who run their own small one-person enterprise.

Of the women workers described as directors and chief executives, 99 per cent were actually self-employed, of which around one-third worked as unpaid family workers. These women were mainly engaged within self-help groups and co-operatives as 'partners', and had thus been recorded as directors or working proprietors, even as their activities for the most part remained confined to food processing and textile and garment manufacturing. A large proportion of self-employed women workers were also engaged in outsourced manufacturing work, typically characterised by low earnings, long hours and lack of any form of social protection.[21]

*

The gulf between the jobs that people want for themselves and for their children and the jobs that are actually available is enormous, and widening. Across age, location, caste and class—in fact, even more so for upper castes and the rich— the first preference of Indians in terms of employment is a government job.[22] A government job offers not just decent pay and respectability, it also offers stability; an estimated 122 million Indians lost their jobs in April 2020 when the country went into lockdown, demonstrating just how precarious most jobs are. Asked to choose between a permanent job with a relatively low salary, a job with like-minded co-workers, a well-earning job, or a job with high job satisfaction, Indians are most likely to choose job stability. This explains why public-sector employment remains so sought after among the youth.[23]

The attraction of a government job has not shown any signs of declining—the majority of India's youth (65 per cent) would prefer a government job, if given a choice. Setting up one's own business comes a distant second (19 per cent), followed by a job in the private sector (7 per cent). The appeal of a government job has, in fact, increased slightly over the last decade. In 2007, in response to the same, 62 per cent of the youth had said they would prefer a government job.[24]

Asked in a 2017 survey to indicate which kind of job would they give most priority to—a permanent job even if it meant drawing a little less salary, a job with an opportunity to work with people of their liking, a job with good income in which one didn't have to worry about money, or a job that gave them a feeling of satisfaction—33 per cent of young people accorded the greatest priority to having a permanent job, even if it meant drawing a little less salary.[25]

Among young Indians, one of the biggest expectations from the Modi government is to create more government jobs: a 2019 survey found that more than 80 per cent of millennials (those aged between twenty-three and thirty-eight) wanted the government to create more jobs in the public sector.[26] This craving for government jobs is also reflected in applications—the same year, a railways recruitment drive for filling 127,000 vacancies attracted applications from twenty-three million candidates.[27]

Among some groups of young people, the desire for white-collar jobs in particular runs deep. A survey of teenage girls found that the top jobs in their minds were skilled professional jobs: teachers, tailors, doctors, policewomen and nurses.[28] Another survey of young girls found that a quarter wanted to become teachers, followed by doctors or nurses, while just 1 per cent of rural youth wanted to work in agriculture.[29] Anju Singh, a seventeen-year-old, lives in a slum in south-central Delhi, and her mother works as a domestic worker. After passing her Class XII exams from a government school, Anju came to me for help for a job. What sort of work do you want to do? I asked her. One in which I have to wear a salwar-kurta and carry a file to office every day, she told me.

But these jobs are rare. Instead, in rural India, half the male workers and over 70 per cent of women workers are employed in agriculture. Another 15 per cent of male rural workers work in construction. The most common job for urban Indian women is domestic work, followed by clothing manufacture, teaching and saleswomen positions in grocery stores. The most common job for urban Indian men is in construction, followed by salesmen positions in grocery stores, taxi and auto driving, clothing manufacture and public administration.[30] (Fig. 7.3)

There were 19.5 million jobs in the public sector in 1992-93, when India's population was 839 million. While there are 1.2 billion Indians now, the number of jobs in the public sector has shrunk to 17.6 million.[31] Fewer than 10 per cent of households in rural India have a family member with a salaried job and fewer than 0.05 per cent have a family member with a government job.[32]

Moreover, while the major attraction of a government job is the security and stability it provides, government jobs may increasingly not be providing this security. A growing proportion of jobs at Central public-sector enterprises are increasingly filled by contract workers who do not receive the benefits that permanent workers enjoy.[33] In the manufacturing and services sector, there has been an increase in government jobs with contracts of less than a year at the cost of jobs with contracts of three years or more.[34] Including all of the government's contractual employment and employment at state-government level suggests that overall public-sector employment may be increasing, but this employment is skewed towards low-skill jobs.[35]

Yet, in addition to some stability, these jobs also offer better pay. At all levels, but particularly at the lowest education and skill levels, private-sector salaries are below public-sector salaries. Due to a guaranteed minimum salary in government service, a cleaning worker in a government office is likely to

Figure 7.3: Blue-collar nation

The most common job that working women in urban India do is that of domestic help...

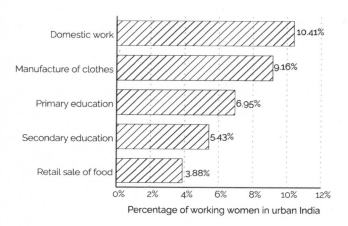

Percentage of working women in urban India

- Domestic work — 10.41%
- Manufacture of clothes — 9.16%
- Primary education — 6.95%
- Secondary education — 5.43%
- Retail sale of food — 3.88%

...while for men it is construction work

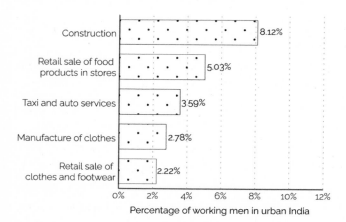

Percentage of working men in urban India

- Construction — 8.12%
- Retail sale of food products in stores — 5.03%
- Taxi and auto services — 3.59%
- Manufacture of clothes — 2.78%
- Retail sale of clothes and footwear — 2.22%

"Job" - industry 4-digit code industry code as per NIC-2008 classification
Source: Periodic Labour Force Survey, Ministry of Statistics and Programme Implementation, GoI, 2020

earn far more than a domestic servant doing the same work in a private home or business, the IHDS shows. In 2012, a rural agricultural wage labourer could expect to earn about Rs 17,500 per year, while the urban non-agricultural labourer could expect to earn about Rs 60,000. But an illiterate male working in a salaried government job could expect to make Rs 144,000 per year.[36]

Government or public-sector employment also serves as a moderating influence on other forms of social inequalities that market forces exacerbate. While women earn lower salaries in both public and private sector, the ratio of female to male salaries is considerably higher in the public sector than in the private sector. Similarly, salary inequalities among various social groups are larger in the private sector than in the public sector. Regardless of the sector, forward castes have higher salaries than OBCs, Dalits, Adivasis and Muslims. But the differences in government salaries by social group are lesser in the public sector at both lower and higher skill levels.

This disparity between the government and private sector contributes to the squeeze on decent jobs that is at the heart of the conversation around reservation in India: the demands for greater reservation by OBC groups and Muslims in some states, the upper-caste pushback against existing reservation, the demand for reservation for economically poor upper castes and an escalation of demands from relatively privileged groups like Jats, Gujjars and Patidars for reservation.

These latter castes, whose protests have posed difficult questions for politics in the last ten years, do not see their future in agriculture because of the attraction exerted by the city and because of the crisis in rural India, particularly the collapse in rural wage growth, according to Christophe Jaffrelot.[37] Some from landed castes who owned land next to big cities could sell it to developers—this is the story of the Maratha farmers of Magarpatta on the outskirts of Pune, for instance, or the Jat farmers who sold land to Greater Noida developers. But most of the migrants who left their village to try their luck in the city are disappointed by the job market, Jaffrelot argues. 'In contrast to the middle class inhabiting urban centres for generations, they have not received the kind of English-medium education that gives access to the services, the sector (especially in IT) offering opportunities. While they have sometimes run heavy debts to get some private, not-so-good education, they have to fall back on unskilled jobs,' he says. These jobs are precarious and badly paid, while those in the public sectors are much better paid, so the dominant castes want to be counted as OBCs to benefit from job reservation.

In objective terms, this sense of victimhood is not based in fact. For the most prestigious category of white-collar jobs, caste hierarchies have remained largely static over the past five decades.[38] The share of men who are in professional or salaried jobs is already by far the highest among Brahmin, and then non-Brahmin forward-caste men, even with reservation in place for those from backward castes and no reservation for upper castes, on account of the disproportionate access historically high levels of education and income give to the upper castes.[39]

Much of this can be explained by the difference in educational attainment. But this is not a full explanation. In a classic experiment, the economists Sukhadeo Thorat and Paul Attewell found that Dalit respondents to job advertisements were less likely to be called than upper-caste respondents with the same qualifications.[40]

For the aspirations of marginalised groups, who suffer from a lack of social and human capital in addition to discrimination, as well as those from socially privileged groups but without the education and skills to get them the jobs they want, an expanded public sector as well as higher minimum wages could help reduce the vast gulf between the private and public sectors, and leave even less room for reservations for the marginalised to be a convenient bogey.

*

Since 2011-12, the government has not published a full Employment and Unemployment survey, as the NSSO reports are called, but has moved from 2017 to the PLFS. This aims to provide higher-frequency (quarterly) employment and unemployment data, but statistical aims are at the mercy of political forces. The first PLFS annual report was expected in December 2018, but the government delayed its release until after the 2019 Lok Sabha elections, presumably because the numbers were bad.

This isn't to say that the NSSO couldn't do a better job of collecting data from the informal sector (just as it should do a better job of obtaining data on the professions of the super-rich). The NSSO has itself constituted numerous committees which have come out with dense reports on ways to improve its informal-sector data. The PLFS, which the government has largely ignored thanks to its unflattering numbers, was supposed to be one step in this direction.

The origins of the PLFS lie in the recommendations of a committee set up by the NSC in 2009 and headed by one of its members, Amitabh Kundu. The Kundu committee's task was to establish a framework for collecting high-frequency (monthly or quarterly) labour-market data for the urban areas of the country. Based on the pilots suggested by the Kundu committee and feedback from other committees that looked into the issue, the NSC recommended a survey questionnaire that was similar to the quinquennial employment–unemployment surveys. It would provide quarterly estimates for urban areas, and annual estimates for both urban and rural areas, setting the stage for the launch of the PLFS in 2016.

But when the report was finalised, it dawned upon the government that it showed a steep spike in unemployment rates compared to the past quinquennial rounds, and so it was held back, prompting the resignations of two NSC members. Government officials such as NITI Aayog chief executive Amitabh Kant expressed scepticism about the findings of the report and raised questions about the methodology. Following Somesh's leak of the data, the NITI Aayog, a government think tank, and then finance minister Arun Jaitley classified the report as a 'draft', while then energy minister Dharmendra Pradhan said that 'no such report existed'. One day after the Modi government came back to power, they released the report, and every word of Somesh's account was found to have been accurate. Once the 2019 elections had come and gone, the government went back to quietly releasing the PLFS reports regularly and without much fanfare or controversy.

All of this was pre-pandemic. Although the PLFS was meant to be, there was no labour data available right through 2020 up until August 2021, as the pandemic threw not just lives and jobs, but also administrative systems out of gear. As a result, many economists have turned to the CMIE, a large sample panel survey that is private, paid and closed. Modi and his administration, on the other hand, have chosen to point to administrative data like payroll statistics.

Modi is right—there is a problem with jobs data. But it isn't the one he claims, that the data doesn't capture jobs. The problem is that the government is neglecting its own data mechanisms, which can capture all the data about real Indian jobs, and suppressing them when they prove inconvenient. India's jobs crisis is two-fold—not enough jobs and suppressed data.

VIII

HOW INDIA IS GROWING AND AGEING

India's population growth has slowed much faster than earlier anticipated, but old narratives persist and no one seems prepared for what the generations of the future will need.

Zeenat Shaikh has five brothers and four sisters; Zeenat is the youngest child, born in her grandmother's home in a village in the western state of Maharashtra in 1950. She went to the local primary school and her education was discontinued after she was ten. Married at sixteen, she has three daughters and a son, all of whom have basic college degrees. 'My oldest girl has one daughter and has told me she does not want any more children—she wants to educate her daughter in the best colleges!' Shaikh says.

In the span of two generations, the lives of the women in the Shaikh family have undergone an incredible transformation, with the economic and social pressure to have large families receding, and the freedom to study and work making an entrance. Yet, Shaikh often finds herself wondering about the world her granddaughter will grow up in.

When India's Midnight's Children[1] were born, they emerged into a new country, one that would be almost unrecognisable today. The average woman in 1950 had more than six children, as against the average Indian woman in 2020, who will have just 2.2 children on average.

The country in all had 376 million people, a billion fewer than today.

At Independence, the median Indian was twenty-one years old (making half the country immediately ineligible to vote at the time) and just 5 per cent of the population was over the age of sixty. The median Indian is now over twenty-eight, and the share of Indians over the age of sixty has doubled.

But within these familiar headlines lies a much stranger, much more unexpected story, and coming to grips with it will shape our preparedness for the future.

The Bomb That Fizzled Out

A majority—57 per cent—of India's 376 million people in 1950 were under the age of twenty-five. Over the next decades, India's population grew quickly; from the early 1960s, the country's population grew at over 2 per cent every year, right until the early 1980s. Between 1950 and 1985 population doubled, growing at a faster rate than even that of China. The phrases 'population explosion', 'ticking time-bomb', and 'demographic disaster' frequented magazine articles; the writer Paul Ehrlich opened his 1968 book, *The Population Bomb*, with a description—of a cab ride that he and his family took in Delhi, in an 'ancient taxi', its seats 'hopping with fleas'— representative of popular opinion. He wrote:

> The streets seemed alive with people. People eating, people washing, people sleeping. People visiting, arguing, and

screaming. People thrust their hands through the taxi window, begging. People defecating and urinating. People clinging to buses. People herding animals. People, people, people, people . . . [S]ince that night, I've known the feel of overpopulation.[2]

But from the early 1980s onwards, annual population growth began to decline steadily, falling first below a 2 per cent annual rate of increase, to 1.5 per cent by 2005, and now to under 1 per cent in 2020.[3] This places India's annual growth rate below population growth rates in Iran, Chile, Australia and Ireland. Population growth has slowed quicker than the United Nations (UN) projected and new forecasts for India are the lowest they have been since the UN first began these projections a decade ago. While the country's population increased by 21.5 per cent between 1991 and 2001, population growth slowed to an increase of 17.7 per cent between 2001 and 2011. According to the Indian government, the population is expected to grow by only 12.1 per cent between 2021 and 2041.[4]

Since 1931, the first Census for which this data is available, the population growth rate of India's Muslim minority—among whom income, health and education indicators are among India's worst—has exceeded that of its Hindu majority. But as per the most recent 2011 Census, Muslim growth has slowed faster than Hindu growth, indicating that convergence between the two communities is on its way.

Behind these downward revisions is the story of India's rapidly accelerating demographic transition, a phenomenon whose pace has defied global expectations. Population projections emerge from the expected direction for trends in births and deaths in a given country. Changes in the fertility rate—the expected number of children that a woman will have in her lifetime if she continues to experience the currently prevailing age-specific fertility rates—affect the birth rate, while changes in disease environments—the decline in maternal mortality and the reduction in deaths from communicable diseases, for instance—affect the death rate. India's fertility rate has fallen faster than earlier predicted by international agencies, on the back of a remarkable turnaround led by some of India's most marginalised women.

Not that you would know it from the headlines. In his 2019 Independence Day address, Indian Prime Minister Narendra Modi warned of a 'population explosion' in the country and called for schemes to address the challenge. Modi said that India's population growth was a hindrance to development and he praised those with small families as undertaking an 'act of patriotism'.[5] On family WhatsApp groups and college alumni Facebook groups, it doesn't take long for someone to trot out the theory that India's only problem is that there are too many people.

After a parliamentarian from Modi's ruling BJP introduced a Private Member Bill seeking a 'two child rule' in India in 2019,[6] other BJP members of Parliament urged the government to bring in such a law.[7] Speaking on World Population Day in 2019, a minister in Modi's cabinet advocated for a population control law; in 2018 he had said that 'one particular community' was responsible for increasing India's population.[8]

While any government is unlikely to bring in a coercive law of this kind at the national level, fear-mongering about high population growth, especially among Muslims, remains an integral part of right-wing Hindu propaganda and has begun to inform policy in terms of punitive measures passed by various states. All the while, India's women, and notably its Muslim women, have scripted a quiet success story.

India's Stunning Fertility Transition

Growing incomes and better access to health and education for women have shrunk family sizes even faster than many had predicted. By the middle of the 2020s, India will have hit replacement fertility levels, after which population growth first stabilises and then gradually begins to shrink. Even among high-fertility social groups—the most prominent and widely discussed of which are Muslims—fertility is falling faster than anticipated.

In demographic terms, 2.1 is considered the 'replacement level of fertility', meaning that if every woman has 2.1 children on average, the population will remain of the same size. By 2013, India's total fertility rate (TFR) was already down to 2.3 children per woman, a further decline from 2.4 in 2012. The earlier UN population projections estimated a higher fertility rate for this period and this threw their projections off. The TFR in twenty-three states and union territories, including all of the south, is now below replacement level, and among the major states only Bihar still had a TFR of above three children per woman as of 2018.[9] (Fig. 8.1)

Muslims in India continue to have a higher fertility rate than Hindus, as they have had since the relevant Census data began to be recorded. However, Muslim fertility is falling faster than Hindu fertility and the gap between the fertility rates of the two communities is closing.[10] States that are doing an overall better job on reducing fertility are also doing a better job of closing the gap between the two communities' fertility rates—as these states get richer, better educated and healthier,

Figure 8.1: Barring eight states in the north and east, all states have achieved replacement fertility in India

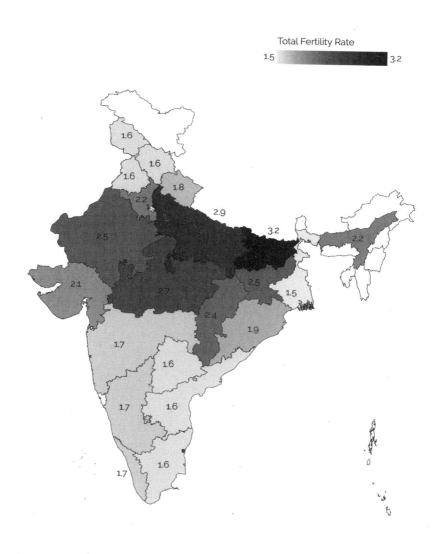

Total Fertility Rate (TFR) is the average number of children that a woman will have in her lifetime. A TFR of 2.1 is considered the replacement level.
Source: Sample Registration System Statistical Report, Office of the Registrar General of India, 2020

the women are beginning to have fewer kids. In every state and every age group, educated women have the lowest fertility rates—women who have completed their schooling have their first child five years later on average than those who have finished less than five years of schooling. As a result, Muslim women in the southern states have a lower fertility rate than Hindus in the Gangetic-belt states; high Muslim fertility is only a problem in states with high levels of fertility for all women.[11] (Fig. 8.2)

In Europe and North America, the fertility transition means that women are having children later than ever; both the median British and the median American woman is now over thirty on average when she has her children. In India, declining fertility has meant, counter-intuitively, a decrease in the mean age at childbirth for women; in 2020, Indian women had their children two years on average *earlier* than women in 1950, contrary to the common belief that Indian women are having children later than ever. The reason behind this is that women in India still have their children relatively young—they just *stop* having more children sooner. Earlier, large family sizes meant that women continued having children well into their forties. With two or three children now the norm, the average Indian woman finishes having her children far earlier than before.

Between 1950 and 1970, the largest share of children were born to women in their late twenties. As women began to limit their family sizes, they began to have most of their children in their early twenties. Only from the middle of the 2020s is this trend expected to once again reverse, as India begins to follow the trajectory more commonly seen in industrialised nations.

Figure 8.2: The Muslim growth bogey

Muslim population growth is slowing rapidly...

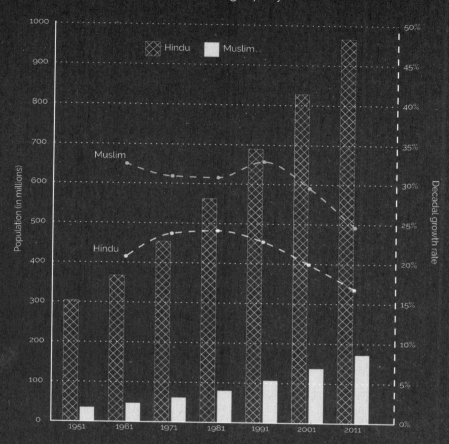

....and in states like Kerala, Muslim population growth is slower than that of Hindus in UP

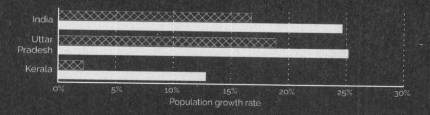

Sources: Census and International Institute of Population Sciences

Fewer Children Means Even Fewer Girls

There is a dark side to this stunning transformation, however.[12] India may be going through a radical demographic transition, but one thing remains the same—the desire for a male child.

The most recent decennial Census, conducted in 2011, clearly indicates that families are choosing to restrict the size of their families. Nearly half of the children born in 2000 were the third, fourth, fifth, and so on in the family. In comparison, in 2011, just a third of children born in the preceding year were the family's third, fourth, fifth, and so on. In fact, the absolute number of first and second-borns only increased between 2000 and 2010, while the number of later-born children declined.

But while the number of children born every year is slowing rapidly in India, the slowdown is faster for girl babies than for boy babies. Just under 2.1 crore children were born in 2010; in 2000 in comparison, 1.98 crore children were born. However, the growth in the number of male children born was higher at 5.44 per cent, while the growth in the number of girls born was far lower at 4.69 per cent. The sex ratio at birth as a result was slightly worse in 2011 than it was in 2001.

The two processes—declining fertility and a preference for male children—are going on simultaneously. 'Fertility is declining faster than expected in India, and when fertility declines, we see an increase in the intensity of preference for male children,' Dr P. Arokiasamy, a leading demographer and head of the Department for Development Studies at the Mumbai-based International Institute for Population Sciences, agrees. This can be through sex-selective abortion, or the 'stopping principle', where families stop having children as soon as they've had a boy.

Smaller families are less gender equal in India. Around

290 million women have had at least one child with two children being the most common family size and large families relatively uncommon. Bring in gender dynamics, however, and an extremely complicated picture emerges. Among families with one to four children, more boys than girls are born. The unnatural advantage for boy babies is particularly sharp among families with two children—half of such families have one boy and one girl, a third have two boys, and just one-sixth have two girls. Even given the slight birth advantage that boys enjoy (in nature, there is a slightly higher likelihood of boys being born than girls), such sharply skewed sex ratios are a clear indication of unnatural processes, most likely pre-natal sex-selective births.

What's more, it's clear that as family sizes have got smaller over the last decade, these processes have only intensified. The magnitude of disparity between small families with more boys than girls and large families with more girls than boys has sharpened between 2001 and 2011. The decline in fertility could, in fact, explain one-third to one-half of the recent increase in India's sex ratio in favour of boys.[13]

Families where a son is born are more likely to stop having children than families where a girl is born. Girls are far more likely to be a part of large families, while boys are much more likely to be part of single-child or smaller-sized families. The male-biased Indian sex ratio at birth is distinctly sharpened for the last child of the family. This is not a trend that occurs naturally; as a comparison made with Indonesia shows, sex ratios in a population do not normally change significantly with birth order, signalling that there is something 'unnatural' going on with Indian fertility.[14]

Some of this could be attributed to families which continue

to have children until they have as many sons as they would like. However, in-utero sex selection definitely plays a part too. With the spread of ultrasound technology that allowed for pre-natal sex determination, the likelihood that third- and fourth-order births would be girls in families that had not yet had a son declined sharply after the mid-1980s.[15] By the mid-1990s, ultrasound access was even more widespread, but the desire for small families was growing too. As a result of these two phenomena, families were no longer waiting for third and fourth births to intervene, and even second-order births began to be less likely to be those of girls.

Further complicating the issue is the fact that multiple Indian states are now experimenting with 'incentivising' small families, a policy decision that could actively worsen India's sex ratio. Whether population control is introduced through coercion or incentives, in patriarchal societies it leads to a worsening of the sex ratio. Areas in China that enforced fines for second births more strictly during the one-child policy regime had lower fertility but worse sex ratios than areas that enforced fines less strictly.[16]

A similar pattern developed in Haryana, when a scheme launched by the state government in 2002 offered financial incentives to families that had fewer children, with the highest cash incentive to those having one daughter only and a lower amount to those having one son only or two daughters only. The result was a decline in fertility, as evidenced by the share of families with only one child. However, this decline was driven almost entirely by families having only one boy. There was no increase in families with only one daughter, despite the financial incentives being highest for this outcome. There was also no consistently significant increase in families having two daughters only, despite the financial benefits for such families being the same as for those who had one boy only. The scheme did encourage smaller families—but only among those who were able to have one son only.[17]

In general, families tend not to sex select before their first child.[18] If the first child is a girl, the likelihood of sex selection rises prior to the second birth. However, with the introduction of financial incentives for having just one child, coupled with latent preference for sons in Indian society, families began to sex select before the birth of the first child as well, resulting in the worsening of the state's sex ratio at birth.[19]

Even schemes with less mass impact than that in Haryana have had similar effects. Starting with Rajasthan in 1992, several states began to enact laws debarring candidates with more than two children from contesting local-body elections. Researchers looked at eight such states and found that these laws did reduce fertility, but again, this came at the cost of a worsening of the sex ratio, as families tried to ensure their future eligibility for public office, while still having their desired number of sons.[20]

India has had remarkable success in lowering fertility to the extent that its southern states have now reached replacement levels of fertility, at which population growth will stabilise and the population as a whole will stop growing. What is all the more admirable is that this change has come largely without coercive measures of the sort adopted by China and is driven by the belief that education, access to health and economic prosperity, particularly for women, automatically drives down female fertility among all social groups. However, there is growing evidence that in the absence of genuine transformation in gender relations, the push for smaller families is making pre-natal sex selection more common. While families might have chosen in the past to have repeated pregnancies until a male child was born—as borne out by the far higher likelihood of the youngest children of a large family being boys—as smaller families become a social norm, families are being pushed towards artificial methods of ensuring a male offspring.

According to the latest NFHS, 89 per cent of women aged fifteen–forty-nine with two sons and no daughters were content with a family size of four. But for women who had daughters but no sons, a larger family was on the cards. Among women aged fifteen–forty-nine with two living daughters and no sons, far fewer (63 per cent) wanted no more children, in comparison. With no real evidence that the Indian preference for at least one son is going away any time soon, for the near future, slowing population growth may continue to mean that families, as far as possible, attempt to have fewer girls.

One Country, Two Speeds

Single narratives have never been able to explain all of India. The larger story for India might be one of falling fertility, but peel back the layers and the story runs on two distinct levels, with untold consequences for the future of Indian society, economy and politics.

A TFR of 2.1 is considered to be an important milestone for developing countries seeking to slow down their population growth. In India, it's also intensely political, because of the wide gap in TFR of southern states—that have better education and health outcomes, and have long reached replacement fertility—and northern states, which are still some way off.

India's TFR now stands at 2.2. All of south and west India have already achieved replacement fertility, while the states of the Gangetic plains are still some way off. As of 2018, Bihar is now the only Indian state where a woman is likely to have over three children in her lifetime. Among states that have not yet reached replacement fertility, Bihar has seen one of the slowest reductions in TFR over the last ten years. By 2036, it will still be the only state that has not achieved replacement fertility, projections say. Over four decades separate India's most developed states from its least developed states in terms of this fertility transition: Kerala achieved replacement fertility in 1998, while Bihar will get there only in 2039.

Many factors could explain why this is the case, in addition to progress that is yet to be made on economic growth and access to health and education for women. With agriculture remaining dominant, families might not yet be seeing the advantages of smaller families. States that have weaker administrative capacity might also be less able to enforce the aggressive female sterilisation measures that have dominated family planning in practice in India. Cultural factors play a role too—women who might want to practice contraception might not want to necessarily subject themselves to the irreversible surgery that is often offered as the only option.

Meanwhile, among the major states, fertility in the south has fallen well below replacement levels. Additionally, save for Bihar, Rajasthan and Uttar Pradesh, the urban areas of all states are now at replacement or below-replacement fertility, which means that these urban areas will only grow as long as mortality improves and there is some in-migration. In fact, the TFR in urban India as a whole has now fallen to levels that in some countries are taken as a cause for concern. The

TFR in urban India fell to 1.7 as of 2017, comparable to that of Belgium, Iceland and Norway, and lower than that of the United States or the United Kingdom (1.8). Japan, which is regarded as being in the grip of a demographic crisis with too-low fertility rates, is some distance behind urban India, at 1.4 children per woman. Some other less affluent states are at Japan-like 'crisis' levels—urban Odisha, West Bengal (1.3), Jammu and Kashmir (1.2) and Himachal Pradesh (1.1) have a TFR lower than that of Japan.

'It *is* a crisis,' says Dr Arokiasamy, 'except that nobody is talking about it.' The focus on above-replacement fertility in the northern states has dominated the national dialogue around fertility to the detriment of the southern states and urban areas where fertility is falling far faster than expected, Dr Arokiasamy says. In addition to the natural demographic transition—by which populations get richer, women get better health and education, child survival rates improve and families choose to have fewer children—the south is also seeing the impact of aggressive family planning 'target-setting' by southern state governments and health officials, he believes. These states should 'now wind up their family-planning efforts' and focus on ageing instead, he says.

As fewer children are born and the developed southern states age rapidly, the average Tamil man will be over twelve years older than the average Bihari man by 2036. Meanwhile, as fertility falls slowly in the north, the average Bihari woman will have more children than women from Kerala did forty years ago. By 2036, Tamil Nadu will be India's oldest state, with a median age of over forty, older still than Kerala, which, with a median age of 31.9 years, was the oldest Indian state in 2011. Bihar was and will remain India's youngest state, the only state where the median individual will be under thirty even in 2036, population projections show. The median Indian will be 34.7 years of age in 2036. (Fig. 8.3)

Meanwhile, over one-third of the total increase in India's population between 2011 and 2036 will come from two states alone—Uttar Pradesh and Bihar—while all of the southern states will see their share in the population declining.

Fertility as a Political Flashpoint

This two-speed transition is at the heart of a deep polarisation between India's poorer northern and richer southern states. The grievances are many—the growing use of Hindi, the language spoken in a large part of northern India, at the cost of the southern languages; the wide disparity in the income generated by the southern states as against the share of federal revenue they receive in return; a debate over political representation—but at the heart of it all is a question of demographic change.

Within the next four years, Bihar will surpass Maharashtra to become India's second-most populous state after Uttar Pradesh, and Rajasthan will grow bigger than Tamil Nadu in population size. In fact, people from the four most populous southern states put together will account for fewer people than from Uttar Pradesh alone. These changes, the public and politicians from southern states are well aware of, come as a result of these states doing a better job of lowering fertility than their northern counterparts. And, they now feel they are being penalised for this, being made victims of their own success.

The Indian Constitution regulates the total number of seats in Parliament. To divide the 545 seats in the Lok Sabha proportionately, Article 82 of the Constitution calls for the

Figure 8.3: By 2036, the age gap between Indian states will widen further

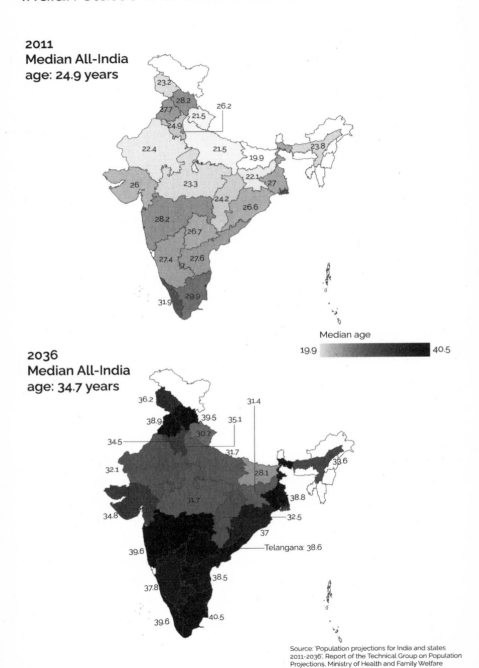

2011
Median All-India age: 24.9 years

23.2
28.2
27.7
26.2
21.5
24.9
22.4
21.5
19.9
23.8
26
23.3
22.1
27
24.2
26.6
28.2
26.7
27.4
27.6
31.9
29.9

Median age
19.9 — 40.5

2036
Median All-India age: 34.7 years

36.2
31.4
38.9
39.5
35.1
34.5
30.7
31.7
32.1
28.1
33.6
31.7
38.8
34.8
32.5
37
39.6
Telangana: 38.6
38.5
37.8
39.6
40.5

Source: 'Population projections for India and states
2011–2036'. Report of the Technical Group on Population
Projections, Ministry of Health and Family Welfare

reallocation of seats after every Census based on updated population figures. However, the Forty-Second Amendment enacted in 1976—during the twenty-one-month Emergency rule by then prime minister Indira Gandhi—suspended the revision of seats until after the 2001 Census. One impetus for the freeze was Gandhi's desire to promote family-planning policies by ensuring that states that managed to lower their fertility rates (and hence limit their population growth) would not be punished. In 2002, Parliament delayed reallocation even further, passing the Eighty-Fourth Amendment and extending this freeze until the next decennial Census after 2026 (which will take place in 2031). Though the Eighty-Seventh Amendment (2003) did allow for redistricting within states based on 2001 population figures, the total number of seats assigned to each state could not be altered. By 2031, the population figures used to allot parliamentary seats to each state will be six decades old.

This unwillingness to acknowledge India's changing demographics has come at a cost. States with slow population growth, such as the southern states of Kerala and Tamil Nadu, argue that they should not be punished for curbing population growth more effectively than states with ballooning populations, such as the northern states of Bihar and Uttar Pradesh. The northern states, in turn, argue that they have been shortchanged; after all, the notion of 'one person, one vote' is a central tenet of democratic representation.[21]

The same argument holds when it comes to revenue-sharing. Facing opposition from southern states over their share of the tax-revenue pie dwindling, the Finance Commission, which determines the parameters of revenue-sharing, added an indicator to the index it uses to calculate a state's share: demographic performance. Using this, states with lower fertility would gain points in the index to help ease the blow from lower devolution.

How far this works will depend on nimble political manoeuvring, but also on the belief that as population growth rates between the north and south eventually converge, these fault lines will close up.

Millennium's Children

One thing is certain: the generation born at the turn of the new millennium looks very little like the midnight's children, and planning for this generation will need a radical reimagination.

Since the 1950s, the mantra driving public investment in education was this: a demographic dividend was on the way. This meant that as India grew older, its working-age population would peak, creating a pool of workers for the Indian economy to benefit from. That phase is now comprehensively here.

As of 2018, India's working-age population (people between fifteen and sixty-four years of age) has grown larger than the dependent population—children aged fourteen or below as well as people above sixty-five years of age. This bulge in the working-age population is going to last till 2055, a period of thirty-seven years, and could mean a time of growth.

However, this growth will depend on those in the working-age population actually having gained the skills that today's jobs market needs, and then actually working. India's labour force participation rate is declining, especially among rural youth (fifteen to twenty-nine-year-olds) and women. For India to harness the power of its favourable demographics, it is critical that this is addressed, and that India's labour force is empowered with the right skills for the modern economy.

Having just passed the height of its 'youth bulge', the Indian electorate is surging with young voters. In 2015, the share of the voting 'youth' (aged twenty–thirty-four) grew to 26 per cent, its highest point since Independence, and will now begin to taper off as fertility slows and India begins to age.

Young people will need jobs and are impatient for change. Alongside the potential sociological pitfalls for a country with a large, unemployed youth cohort, the new millennium's children will also exert significant pressure on democratic processes. Over the next few decades, as the pyramid first becomes more diamond-shaped, and then slowly but surely inverts itself, the perspective will need to change too. 'Population explosion' will need to be sent into retirement along with other Malthusian fears. As families get smaller, the sex ratio could worsen. For the growing band of fifteen–twenty-five-year-olds, the economy will need to produce jobs, and fast. Families and social welfare will have to align quickly to the burgeoning cohort of elderly people.

The changes could come even quicker than anticipated; once changes are established in some demographic groups and states and the advantages of lowered fertility like better incomes and health outcomes are visible, the aspiration of other groups too to reduce family size increases, demographers find.

The aspiration to give their children a better future could be driving a big part of this change. Smaller families are able to invest significantly more in children's education. Expenditure on children's education was 40 per cent higher in one-child families than in families with three or more children. 'Only' children were over one-and-a-half times more likely to be enrolled in a private school than children from families with over three children, and children from two-child families were 1.4 times as likely to.[22]

The change is happening on its own. What needs attention now is ageing. As the working-age population declines in India, supporting a dependent older population will become a growing burden on the government's resources. Family structures will be recast and elderly persons living alone will become an increasing source of concern.

In 1951, the Indian government began what would become the world's biggest 'family-planning' programme, and sterilisation as a form of birth control was aggressively pushed in the subsequent years.[23] When then prime minister Indira Gandhi suspended democratic rights to impose an 'Emergency' in 1975, her son, Sanjay Gandhi, personally led a campaign of forced sterilisation of men in some of northern India's poorest communities.[24] By 1992, when the first data was available, female sterilisation was already by far the most commonly used form of contraception.[25]

Despite well-established socio-economic processes producing transformational change in India, the rhetoric is stuck in the 1970s—population explosions, two-child families, sterilisation, control. On the other hand, no Indian state has a ministry for the ageing or the elderly, and social protections for the elderly are not universal.

A large proportion of elderly households depend on income from salaried or wage work, numbers that are not surprising, since only formal-sector workers have access to some form of pension. Self-employed or casual workers do not have this benefit and their continued employment is mainly driven by lack of alternative income in the form of pension. Income from property and pension are highest among the better-off segment of population, namely educated, affluent, high-caste Hindus/other religions, and those residing in urban areas.

When I met him in Delhi's Trilokpuri slum in 2012, Ramkumar Gupta was older than his country. Originally from Bihar's Bhojpur district, Gupta and his wife, Shanti Devi, left their son and village behind when they were in their forties and could no longer make ends meet from agricultural labour on the fields of the landed. The elderly couple had lived in and around Trilokpuri, a low-income area in east Delhi ever since, frequently moving house when rents rose, with no real paperwork to their name. Gupta made a living selling fruit that was of slightly lower quality, and so was slightly cheaper, to Trilokpuri's labourers, construction workers, maids and hawkers. His eyes lit up while he spoke to me, reminiscing about the sweet litchis of his childhood. Save for his twice-weekly trips to the wholesale market, Gupta sat from 9 a.m. to 9 p.m. every day and sold seasonal fruit, moving across the road with the shifting shade. His biggest worry at the moment was the uncontrollable shake that his left hand had recently developed—if it got any worse, they would starve. His son lived back in the village and had his own family to take care of, he said.

For these vulnerable elderly people, state protection becomes vital: 42 per cent elderly households depend at least to a small extent on the modest old-age pension the Indian state currently pays out. Experts recommend a universal modest social pension program that benefits all elderly.[26]

Zeenat's granddaughter Farzana is nineteen and a budding graphic artist. By that age, her grandmother had already had two children. Farzana participated in anti-government protests in 2019 and 2020, while her grandmother had never left the house without a male chaperone. Zeenat remembers her fears for the country being over whether everyone could be fed and clothed, and whether there would be war. Farzana doesn't worry that India has too many people—she worries about the government being cruel to its people. She'd like to study in the US—but she'll worry about her grandmother back home, alone.

Newly independent India had a great deal of growing up to do. Working-age India will now need to get the job done.

IX

HOW INDIA LIVES AND WHERE

Every narrative about India's urbanisation and growth has become outdated and inaccurate. We need to look at the data to get it right.

In 1947, when Mahatma Gandhi famously remarked that 'true India lies in its seven lakh villages', he was statistically accurate. In 1951, eighty-three of every hundred Indians lived in rural areas; the median Indian did live in a village.

Few would believe that holds good today—the face that India shows the world is of fast-paced megalopolises and aspiring smaller towns. Villages are emptying, it would seem, as an exodus of migrants pours into fast-urbanising cities, engines of growth that are expanding faster than ever. The truth is that this fundamental misunderstanding of where and how India lives is driving both public conversation and policy in a misguided, data-free direction.

Even today, the median Indian lives in a village. As of 2011, India had a little less than 600,000 villages and a little under 8,000 towns. By 2011, the share of Indians living in rural areas had declined—but not by much—to sixty-nine of every hundred Indians. Thirteen of every hundred Indians live in a village of fewer than 1,000 people. Forty of every hundred Indians live in a village of 1,000–5,000 people. The remaining sixteen rural residents of every hundred Indians live in a village of more than 5,000 people.

That leaves just thirty-one of every hundred Indians living in a city. Of these, twenty-two live in big cities of more than 100,000 people, so just nine of every 100 Indians live in a relatively small town (of fewer than 100,000 people). Over 13.7 million people—or over 17 per cent of India's urban population—live in slums.[1]

*

Life Inside the House

Data offers us a granular picture of what life inside the average Indian house looks like. The average Indian family lives in a house that's less than 500 square feet in size. What do these houses look like? Nine out of ten rural households live in single-storey, independent houses. In urban areas as well, the majority of houses are classified as 'independent houses'. One in three urban households lives in a multi-storeyed flat. On average, urban houses have two 'living rooms', which include bedrooms, halls and dining rooms, and two 'other rooms', which include kitchens, bathrooms and store rooms. Only half of rural households have a separate kitchen, and as of 2018, fewer than half used LPG for cooking, with the rest using firewood, crop residue and animal dung as fuel. Three-quarters of urban households have a separate kitchen and 87 per cent of urban households use LPG for cooking.[2]

Virtually everyone in rural India owns their house; in urban India, one in three households rents their house. Urban renters pay just over Rs 3,300 per month for rent on average. Nearly one in ten urban households live in a house that doubles up as a commercial unit during the day.[3]

Despite how it may seem to those trying to buy a house at the high end of the price spectrum, the urban housing market is actually still very modest in scale. Among the small subset of people who constructed or bought a house in the year before they were surveyed, the average amount spent was under Rs 2.5 lakh. These house constructions and purchases were funded through savings and borrowings from friends and relatives—just 14 per cent took a bank loan.[4]

The average rural Indian household now has 4.5 people, with the southern states (except Karnataka) averaging fewer than four people in a household and rural Uttar Pradesh and Bihar having more than five people per household. The average urban household on the other hand has fewer than four people.[5] What this means is that India is now a comprehensively 'nuclear' country; on average, every household has one married couple only.[6] That is a big change in terms of the privacy afforded to most Indians: in seven out of ten households, each married couple does not get a room to themselves even now.

When Rampujari Kushwaha was a young bride, she remembers stepping around her sleeping older sisters-in-law and mother-in-law at 4.45 a.m. to wash her face and start the chulha every morning. The three older women and the two young children of the household slept in the kitchen, while their husbands slept in the covered area just outside the door to the house, where they could keep an eye on their cow and goats. Rampujari, then seventeen, and her husband, Sailesh, were given the house's sole bedroom as the newly married couple.

By the time Rampujari's own son got married in 2020, those days were a distant memory. Sailesh's father had passed away, the oldest brother had moved into a house he had built for himself in Tikamgarh town in Madhya Pradesh, another brother had fallen out with the family and moved to another part of the village, while Sailesh remained in the family house in Baori village to look after the family farm. Their son Sooraj had not lived under their roof since he was nineteen, and his new wife had only spent a handful of nights there before she joined her husband in Bhavnagar, Gujarat, where he worked on construction sites. 'From eleven mouths to feed to three— even if I wake up after sunrise, all the work is done before it's time to go to the fields,' Rampujari, now forty-two, chuckles. Under a government scheme, the Kushwahas converted their one bedroom-one kitchen thatched house into a concrete whitewashed house with two bedrooms, a small hall and a separate kitchen in 2013. 'Now we have all the space and no one to live in it,' she says, laughing.

*

The most widely accepted narrative about where India lives and where people will live in the future is that there is an urban boom.

In 1901, a quarter of India's urban population lived in big cities of more than 100,000 people. By Independence, this was up to 45 per cent of the country's urban population. By 2011, over 70 per cent of urban India lived in big cities. (Fig. 9.1)

Figure 9.1: India's urbanisation story is overwhelmingly a big-city story

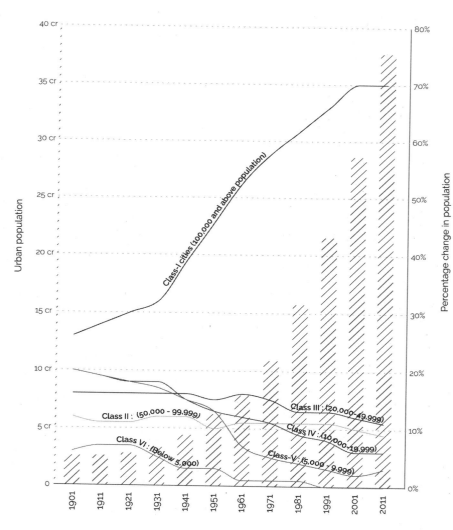

Source: Census of India, Office of the Registrar General of India, GoI, 2011

India now has 298 urban agglomerations—contiguous areas made up of multiple municipalities and/or towns—and 170 towns of more than 100,000 people. Of these, fifty-two are megacities of more than a million people. Officially, the Greater Mumbai Urban Agglomeration is India's biggest city with over eighteen million people, followed by Delhi with sixteen million people, Kolkata with fourteen million people, Chennai with 8.7 million people and Bengaluru with 8.5 million people. 160.7 million persons (or 42.6 per cent of the urban population) live in these million-plus urban agglomerations and cities, eighteen more such cities than there were in the 2001 Census. Of the 8,000 or so towns that India officially has, 6,166 are parts of urban agglomerations of different sizes. Only 1,770 towns are independent towns.[7]

All of this sounds like an urban explosion and there's certainly a narrative—in the media, among global think tanks, in the minds of many of us—that India is experiencing rapid urbanisation. But the truth is that India has been punching below its weight all this time and a question that has puzzled India-watchers is why urbanisation has not, in fact, exploded in the country. India is less urban than it is perceived to be and is urbanising slower than anticipated. India's urbanisation rate is a little over ten percentage points lower than the rate predicted for its level of per capita income[8] and the pace of urbanisation has been slower in India than in many other countries. Between 1971 and 2011, the share of India's urban population increased from around 20 per cent to 31 per cent. In the same time period, many Asian and African countries more than doubled their urban population shares from similar starting points and China became more urban than rural.

For a long time now, we may have been misunderstanding

the determinants of urban growth in India, but if we looked closely at them, we'd have a good sense of why urbanisation is moving so slowly.

How does a country urbanise? For one, the urban population may have more children and fewer deaths, and so have a higher natural growth rate than rural areas. This is intuitive, but gets very little play in the discussion about urbanisation. The historian Chinmay Tumbe has noted that 50 per cent of the observed gap between India's actual rate of urbanisation and that predicted at its level of income can be explained by high rural fertility—the number of children a woman will have in her lifetime on average. This explains the 'slowness', he says, along with the highly gendered nature of work-related migration that leads to considerable return migration from cities to villages.

In the 1970s, urban families had fewer children than rural families, but they also had fewer deaths than rural families, making the natural growth rates in rural and urban areas identical. But since then, rural and urban natural growth rates have diverged; the poorer northern states like Bihar, Madhya Pradesh, Rajasthan and Uttar Pradesh as well Assam have seen natural growth rates fall in urban areas and rise in rural areas, Tumbe found. The data on birth and death rates make it clear that the reason for this is that while the difference in death rates between urban and rural areas is now small, the difference in birth rates is still large. Among rural areas, those with relatively lower agricultural productivity and rural literacy rates are associated with higher rural–urban fertility differences.[9]

There is a significant north versus south angle too: northern cities are growing faster than southern cities on account of higher fertility rates but urbanising slower than the south because northern villages are also growing much faster than southern villages.[10] Since 1971-81, the rate of growth of population in the southern and western states has been declining. Only since 2001-11 has this change reached the north too: even in the poorer northern, eastern and central Indian states, the population now grows slower with every passing decade.[11]

A second pathway to urbanisation is through migration, and in the popular imagination, this is what is driving Indian urbanisation. But what is actually happening is both more migration than we imagine, and less—just not in the way we usually picture it.

Migration

There are three important stories about Indian migration that contribute to why it is not resulting in much more urbanisation. One, that there isn't that much migration—in statistical terms—at all. Two, many migrants don't move away from their villages permanently. And lastly, you need to be relatively well-off to migrate.

The defining trend of Indian migration remains that people do not yet move a lot, and those who do, do not, on the whole, move very far. The Indian Census takes a migrant to be a person who is at a different place from his or her 'usual place of residence' at the time of the Census enumeration. In all, 455 million Indians, or over one-third of the population could be classified as 'migrants'.

If you do not live in the place where you were born, you are already an outlier—just 5 per cent of the country lives outside of the state that they were born in. Sixty-three per cent of people live in the same place they were born. Among those who have moved away from their birthplace, 59 per cent live within the same district.

Most states—including those that are seeing the rise of strong anti-'outsider' sentiment—have an extremely low share of actual 'outsiders'. Richer western and southern states might tell themselves that migrants from the north are flooding their states, but in reality just 9 per cent of people currently living in Maharashtra, 6 per cent in Karnataka and 2 per cent in Kerala were born outside the state. In all, 455 million Indians, or over one-third of the population, could be classified as 'migrants'.

Domestic migration in India remains a story largely of proximity. Moving to another state, especially over a large distance, like from the north to the south or west, is relatively uncommon. Internal migrants seek a better life, but as close to home as possible. The median migrant has moved out of her village but remains within her district. Inter-district but within-state migration is the next most common flow, followed by inter-state migration. This is changing with time—the most recent migrants are more likely to have moved out of their state. However, even now, Delhi gets most migrants from the northern states surrounding it, while Mumbai sees most migration from Maharashtra and substantial migration from neighbouring Gujarat and Karnataka.[12]

Rural–rural migration, moving from one village to another, dwarfs rural–urban migration. (Fig. 9.2) In fact, between 1991 and 2011, the share of rural–urban migrants among all migrants actually fell, while the share of urban–urban migrants rose. Part of the reason that rural–rural migration is such a big part of the Indian migration story is because migration, overall, is overwhelmingly a female tale. Migration

Figure 9.2: Despite dominating public debate, rural—urban migration is a slow-growing stream...

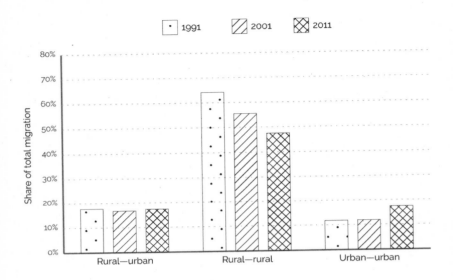

... and the Indian migration story is still one of proximity

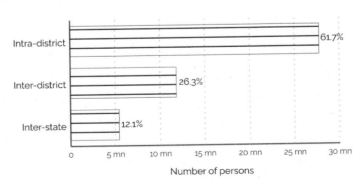

Source: Census of India. Office of the Registrar General of India. GoI. 2

as it is usually understood in India is the movement of people (usually men) in search of jobs. But the truth is that migration in India is an overwhelmingly female phenomenon because of the sociological nature of marriage in the country, which tends to follow the norm of caste endogamy (marrying within one's caste) but village exogamy (marrying outside one's village). Women make up 68 per cent of all migrants in India and 66 per cent of them migrate because of marriage. There are more female migrants at all geographical combinations than men, including more inter-state female migrants than male migrants.

The only two states sending out more men than women are Uttar Pradesh and Bihar. The male migrants heading out of these two states are undoubtedly seeking work—over half of the male out-migrants from Uttar Pradesh and Bihar cite 'work or employment' as their reason for migration. On average nationally, however, work migrants comprise just a quarter of all male migrants; most of the rest are counted as 'migrants' because their household moved at some time after their birth.

It is a fact that migrants from Uttar Pradesh form the largest share of inter-state migrants to both Delhi and Mumbai. However, there are many nuances here that the anti-north sentiment misses. For one, Mumbai now gets almost as many migrants from other parts of Maharashtra as it does from other states. Secondly, migration from Uttar Pradesh and Bihar to Maharashtra and Delhi has not grown as fast as it has to the southern states, where the total number of migrants from those two states is still relatively low. Migrants from Bihar go more to other northern states—more Bihari migrants go to West Bengal and to Uttar Pradesh than to

Maharashtra. The greatest increase in Bihari migrants, too, is in the southern states.

By the Census's definition, such economic migrants make up less than a tenth of all migrants at just over forty-five million. But official estimates undercount short-term migrants; by other estimates, India's total migrant workforce could have been over a hundred million in 2016.[13]

This underestimation lay exposed in 2020 when floods of migrants began the long walk home after Modi announced that the country was going into a full lockdown on 25 March, giving people only a few hours to set in place a plan or gather emergency funds. Why were they returning home and not waiting out the lockdown in big cities? some commentators asked. The question exposed not just the lack of understanding over how precarious the lives of these migrants are, but also the fact that the big cities were not actually 'home'. Left out of Census estimates is this circular or seasonal migrant, who might go to a city to work for a period of time and then return home or go to a new place. The Census only asks people in a village or town if their 'usual place of residence'—somewhere they have lived for over six months—is different from where they are now. Hence, it misses all those people who undertook a migration but then returned.

One survey that directly asked households if any family member had gone to another city or town in the preceding five years for work for a period of at least ten days found that 4 per cent of rural males of working age had taken part in such short-term migration (separate from long-term migration) in the five years before the survey, though even this was likely to be an under-estimate.[14] One such well-documented seasonal circuit is the short-term migration of labourers from districts in Bihar to the rice-growing regions of Punjab in June for the backbreaking work of transplanting paddy. In June 2012, I interviewed over a hundred migrant labourers as they worked in the fields in Sangrur and Patiala districts. Earlier, the men would make the journey to Punjab in April–May for the wheat harvest and do odd jobs, including driving rickshaws in Ludhiana city, until it was paddy transplantation time in June. But over time, wheat farming became almost completely mechanised in prosperous Punjab, and farmers could make do with family labour for the wheat harvest. 'We are not needed for wheat any more. So we fixed up with the farmer over the phone and came in time for the paddy transplantation,' said Gugli Sahni, a worker from Motihari in Bihar, who was working on the fields of brothers Gamdoor and Parpoor Singh in Patiala district's Gajju Majra village. 'After planting rice in Patiala, we will go to Haryana, then Madhya Pradesh and finally back home to Bihar, where we will plant rice in our own small fields,' said Saini Sada a worker from Supaul district who was transplanting paddy in Khedi Malan village. Across the two districts, workers spoke of a similar journey that they would make, planting rice as they went, until they returned home to wait out the monsoons. If a surveyor had asked the men, back in their villages, in August if their usual place of residence was different from where they now were, she would have missed this entire epic journey.

Contrary to popular belief, migrants are not the poorest Indians. Migration is in fact least common among the poorest.[15] But short-term migrants are considerably worse off than long-term migrants; they are in cities not so much to make a better life for themselves as to survive. 'Migration of this sort is discouragingly unpleasant,' one survey noted, 'but it is not financially costly.'[16] Long-term migrants come from both wealthy and poor states but short-term migrants are mostly located in poorer states such as Uttar Pradesh, Bihar and Chhattisgarh. Long-term migrants are more likely to be educated, come from upper-income groups and belong to a forward caste. In contrast, short-term migrants are less educated, tend to be Dalits or adivasis and come from the poorer sections of the society. Of the households that reported at least one short-term migrant, 45 per cent were either Dalits or adivasis. In 85 per cent of households which reported short-term migration, the household head was either illiterate or had only completed primary education.

More than a reflection of The Great Indian Dream, the story of short-term migration is one of desperation. They leave because there is no decent paid work in the village—long-term migrants are more likely to be from villages with higher wage rates whereas short-term migrants tend to be from villages with lower wage rates. Villages in which very little manual work is available also seem to show higher short-term migration.[17] Unlike overall migration, where the intra-state variety occurs far more than inter-state, short-term migrants are more likely to migrate between states. This explains why so many of the journeys on foot during the lockdown were between states—short-term migrants move largely to urban areas and over longer distances than long-term migrants.[18] One-third of short-term migrants were employed in the construction sector and contractors played an important role in arranging for work. Around half of all short-term migrants migrated with the help of a contractor, indicating that when work fell through, returning home would have been an unfamiliar journey for the migrant to plan by himself or herself.

Some channels of migration are even more ephemeral: nearly 12.5 million workers cross the rural–urban boundary for work every day, while 12.2 million workers report not having a fixed place of work.[19]

It's not surprising, then, that migration isn't leading to a surge in urbanisation—there's not that much of it, what's there isn't of the permanent sort that would inflate the urban population, and those who move for good to cities need to be relatively well-off, which the majority of the country is not.

Growth by Definition

Net rural–urban migration, then, only has a small impact on urban growth.[20] In numerical terms, a bigger contributor to urban expansion is the reclassification of an area as 'urban', a process that has been described as in situ urbanisation in the case of China.[21] Reclassification, or a rural area slowly taking on more urban characteristics, empirically has a greater impact on the nature of population redistribution and urbanisation compared to net rural to urban migration.[22]

There are two ways for an area to become urban in the eyes of the Indian Census. The first is by becoming a statutory town. The Indian Census defines statutory towns as all places with urban governing structures—a municipality, corporation, cantonment board or notified town area committee. But these classifications of urban and rural can be influenced by social and political factors too; urban status is often favoured by the social groups involved in commercial and services sectors and resisted by the residents still involved in farming.

In the 1990s, the temple town of Shirdi near Pune was expanding rapidly. In 1995, the Shirdi village panchayat was converted into a municipal council and elections to the council were announced. In protest, residents boycotted the elections and not a single nomination was received. The state made four more attempts to hold elections so as to constitute a council, but on every occasion, the election could not be held. Finally, the state government had to first reconvert the council to a village panchayat and immediately thereafter to a nagar panchayat, one stage up from a village panchayat but down from a municipal council. Only then could an election be held.[23] Similarly, in June 2004, 566 town panchayats (small urban local bodies) in Tamil Nadu were reclassified as rural panchayats due to local resistance to urban taxation.[24]

In Maharashtra, the researchers Amita Bhide and Smita Waingankar found multiple examples of misclassification of urban areas. In many cases, this was the real and intentional effect of concerted organising by rural residents who feared the impact of being declared urban.[25] In July 2009, for instance, the Maharashtra state government issued a notification announcing that the municipal councils of Nallasopara, Virar, Navghar-Manickpur and Vasai, along with fifty-three adjoining villages, would be merged to create the new municipal corporation of Vasai-Virar, in some ways an extended suburb of Mumbai. The news caused a furore across the villages, and multiple community and political outfits sprang up to fight against urbanisation; in the ultimate example of trying to fight from within, one of the key organisations fighting against municipal status nominated candidates to the local civic elections to oppose municipal status for the villages.[26] While some villages were able to get the state government to exclude them from the new municipal corporation, the situation on the ground shows how much rurality and urbanity are states of mind.

Many of the villages of the area saw municipal money roll

out better roads and introduce amenities like garbage collection, while the increased taxes and rampant concretisation they feared have yet to unfold. By 2015, Wagholi village, which witnessed violent protests against a local politician pushing for municipal status, had come around. Resident Atmaram Patil now sees paver blocks, water supply and transport as services that can only be provided by a municipality. Mulgaon resident Milind Mhatre earlier had doubts about his part of the village joining the municipality; now he sees urbanisation as inevitable. 'More than half of the fertile farms are lying vacant,' said Mhatre, who remembers what an agricultural life had once been like, travelling to Bhuleshwar in the heart of Mumbai with his father in the 1980s to sell flowers from their farm. But Mhatre himself chose to teach instead of farm and now runs a local coaching class. His college-going son Chaitanya may enjoy plucking mangoes with his friends, but he certainly does not want to become a farmer. Chaitanya intends to get an MBA and work in Mumbai. Others attempt a more delicate balancing act: Tulsidas Mhatre commutes from Nirmal village in Nalasopara to the MTNL office in Vile Parle, but continues to invest in his farm. 'My children are studying but I am encouraging them to take up farming at least part-time,' he said. He remains unconvinced about urbanisation—'Joining the municipality will mean taxes on every single tree we own.'[27]

The other pathway to urbanisation in the eyes of the Indian Census is more organic. Urban areas that do not have statutory status are called census towns. These are essentially villages that have shed a large part of the agrarian economy. To be officially classified as a census town, a former village must have a minimum population of 5,000 people, at least 75 per cent of the male main workers must tell Census surveyors that they are no longer in agriculture, and the area's population density must be at least 400 people per sq km.

Between 2001 and 2011, the major change really took place, at least statistically, in these census towns. City growth rates peaked in the 1980s and the growth in population in megacities has slowed down considerably. The Greater Mumbai Urban Agglomeration, which had witnessed a 30.47 per cent growth in its population between 1991 and 2001, found its growth rate cut to less than half, at just 12.05 per cent, between 2001 and 2011. Similarly, population growth in Delhi (from 52.24 per cent to 26.69 per cent in 2001–11) and Kolkata Urban Agglomeration (from 19.60 per cent to 6.87 per cent in 2001–11) also slowed down considerably. Some wards in Kolkata saw population declines between 2001 and 2011.

While India added just 242 statutory towns between 2001 and 2011, it added 2,532 census towns over the decade, more than in the previous ten decades. Research finds that the majority of census towns appear as small 'market towns', providing trade and other local services to the nearby rural market. Whether the explosion of census towns points to urban opportunity or rural collapse is a matter of debate. Some researchers claim that agrarian distress drives the growth of the rural non-farm sector and is the main reason for the enormous increase of census towns in a state. Others point to Kerala, which many observers describe as 'one big city' to say that the census town reclassification is organic—between 2001 and 2011, the total number of census towns and statutory towns increased from 159 to 520 in Kerala, driving it from 26 per cent urban in 2001 to 48 per cent urban in 2011.

Where Will the Indians of the Future Live?

Among inter-state migrants in the country the top destination states of all time are Maharashtra, Delhi, Uttar Pradesh, Gujarat and Haryana. In recent years, i.e., those between the last two Census years of 2001 and 2011, Maharashtra and Delhi have remained the top two destinations. After Gujarat and Haryana, Karnataka has come in at fifth and UP has slid to the sixth spot.

The southern states are clear growth magnets. But the slow rate of falling fertility in the north means that more and more Indians will live there. In 1951, more than eight of every hundred Indians lived in Tamil Nadu. By 2011, this was down to fewer than six of every hundred Indians. By 2036, Tamils will account for just five of every hundred Indians. In the north, Bihar has followed the opposite trajectory in this duration. In 1951, Bihar accounted for a little over eight of every hundred Indians. By 2011, this was up to nearly nine of every hundred Indians. By 2036, every tenth Indian will be from Bihar—double the share of Tamils in the population.

Apart from what this means for infrastructure, quality of life, political representation and climate change, it also has a significant impact on language. What language will most Indians of the future speak?

As a result of the growing northward skew of India's population, Hindi is by far the most widely spoken first language in India, and growing. In 2001, forty-one of every hundred Indians reported to the Census that Hindi was their mother tongue. By 2011, this was up to forty-four of every hundred Indians.

But 'Hindi', as defined by the Census, is not simply one language; it is also an umbrella term. Hindi is the most widely spoken first and second language in India, but it includes over fifty so-called dialects, including Bhojpuri, which is spoken by over fifty million Indians.

English is the primary language (the 'mother tongue') of 250,000 people, making it just the forty-fourth most widely spoken first language. But it is also the second language of eighty-three million people and the third language of another forty-six million people, making it the second most widely spoken language after Hindi overall. Between mother tongue, second and third language, the 2011 Census recorded that over 10 per cent of Indians reported being able to speak some English. It is the only language which more speakers use as a second language than a first language. Between 2001 and 2011, the share of Indians reporting Hindi as their second language increased by over 40 per cent and the share of those reporting English as their third language grew substantially.

Talli Imchen remembers her mother being able to speak only one language—the Mongsen Ao language spoken by their Ao Naga tribe in Nagaland's Mokokchung district. Talli, now a grandmother, learnt an additional language in school—Chungli Ao, the language of the local church, which she said would have been her 'second language'. Her daughter, Merenla, grew up with Chungli Ao and picked up Nagamese, the market language of Nagaland's bigger cities once she moved to Dimapur for a government job; that would have been her second language. Merenla's daughter, Mellie, speaks English more than any other language at her job as a hairstylist in Bengaluru. She would definitely count it as her second language after Nagamese. Her brother Teddy moved to Delhi. He would count Hindi as his second language and English as his third. As people move further away from home, the dynamics of language change too.

How much of this future population will live in villages and how many in cities is a matter of some debate too. The 2011 Census, for the first time since India's independence, found the absolute increase in surveyed population to be more in urban areas than in rural areas. It also found that for the first time since 1971–81, the rate of growth of the urban population was faster than in the previous decade. Seventy per cent of the total population increase between 2011 and 2036, a government report estimates,[28] will be in urban areas. India's urban population will increase from 377 million in 2011 to 594 million in 2036—a growth of 57 per cent. So, while 31 per cent of Indians were living in urban India in 2011, that will grow to 39 per cent by 2036. Delhi, which was 98 per cent urban in 2011, will be 100 per cent urban by 2036. In addition, Tamil Nadu, Kerala, Maharashtra, Telangana and Gujarat will all be more than 50 per cent urban, the report predicts.

Data Issues

Underlying all of these numbers and calculations is one belief—that the Indian Census does a perfect job of counting every Indian and accurately representing where they live. This is taken as something of an indisputable fact, particularly by those with faith in the Indian state and its statistical system. To be sure, the Census does an incredible job. But it is not infallible, and putting it on a pedestal will mean turning a blind eye to those who it misses—those on the periphery and those who are already the most marginalised.

After the Census is completed, the Office of the Registrar General of India that conducts the exercise undertakes a post enumeration survey (PES), a sample survey to estimate the extent and type of under- and over-counting errors. The 2011

Census PES found that the net omission rate (undercounting after duplications are removed) was twenty-three persons per 1000 enumerated persons. This rate had not improved since the previous Census and was significantly higher than, for example, the US Census's net over-count rate of 0.001 person for every 1000 persons. For 2011, India's Census missed 27.85 million people, a population roughly the size of the state of Punjab at the time.

The overall rate of omission is worse in urban India than in rural India, but has slightly improved in urban areas, while consistently worsening in rural areas—the Census has missed more and more people in rural areas every decade. The post-2011 PES finds that the central and northern zones of the country have higher omission rates, particularly in the urban areas of cities in the northern zone. This could be a result of high mobility on account of migration for work, the report suggests. Illiterate men and women in urban areas have the highest omission rates. The immediate head of the household and his or her spouse and children are more likely to make it to the Census, while other relatives and unrelated persons living in the housing unit are more likely to get left out. Just as in the US Census, the highest omission rates are of children aged 0–4 years.

The US post-census Census Coverage Measurement report has much more detailed data on who exactly gets missed, and it shows that the US census undercounts racial minorities and over-counts white people. The hypothesis around the undercounting of young children in the US is that young children are more concentrated in poorer, minority households which have higher fertility rates but are being undercounted at a higher rate. This, unfortunately, is not something we have information for in India.

In India, these estimates only come from smaller studies. Vikas Kumar, an assistant professor of economics at Azim Premji University, has been studying errors in official statistics, particularly in Nagaland and Jammu and Kashmir, for nearly a decade. Working with Ankush Agarwal, an assistant professor of economics at IIT Delhi, Kumar found that Nagaland first inflated its population count in 2001 and then corrected for it in 2011 by showing a population decline that could not be explained by any normal processes. Both states were also inadequately counted by the NSSO, resulting in a severe under-estimation of Nagaland's poor.[29]

And it is only going to get worse.

The Future

In 2011, the government first collected data for a new National Population Register (NPR) alongside the Census house-listing data, the first round of the Census. The objective of the NPR 'is to create a comprehensive identity database of every usual resident in the country', including demographic as well as biometric information. Its questions include demographic details such as name, age, sex, relationship in household, nationality, educational qualifications, occupation, date of birth, marital status, residential address, birthplace and mother tongue. Crucially, the NPR also asks respondents where their parents were born. The rules of the amended Citizenship Act, 1955 make it clear that the NPR will lay the ground for a National Register of Citizens (NRC)—the NPR will create a list of all the residents of the country, which the NRC will then use to identify people of 'doubtful citizenship'. In its 2019 manifesto, the BJP promised to implement an NRC for the whole country.

But given the widespread distress and suffering that the implementation of the NRC caused in Assam—lakhs of people, many of them old and infirm, were forced to dig up documents and convince tribunals of their status as citizens, despite having lived there for years and in some cases generations—the passage of the Citizenship Amendment Act (CAA) in December 2019 set off a firestorm of protests across the country. These were directed against not only the CAA but also the NRC, which would bestow citizenship, and the NPR the NRC would, in turn, be based on.

India's Census Act makes it legally mandatory for every citizen to respond to the Census. Before the pandemic hit India in early 2020, a strong movement had built up across the country, particularly among Muslim citizens, against the NPR. When the delayed 2021 Census is picked up again, all indications are that the NPR will be conducted alongside it. The government has said that provisional data for the 2021 Census and NPR will be available before the next general elections in 2024.

The United States has found that adding a question on citizenship depressed response rates among minorities.[30] For India, the combination of the Census and the NPR questionnaire will prove a massive counting challenge.

Many leading statisticians believe that India's 2021 Census will produce deeply contaminated results. 'Exercises to establish citizenship or prepare citizen registers for the population will have a bearing on the reportage of migration related issues. Migration reporting including period since migration is also likely to be affected if the respondents have concerns of their ultimate use by government agencies for possible administrative and political purposes,' P.C. Mohanan says. Pronab Sen agrees. He cannot picture how the 2021 Census can maintain data integrity, how its findings can be trusted, and how all the future planning and statistical exercises that it rests on can be trusted. 'I see only one solution. Completely de-link the NPR, NRC and CAA from the Census and maintain the integrity of the Census because it is vital for India's democratic future,' Sen told me.

Even that might not be enough—the seeds of suspicion have been planted deep. If the delayed 2021 Census produces unexpected estimates of where Indians live, it's going to be hard to tell if what changed was the country or the trust that allowed people to tell the country their truth.

X

HOW INDIA FALLS SICK AND GETS BETTER

India undercounts its sick people, misunderstands how the poor access health, and is stuck in an ossified Left/Right binary over healthcare. The coronavirus pandemic showed up the dangers of planning using bad data.

When we misread data, the consequences can be serious—we may form false narratives around what women are voting for (chapter 3)—or amusing—we might make movies for a middle class that doesn't exist (chapter 5)—or a colossal waste of money—we might design commuter policy for a white-collar workforce that is much smaller than we thought (chapter 7). But when it comes to health, our misunderstandings of the data have, and have had, the potential to kill.

With one of the lowest levels of government spending on healthcare and one of the highest levels of out-of-pocket expenditure on health in the world,[1] India continues to have the largest number of undernourished children, a number that grew in 2019, in a shocking reversal of decades of progress.[2]

India had been struggling with a still-high burden of infectious diseases, particularly in its poorest states, alongside a rising tide of non-communicable or 'lifestyle' diseases when the novel coronavirus pandemic hit.

As a country, we went into the pandemic with a faulty understanding of the situation, based on bad or misunderstood data. The failure to properly understand who gets sick and who reports sickness led to some of the most vulnerable being overlooked and confusions over India's national data. The enormous gaps between states in terms of capacity exposed both how different numbers and outcomes could be depending on where in India you lived. The long-ignored deficiencies in how India records deaths left the country's experts unable to fully grasp the extent of deaths from COVID. The Left/Right binary over public versus private healthcare, solidified over decades, led to many patients having to experience the worst of the government system and the worst of the private system. The absence of a culture of transparency over inconvenient data made the most basic data about the pandemic unavailable to most Indians and contributed to dubious decision-making on drugs and vaccines.

For things to get better, for the pandemic to at the very least leave in its wake the blueprint for a better health architecture for the future, we must begin by accepting all that India has read wrong.

Who Falls Sick in India and from What?

India collates its official statistics on incidence, prevalence and mortality rates of different diseases in the National Health Profile (NHP), published by the health ministry's Central Bureau of Health Intelligence. These are such severe underestimates that they are nearly unusable. The NHP figures fail to capture the real extent of disease and death in a country where more people visit private healthcare providers than public ones.[3] Further, a whole host of diseases, much like COVID-19, have a strong component of asymptomatic infections that data gathered from hospitals will miss. In 2019, for instance, a national sero-survey for dengue noted that 75 per cent of dengue infections in India were likely to be 'subclinical', meaning asymptomatic and undetected. The government is aware that its officially reported numbers represent an under-estimate, which it attributes to public sector versus private sector reporting issues. 'Since the reported Data is by and large from Government health facilities, it may have limitations in terms of its completeness as Private Medical & Health Care Institution still need to strengthen their reporting to their respective Government Health units (sic),' stated the most recent NHP in October 2019.

One way to know if these are 'true' estimates is to compare them against other numbers. For this there's limited data. The Global Burden of Disease (GBD) project is a mammoth global collaboration led by the Institute for Health Metrics and Evaluation in Seattle, USA, that uses multiple sources to estimate the true burden of disease and death in 195 countries, from 1990 onwards. It has its critics: 'The GBD uses assumptions about things that we simply do not know enough about, and these estimates are then presented as fact, while they are in fact at best informed guesses, and at worst quite faulty guesses,' Aashish Gupta, a demographer and economist who works with health data told me. While remaining mindful of these assumptions, a comparison between officially reported data from the NHP and GBD estimates reveals the extent of undercounting for both reported infections of and deaths from several diseases. The NHP, India's official source of health data, estimated 194 deaths from malaria in 2017, while the GBD initiative, which uses multiple sources, estimated 50,000 deaths for the same year. Estimates for tuberculosis and typhoid incidence were ten times the official numbers.

In epidemiological terms, India is at the cusp of a major transformation. As states or countries grow richer, their burden of disease tends to shift from communicable diseases to non-communicable diseases, a process that is known as the epidemiological transition. India is right at the point where this change occurs. The top two causes of mortality in Indians are now non-communicable diseases, though three of the five biggest causes of mortality are still infectious diseases. Between them, the top five diseases—ischemic heart disease, chronic obstructive pulmonary disease, diarrhoeal diseases, lower respiratory infections and drug-susceptible tuberculosis—kill over 11,000 Indians every day. (Fig. 10.1)

India's richest states, including Kerala, Delhi and Goa, are far along in this epidemiological transition and hence face a higher risk of non-communicable diseases like diabetes, hypertension and kidney disease. Even so, India's poorest states have witnessed a faster growth in these non-communicable diseases than the richest states, yet the non-communicable disease epidemic in these states remains a silent crisis. This is in the background of an already high rate of communicable diseases in the poorest states, which have a far higher burden of communicable diseases. States like Bihar thus face a 'double burden of disease'.

Simultaneously, the health infrastructure in the poorest states is in the most precarious shape. India has just six hospital

Figure 10.1: India has made an epidemiological transition: non-communicable diseases now kill more people in the country

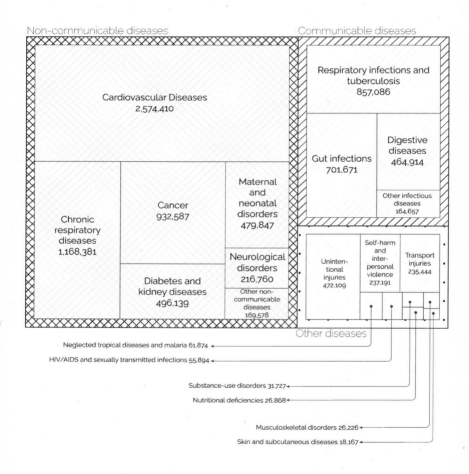

Source: Global Burden of Disease Collaborative Network. Global Burden of Disease Study 2019 (GBD 2019) Reference Life Table. Seattle, United States of America: Institute for Health Metrics and Evaluation (IHME), 2021

beds for every 10,000 people, against the global threshold of eighteen beds for every 10,000 people. There are just twenty-eight healthcare workers for every 10,000 people, as against the global norm of forty-five healthcare workers. The average is driven up by richer states: Bihar has just one hospital bed for every 10,000 people and just four doctors for every 10,000 people.[4]

Health in India is deeply divided territory. The general belief in India is that richer people's lifestyles—more sedentary time, richer and fattier foods—make them likelier to suffer from non-communicable diseases, including high blood pressure, diabetes and heart disease. Richer people do have a higher likelihood of having these non-communicable diseases. But living in a richer household is a considerable safeguard against death from disease—the well-off are less likely to die from non-communicable diseases than poor people with non-communicable diseases. The overall mortality rates of the rich are also lower than that of the poor.[5]

Most standard health indicators in India, in fact, cannot be explained in purely medical terms because they represent the culmination of generations of deprivations and discriminations.

The 'Mystery' of Indian Heights

Health status has many determinants—while higher incomes typically correspond to healthier people, the relationship isn't linear.

One of the 'mysteries' about India is why Indians are so short. Height is of particular interest to demographers, nutritionists and economists. Children who do not get adequate nutrition in the first two years of their lives are shorter than they could have been, i.e., their genetic potential. Lack of access to proper sanitation and the poor social and health status of women affects the nutritional status of children, thus leading to their being shorter in height.

Indians are among the shortest people in the world. For its per capita income, India has stubbornly higher than expected levels of stunting among children and adults. For a long time, stunting was believed to be purely an outcome of not getting enough food. While many of the earlier discussions, including influential work by Nobel laureate Amartya Sen, focussed on food availability and consumption, there has been a growing acknowledgement, including by Dr Sen himself, that food consumption alone does not explain the scale of India's under-nutrition.

Nor is it a question of genetics alone. On the right, economists like Arvind Panagariya have attacked the data itself and suggested that the answer is genetic; Panagariya was on one side of a debate fought in the pages of the *Economic and Political Weekly* in 2013. But the consensus is that genes contribute to only a small portion of adult height, while environmental factors, including the mother's health, infant and child nutrition, sanitation and environmental pollution, explain the bulk of the difference in growth in height between groups. In India, forward-caste men are the tallest, and SC and ST men the shortest. A study compared the heights of children in West Bengal with those in what was East Bengal, i.e., Bangladesh. There could not conceivably be much genetic difference between these two neighbouring populations, which became part of separate nation states relatively recently. The study found that on average, children in West Bengal were taller, but were also richer (average incomes were higher then in West Bengal than Bangladesh). Yet, when you compared children of similar wealth across the border, kids in Bangladesh were significantly taller. A combination of the better social status of women in Bangladesh and better sanitation (less open defecation) statistically accounted for almost all of this difference, the researchers found.

A person whose height-for-age is below two standard deviations less than the median for the reference population is described as 'stunted'. According to the 2015-16 NFHS, 48 per cent of children in India were stunted. One of the most worrying developments has been a recent increase in the levels of stunting in some parts of India, something that is seen rarely in the world. Between 2005-06 and 2015-16, two previous rounds of the NFHS, India made substantial progress, lowering the share of stunted children by nearly ten percentage points. However, the latest, fifth round of NFHS indicates that further progress has been slow. The share of stunted, wasted and underweight children has grown in several states. Rates of stunting have risen in rich states such as Kerala, Gujarat, Maharashtra, Goa and Himachal Pradesh, all of which had lowered their rates of stunting in the previous decade.

Accessing Healthcare

On the whole, the poorest are most likely to face ill-health and the richest the least likely.[6] Women are more likely to report illness than men.[7] The poorest and most marginalised—Dalits and Muslims—are most likely to have experienced respiratory illness and fever recently, and to have been incapacitated by it. When it comes to longer, chronic illnesses, the poorest are most likely to suffer from them, but the richest come next.

But chronic conditions do not incapacitate the rich in terms of days lost to incapacity in quite the same way as they do the poor.[8]

These insights from the well-regarded demographic and sociological survey IHDS 2011-12 are particularly valuable because official statistics based on direct answers to questions on reporting illness can—and do—give the wrong impression. India's official source of statistics on healthcare would appear to show that the richest and best developed states—Kerala and Tamil Nadu in particular—have the highest rates of people reporting illness and of hospitalisation. So does that mean the poorest states are the most healthy? Unlikely; the poorest states have the highest infant mortality rates, seen as a bellwether statistic for the health of a populace, indicating that what's driving up reported illness in richer states is probably greater access to health. Other sources that look at a wider range of surveys and indicators reflect these conclusions—the per-person disease burden, measured by 'disability-adjusted life years' was the highest in poorer states, including Assam, Uttar Pradesh and Chhattisgarh, and the lowest in rich states, including Kerala and Goa, in 2017.[9]

Despite the fact that the rich experience illness less often, they are more likely to access healthcare than the poor. The richest one-fifth of rural Indians made up nearly one-third of all hospitalisations in 2017, while the poorest one-fifth made up just over a tenth of hospitalisations.[10]

Women are also less likely to access healthcare. In 2016, a group of economists studied all 2.3 million out-patient department (OPD) visits to the All India Institute of Medical Sciences (AIIMS) in Delhi, excluding those for gynaecology and obstetrics, which are accessed by women alone. They found a large difference in the likelihood of men and women coming to the OPD. For every visit by a woman, 1.7 men visited.[11]

Belying popular perception, women are actually more likely to experience non-communicable diseases than men,[12] but they are less likely to get treatment. Women are, for instance, less likely to get treated for cancer. In rural Odisha, gender discrimination (and not differential rates of occurrence) could explain 73 per cent of the difference in expenditure on cancer treatments between men and women. Women were also twenty percentage points less likely to get cancer treatment before coming to a tertiary care centre.[13]

Costs are a clear factor when it comes to decisions around seeking medical treatment. For coughs and fevers, the median expenditure remained virtually the same for the bottom 80 per cent of the country despite a wide difference in their incomes. The poor and the middle class accessed treatment for such common illnesses the same way—the majority in private clinics—and were charged the same amount. Only the top 20 per cent of the country, those living in metros and upper-caste Hindus, could pay more for treating such illnesses.[14] (Fig. 10.2)

Medical treatment can and does drive poor families into debt. In 2019, medical treatments formed a greater component of total household debt in poorer households than in richer households.[15] India has one of the world's highest proportions of out-of-pocket health expenditure and the expense per hospitalisation can be catastrophically high, especially for the poor. Even for a common disease like tuberculosis, where free treatment is available in the public sector, patients incur high out-of-pocket expenses.[16] One case of hospitalisation

Figure 10.2: Who falls sick and who gets care is determined by how rich you are

The poor report worse health...

Morbidity per 1,000 from cough/ fever/ diarrhoea

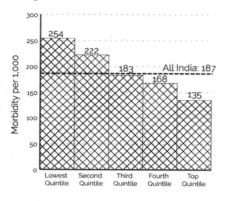

Days incapacitated in last month (if sick)

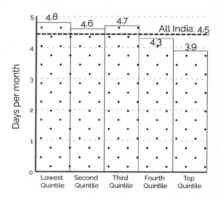

Days lost to sickness per year for whole population

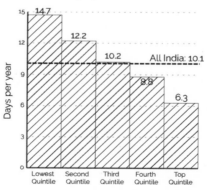

Source: National Council for Applied Economic Research and University of Maryland, 'India Human Development Survey' Round 2, 2011-12

... but the rich are significantly more likely to be hospitalised than the poor...

Share in total hopsitalisation cases in one year (July 2017—June 2018)*

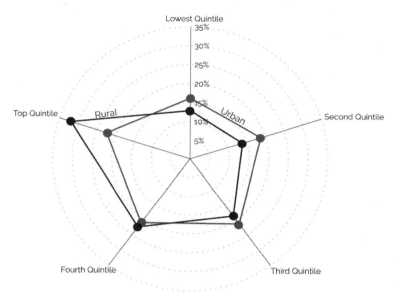

Source: 'Key Indicators of Social Consumption in India: Health', National Sample Survey 75th round, Ministry of Statistics and Programme Implementation, GoI, 2019

... yet medical treatments occupy a greater share of poor households' loans

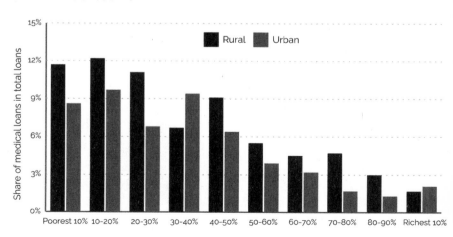

Source: All India Debt and Investment Survey, National Sample Survey 77th Round, Ministry of Statistics and Programme Implementation, GoI, 2021

alone can on average cost roughly the same as the average Indian's consumption expenditure for the year. India's latest push towards health insurance for the poor (the Ayushman Bharat scheme) is relatively new, and at least until now, the availability of public health insurance has not had a significant impact on out-of-pocket expenditure.

However, with the rate of hospitalisation currently at 2.9 per cent (meaning that around three out of every hundred people need hospitalisation, excluding childbirth, during a calendar year), these spending shocks are rarer compared to routine ailments. In the case of medical care that doesn't require hospitalisation expense recurs frequently. In the fifteen days preceding a national survey conducted in 2017-18, 8 per cent of people reported having had an ailment.[17] The high burden of outpatient health expenditure hits the poorest hard in both rural and urban areas. In rural India, the share of outpatient expenses in total medical expenditure has been falling since 2004-05, but it has risen since 2009-10 in urban India.

While these trends hold true across the country, there is wide variation among states in the degree of dependence on private versus public healthcare and the relative share of non-hospitalisation costs in the total basket of expenditure. In general, poorer people report lower levels of ailments and hospitalisations, but despite consuming less healthcare, those in the poorest states don't get cheaper healthcare; treatment costs are higher in many poorer states than in richer states.[18]

Private hospitals are more expensive than public ones, healthcare costs are prohibitive and a health setback can push a family into debt. Surely, then, the solution must lie in building more public hospitals? That's certainly the tone that some of the activism and public-spirited journalism around the pandemic in India took: private hospitals were price-gouging even though governments had set cost caps, and patients, the argument went, would be much better off in public hospitals.

Yet again, a wilful misreading of the data, with disastrous consequences.

The Public versus Private Debate

In May 2020, as the coronavirus raged through Maharashtra, Harshal Nehete's sixty-three-year-old father, Tulsiram, who lived in Jalgaon, a city of half a million people in western Maharashtra, developed COVID-like symptoms and then tested positive. A few days later, Harshal's sixty-year-old mother, Tila, and eighty-two-year-old grandmother Malati also tested positive. They were isolated in a government school and then in a railway hospital. While at the railway hospital, Tila tried to walk to the toilet and collapsed there. No staffer came to help her. After two hours, another patient helped her back to her bed, Harshal said.

On 31 May, Tila's condition deteriorated and she was moved to the Jalgaon civil hospital, a dedicated COVID facility. After six hours of waiting for an ICU bed to become available, she died.

Then, on 1 June, Malati's health deteriorated. She too was shifted to the civil hospital and wrongly put in the hospital's Ward 7, which was meant for suspected COVID cases only, and not confirmed high-risk patients like her.

The next day, at 4.30 p.m., when Harshal called the hospital from Pune, where he was marooned with his heavily pregnant wife, to check on his grandmother, a ward boy told him that

Malati, who Harshal said could hardly walk on a good day, was 'missing'. What followed was one of the most horrific stories of a pandemic in which horror stories have not been in short supply. On 4 June, a hospital doctor informed the family that Malati had been found and that she was stable. But on 5 June, when a relative went to the hospital and showed Malati's photo to a nurse, he was told that she had been missing since 2 June. The family registered a missing person complaint with the police the same day.

Jalgaon city police officials visited the wards and corridors but could not find Malati. 'I told the doctors to check the toilets because my mother had collapsed in one earlier. But no one checked,' Harshal said. A full five days later patients using the bathroom in Ward 7 complained of a smell that was making it impossible for them to use the bathroom. Malati's body was found in the bathroom; she had collapsed while using it on 1 June, and no one checked on her—or cleaned the bathroom—for nine days.

If this had been an isolated incident, it could have been written off as one poorly functioning public hospital in one city. Unfortunately, it was immediately clear that that was untrue. In the two months between Jalgaon's first case and Malati's death, three other patients had died while attempting to reach the toilet of the same hospital.[19] In October, a young man died while attempting to reach the toilet of the isolation ward of a hospital in Mumbai and his body lay undiscovered for fourteen days. The incident led to a review which found that a substantial share of deaths of hospitalised COVID patients in Mumbai were taking place between 1 and 5 a.m., as seriously ill patients were having to remove their oxygen supply, unattended, and make their own way to the bathroom. Nine months into the pandemic, India's richest city's commissioner had to issue a direction that bed pans be provided.

'We are not rich—we are just middle class. But we were prepared to pay for a private hospital. At the time it was not allowed in Jalgaon,' a tearful Harshal said. His father, Tulsiram, was shifted to a private hospital and was the only family member to survive.

There is no doubt that private hospitals can be and are predatory and poorly regulated. The fear of unnecessary procedures is real: the share of babies delivered via caesarean section is far higher in private than public hospitals and in many states, at levels far in excess of even the most developed countries; by 2020, over 80 per cent of all births in private hospitals in Telangana were via C-section, as against the WHO guideline of 10–15 per cent.

Price inflation is real too. Stories of elderly people being held captive until their families cleared their bills abounded during the pandemic. Families who turned to private care were forced to sell assets including homes and livestock to pay bills amounting to lakhs of rupees that accumulated within days. In Agra, shoemaker Shyambabu Nigam worked for years to save enough money to buy a small house. When his wife fell seriously ill with COVID-19 in 2020, the couple turned to a mix of subsidised government hospitals and more expensive private clinics to treat the illness and pay for two open-heart surgeries that followed. The total cost amounted to more than Rs 6 lakh—roughly six times Nigam's annual income. He was forced to sell his modest two-bedroom house, which covered most of that amount, borrow money from friends and sell one of his three leather sewing machines. In Jharkhand, twenty-four-year-old Soni Devi borrowed 10,000 rupees and sold three of the family's six pigs to pay for COVID treatment for her mother and three children and was left with little money to buy rice and feed her family.[20]

None of these horrific stories necessarily imply that either the public or the private sector is all good or all bad. However, the public versus private debate has been so ossified over decades that for each side, the other appears as little more than a caricature. Much of the activism and public-spirited journalism during the pandemic focused on the predatory practices of the private sector while whitewashing the horrors faced by people like the Nehetes in public hospitals, or the reasons why Nigam turned to private hospitals he could ill afford.

The reality of how healthcare is experienced in India does not fit neatly into any of the usual Left–Right debates on healthcare. For one, the fact that private healthcare is not simply what the urban rich choose and private providers dominate rural India is rarely acknowledged. In rural India, most providers are in the private sector (86 per cent), and within the private sector, the majority are 'informal providers' without any formal medical training—one estimate suggests that such informal providers account for 68 per cent of the total provider population in rural India.

Then there is the issue of quality. In 2010-11, researchers sent decoy patients into real-life healthcare settings in rural Madhya Pradesh and urban Delhi. They found that doctors correctly diagnosing diseases were rare, that private practitioners with no formal training were as likely to diagnose correctly as qualified doctors in government hospitals, private providers spent more time per patient than those in government set-ups, and that more expensive private providers were more likely to diagnose correctly but also more likely to recommend unnecessary treatments and medicines. So, public providers were not more caring or better at their jobs, private providers were not better trained, the rural poor were more likely to go to private than public providers, and both got a lot wrong.[21] A similar study on tuberculosis found that while the public sector does do a better job of following tuberculosis protocols (say, ordering a tuberculosis test), the private sector does better on other dimensions (such as the time spent with patient and better history taking).[22]

A major study of rural healthcare found that a better predictor of quality of care was the development status of the state as a whole—more developed states can provide better care to their citizens, whether in the public or private sector, whether via informal or formal practitioners. Formal qualifications were a poor predictor of quality. The medical knowledge of informal providers in Tamil Nadu and Karnataka was higher than that of fully trained doctors in Bihar and Uttar Pradesh. The share of informal providers did not decline with socioeconomic status; instead, their quality, along with the quality of doctors in the private and public sector, increased sharply.[23]

Finally, there is the issue of cost: official national data shows that costs are clearly higher in the private sector. However, there is also a cost-quality trade-off. The rural study showed that better performing states also deliver this higher quality at a lower cost per patient. Northern states suffered from low quality and high per-visit costs while southern states enjoyed higher quality at lower per-visit costs.

Bad Data Meets the Pandemic

Had these dynamics been front and centre in the understanding of Indian health and healthcare access in India, early assumptions about the pandemic could have been challenged and a feedback loop could even have saved lives. Instead, India went into the pandemic without a strong health-data architecture. This has had a profound impact on how India and the world have understood the country's experience of the COVID-19 epidemic.

For one, as we know, India went in without a strong sense of the true burden of disease, given the extent of undercounting of communicable diseases in particular. Then, there wasn't enough understanding of who falls ill and who might need greater attention.

First, take the case of women. Worldwide, more men than women have tested positive for COVID-19 and more men have died. However, there is reason to worry that India's COVID-19 surveillance left out some women. For one, the first one million tests that India conducted showed that while men made up the majority of positive cases, women were slightly more likely to test positive than they were to be tested.[24] Then, even though there were far more men than women in terms of confirmed cases, some sero-surveys, including in Delhi, Madurai, Mumbai and Ahmedabad, showed that more women than men were likely exposed to the virus. This is important because research has pointed to the likelihood of even asymptomatic patients or those with mild forms of the disease contracting lung and heart conditions. Getting left out of the COVID count could have very real consequences for women's long-term health. Then, there is the concern that women are less likely to be accurately counted in death statistics even in 'normal' times. As of 2018, women made up just 40 per cent of total registered deaths and just 38 per cent of medically certified deaths. Additionally, despite making up the majority of healthcare and frontline workers, women substantially lagged behind men in COVID-19 vaccinations. All of this could have been avoided if India had gone into the pandemic with the clear acknowledgement that women are less likely to access healthcare, even when ill.

India should have also gone in armed with the knowledge that the poor have greater exposure to disease but are less likely to get treated. By the middle of 2020, sero-surveys in Pune and Mumbai showed that the virus had blazed through slum areas, where over half of the population already showed antibodies to the virus, over three times what sero-prevalence was in high rises. But people in high rises were four to six times more likely to get tested, Sandeep Juneja, the Tata Institute of Fundamental Research scientist who co-led the Mumbai survey, told me. In the final count, India might well find that the poor paid the price for these costly pieces of missing data.

One of the many enduring puzzles over the pandemic in India is the question of why poorer states saw relatively fewer cases and fewer deaths than richer ones. Problematic assumptions about poorer states and faulty data foundations laid the ground for a dangerous narrative during the pandemic. The go-to explanation became that poorer people and people in poorer states must have greater immunity,[25] even though the evidence for this was wholly absent,[26] and as past data has shown, likely untrue.

Then, take mortality—deaths from COVID—which was initially relatively low in India. There is no doubt that India was undercounting deaths. This is partly because

India undercounts *all* deaths. Only nine out of ten deaths are officially registered, and less-developed states miss more deaths—Bihar registered just half of all deaths that took place in 2019, while Delhi captured 100 per cent. Just 22 per cent of these nationally registered deaths are medically certified, meaning that a cause of death is established by a medical practitioner. Medical certification takes place mainly in urban areas and for deaths that make it to hospitals. More sudden deaths are recorded at hospitals, while more deaths from chronic illness and infectious disease take place at home and never make it to hospital death records.

Even in the minority of deaths which are medically certified, there are major problems with the way doctors arrive at the cause of death. One consistent problem, which has implications for estimates of coronavirus deaths, is that doctors record the mode of death (for example, 'heart attack') rather than the underlying causes ('chronic heart disease' or 'hypertension'). Multiple reviews of death certificates filled in at individual hospitals have shown that underlying and contributory causes of death are incomplete or incorrect.

Additionally, mounting evidence suggests that political compulsions forced most states to attempt to downplay their COVID numbers. States across the country formed audit committees that decided which deaths of COVID-positive persons should be counted as COVID deaths, and in four states, members of these committees told me of the ways in which they were whittling down their numbers. Despite the guidelines of the World Health Organisation and the Indian Council for Medical Research that encourage adopting as liberal a definition of a COVID death as possible, Indian states have systematically adopted an excessively stringent definition—only deaths of people who tested positive for COVID prior to death and died with a typical progression of disease in hospitals are typically counted as India's COVID dead.

As India's first wave began to decline in September 2020, it was clearly a global outlier in terms of mortality data. But instead of wondering if there was something exceptional going on with Indian data, the government-pushed narrative was that it was the country that was exceptional.

On 29 April 2021, India reported over 250,000 new COVID cases and over 3,000 deaths. It was one of the worst-ever days of the country's experience of the pandemic, just ten days away from the peak of its deadly second wave. That very day, the capital city of Delhi was virtually out of space to cremate the COVID dead—the bodies just kept coming in.

That morning, India's then health minister, Harsh Vardhan, visited a COVID hospital in Delhi. In over a year of leading his country's pandemic response, the minister had addressed virtually no press conferences, much like his prime minister. But in a statement delivered to the media after his visit, the minister's main point was one that has been central to the Modi government's messaging: while every death was sad, the minister said, India had one of the lowest mortality rates in the world.

Since the beginning of the pandemic, India's government sought to argue that India handled the pandemic better than most any country, and that this was evidenced by its low COVID mortality rate. This triumphalism was on display in Modi's now infamous January 2021 speech to the World Economic Forum in which he said, 'India is among those countries which have succeeded in saving the lives of the maximum number of its citizens.'

Those on the ground, people who were seeing their hometowns devastated yet unrepresented in official data, knew that the government was not counting every COVID death. For the families of the COVID dead, it was a denial of closure, a denial of dignity to the dead. Public-spirited citizens stepped in to try to fill in some of the gaps. Arun N. Madhavan is a doctor of internal medicine who runs a clinic in Palakkad, Kerala. He led a team of volunteers who scanned the state's media for news reports and obituaries that mention a death from COVID-19 and cross-referenced it against the state's official list. By December 2020, the group found that 45 per cent of the deaths they tallied never showed up in the government's list. By the time the second wave hit, Dr Madhavan and his team had to stop their parallel tallying—newspapers were no longer reporting all deaths either.

As the virus raged through India in the second wave in the summer of 2021, images of ambulances lined up at crematoria, furnaces bent from overuse, and hastily erected makeshift pyres cremating dozens of bodies each day with COVID protocols flooded social media and the airwaves. Newspaper reporters compared the deaths recorded in crematoria and burial grounds with those reported by state governments to charge that there was as much as three to five times undercounting. But crematoria records are poorly maintained and the data was unreliable. There was also no way to be certain that all of those deaths were from COVID.

There are, however, ways to fill in the blanks. Dr Prabhat Jha is the world's leading expert on mortality in India and founding director of the Centre for Global Health Research in Toronto. In 1975, when Dr Jha was growing up in Canada, his family received a report from India that his grandfather had died; the cause was unclear. Jha's grandfather had died at home, without having visited a hospital. Jha's mother was desperate for more information, so she returned to her home village to talk to locals. Years later, when Jha was at medical school, he reviewed his mother's notes and realised that his grandfather had probably died of a stroke.[27]

Dr Jha uses essentially this strategy in his work on mortality in India. He and his team pioneered the use of verbal autopsies, where trained investigators visit a household where a person has died, conduct an interview, and then two doctors oversee those notes to decide upon a cause of death. The Million Death Study that he led found that India vastly underestimated deaths from smoking, snakebites and malaria, among other causes. India could be similarly underestimating the number of coronavirus cases and possible deaths, given this background of low level of death certification and high levels of errors. From the beginning of the pandemic, Dr Jha has been urging the Indian government to conduct such a Million Death Study. Yet, it never took place.

Countries around the world, even those that followed more liberal definitions of a COVID death, accept that they were likely missing some deaths from COVID. To fill in this gap, they turned to estimates of excess mortality as a proxy for confirmed and suspected COVID deaths. South Africa, for instance, estimated the actual number of deaths that had occurred in the country and calculated the number of excess deaths over and above the numbers that would be expected had the historical mortality trends prior to the COVID-19 pandemic continued. In doing so, it found that the cumulative number of excess deaths from natural causes between 3 May 2020 (after the country's first COVID-19 lockdown) and 23

January 2021 (during the country's second surge of COVID-19 infections and lockdown) was greater by 125,000 than the numbers predicted by historical trends.

India last released all-cause mortality data for the year 2019. Yet, I knew that updated data on deaths from all causes in the smallest village to the biggest city were being uploaded to government servers every day. In June 2021, I began to access secret official government portals that held Civil Registration System data for every state. I found that in May 2021—the peak of India's second wave—mortality from all causes shot up to nearly five times the usual average. In Madhya Pradesh, the excess mortality in the first five months of 2021 was over forty-two times the officially reported toll from COVID for the same time period. In Andhra Pradesh it was thirty-eight times. The undercounting for more developed states appeared to be lesser—could it be that all this while the states that appeared to be the worst affected were just the ones doing the best counting?

Behind these statistics is the story of what 'undercounting' means. In May 2021, thirty-two-year-old Rinku Parmar tested positive for COVID in the ninth month of her pregnancy. Within two days, she began to sink before her husband Manoj's eyes, and he got her admitted to a private hospital in Silchar, Assam, where they lived. The baby, a little boy, was delivered via C-section two weeks before the expected due date as Rinku's lungs were on the verge of collapse and the hospital wanted to put her on a ventilator. Three weeks later, without ever having held her son, she was gone. Yet, her death certificate did not mention COVID—the hospital said that it was nearly a month since she had tested positive, the most recent COVID test had came out negative, and the district administration had told them not to count such deaths. 'I had to tell my five-year-old daughter that her mother died of corona,' Manoj told me over the phone, his voice shaking with sobs. 'To think that she didn't even count is an insult to her memory.'

India's Health Data Deficit Laid Bare

When there is so much that India's health data does not capture, the country should have at least gone into the pandemic with the humility to learn. Unfortunately, the pandemic not only demonstrated the acute limitations of Indian state capacity, including when it comes to data, but also exposed a growing opacity that threatens to not just weaken our understanding of health but to weaken democracy itself.

From the beginning, India's official pandemic response was unusual for all that it did not say. India was the only major country not to publish detailed data on its COVID cases; every Latin American country was able to have a high-quality website with downloadable historical data from every city up and running weeks into the pandemic, but India never provided anything more than cumulative state-level counts—no historical data, no district data, no demographic information, little detail on testing. The task fell to public-spirited volunteers who coordinated over the messaging platform Telegram and set up covid19india.org, a crowd-sourced website that used only official data, yet had to be set up privately, and was then used as a resource by every academic and media organisation globally through the pandemic. The group intended to ceased operations by the end of October 2021, but despite a fully functional, meticulously documented website having been already built, the government did not step in to take the baton from them. Instead, the government consistently stonewalled all attempts at providing detailed data, including through Right To Information requests.

In the early months of the 2020 lockdown, it quickly became apparent to me that there was a huge lack of access to routine health services. To put numbers to the crisis, I accessed data from the National Health Mission's Health Management Information System (NHM-HMIS), which tracks indicators on utilisation of health services from over 200,000 health facilities, from primary health centres to district hospitals in every district of the country, and is updated nearly every day. These health facilities are predominantly in rural areas and in the public sector. After I wrote about the severe curtailment in health services in March 2020 as compared to previous months and years, the NHM stopped publishing this data. In August 2020, the NHM-HMIS finally published data for April, May and June. Once again, I wrote about it and within a few days, the portal stopped publishing new data entirely. In July 2021, it was the same dance again: the data reappeared, I wrote about it, and it went offline. This time, I wrote about its disappearance, putting the flimsy official excuse of 'server problems' out publicly, and that weekend the data was restored.

Through both 2020 and 2021, there was very little genuine effort to understand why there were more cases and deaths in some places than others. India knows very little about why cases rose and then fell across the country in September 2020, and then rose sharply in March 2021. States with better healthcare access or testing regimens did not necessarily do better. Not all states with younger populations had an easier time of it, and states like Bihar with poor mask compliance and massive election rallies in October 2020 saw no surge. Then there is the case of Kerala, which saw a later spurt in cases, but had low mortality.

The issue here cuts to the heart of a broader problem with inter-state comparisons on healthcare in India—the wide variations between states in their ability and willingness to report data. Many states to a larger or smaller extent have attempted to under-report data so as not to attract negative media and political attention. Assam's mortality from COVID-19 was among the country's lowest in the first wave, but reporting from the state has shown that its death audit committees reclassified 60 per cent of deaths of COVID-19-positive people as being 'deaths from other causes'.[28] Much as with crime data, comparing states on the basis of their reported numbers and then criticising the states reporting higher numbers is actually not fair, Giridhar Babu, an epidemiologist with the Public Health Foundation of India, told me.

Responses came on predictably partisan lines. Surges were blamed on Muslim and Hindu religious gatherings respectively, without the acknowledgement that any mass gathering, whether for an election or for a Goa rave, was a bad idea. Kerala's initial successes in containing its outbreak were uncritically cheered by those on the Left, while its second wave in December 2020, when numbers had subsided elsewhere, was mocked by those on the right. In April 2021, as Indian cities gasped in the throes of the second wave, the ruling BJP's national spokesperson Amit Malviya sought to argue that warnings about a second wave had been given, but it was Congress-ruled states in particular that had chosen to ignore them, instead of looking for answers in epidemiology or demography.

Where data did not exist because the right studies had not been undertaken, there was sometimes an overselling of limited positive data. In a press conference in late April 2021, the Indian government presented data that appeared to show that only two to four persons of every 10,000 vaccinated with either of the two COVID-19 vaccines being used in India were seeing breakthrough infections (when a vaccinated person gets infected). However, this was based on incomplete data—for nearly three months after vaccination began, the government's COVID-19 test form, used by both government and private laboratories, did not check if those being tested had been vaccinated. Cases of post-vaccination infection would therefore not have been detected and recorded. Even after the form was changed to include vaccination details, the change did not fully make it to the ground—most government websites, hospital websites and labs continued to use the old form. This meant that many people who were testing positive for COVID-19 after getting vaccinated were still not being reflected in ICMR's data on breakthrough infections. Worse still, some, like sixty-nine-year-old B. Sumana from Chennai, had been vaccinated before testing positive, but were never asked—their documentation said that they had not been vaccinated. At best, the government could have said that they had only detected a small number of breakthrough infections and there could have been more. Instead, they chose to claim there were only very few. India was using efficacious vaccines, yet the government chose to put out misleading data to make the vaccines look better than they were. It took research from the UK, which was by then dealing with the same variant of the original virus as India and also using the AstraZeneca vaccine, for true effectiveness data to come out.

It was a thread that had run through the pandemic—the government putting out too little data or misleading data, journalists seeking more information being attacked for working against the country's interests, or for looking for 'bad news'. If there was any hope that the pandemic was to be a turning point, the beginning of increased spending on health, the dawn of a less polarised sphere of debate and the ushering in of openness in data, this fond hope now appears to have been firmly dashed.

Critics of the government have often framed their problems with Indian COVID data in the language of fraud and deceit; the government, in their telling, hid or made up numbers. The truth, however, lies in a combination of five cardinal sins in India's data infrastructure, failings that leave their mark on most official statistics: not collecting essential data, not collating or publishing existing data in usable ways, obfuscating or suppressing some data, overselling data well beyond what it really says and knee-jerk criticism of inconvenient data. Some of these are institutional failings and we can hope that future governments turn things around for the next pandemic. But some of these are all-new and the alarm bells are ringing loud and clear for the future of India's data integrity.

CONCLUSION

Data tells us a great deal about India. It tells us the big stories of who people vote for and how many more women have been voting over the years. Of how some types of reported crime are rising and some states report more crime than others. Of how much people spend, of who is poor and who is rich, and who is getting richer while some are stuck where their parents were. Of what people eat and drink and would like to eat more of if they had more money. Of how many people have jobs and how many are looking for them and what work they do and how much money it makes them. Of how much longer the country will grow and who will age and who will migrate. Of who falls sick and dies and of what.

It also chronicles some of the smaller stories that fill colour into our picture of India. Of what part of the country likes brinjals and which part likes ladies' fingers. Of how much television women watch and how much time they get to spend chatting. Of how many people speak Bhojpuri even though the government may say it is Hindi. Of how many people get Sundays off from work.

What official data alone can sometimes not do very well is tell us the why. That is where high quality privately collected data can step in. It can tell us why young Dalits are voting for the BJP and why young upper-caste people want reservation for themselves. Why crimes rose in one year and fell in another, and why they're higher in some states. Why official numbers seem to be missing so many COVID deaths and why people don't always make it to the hospital in time. Why rich people think they are middle-class and upper-caste people don't want a Dalit person in their kitchen. Why conservative and liberal attitudes seem to coexist in India and, perhaps, what the future could look like.

But for Indian data, particularly official data, to continue to be able to tell us these big stories, there will need to something of a public movement to secure it. India's official statistics are, for the most part, not lying to us, but they are being silenced. A combination of neglect, discredit and dismissal makes the deficiencies in the data seem too big, too fatal to fix. Indian statistics are missing the true story of 'new India', we are being told, and so should be buried, and administrative data, which is directly controlled by the government, be used instead. When inconvenient data is suppressed—as has also been the case—the narrative that is quickly dusted off and shipped off to op-ed pages is this one: official statistics miss too much, so we're better off without them.

Indian data has told us the real story of life in India for decades—not always at the right time, and not always without controversy, and not always the full story. But using official and private sources, we have been able to piece together the story until now. The only way to fix the problems is to accurately identify the flaws and talk to experts about how to fix them. A vague, overly broad scepticism and suspicion about all official data and all inconvenient private data will not help; it will only strengthen the arm of those who seek to suppress it.

Being so bound by ideology that each side refuses to engage with the other is partly what got us into this mess. To get out of it, we're going to have to dig deep and get specific. Properly collected data cannot be junked if it tells an inconvenient story for either side and bad data cannot be defended for its value in preserving political points. More data, better collection, greater openness and more interrogation—that is what will fix this.

Reaching across the aisle isn't always easy or necessary—or even morally right. I might choose not to build bridges to those who don't consider people of all religions and castes worthy of equal respect and protection before the law. But many others who may appear to be ideological adversaries are people who have different political or economic beliefs but might want the same thing—for life to get better for all Indians. Conversation has broken down between India's Left and Right, and in the right hands, data can be that bridge. With investment, upgradation, commitment and independent oversight, India's official statistical systems and public-spirited private organisations can produce the data that gives us a fair idea of how India works and how most Indians are leading their lives. Ideological adversaries can still argue about the best way forward from there, but let the data bring us onto the same page first.

For over 75 years, this data has shaped policy and driven change. It has given rise to passionate debates about growth, development and the trade-offs between them, about the trajectories that different Indian states have set off on, about which government schemes really reach the people and which ones remain on paper, and about how people's most intimate thoughts and beliefs are changing. These conversations have helped us decide—or at the very least, argue about—who we want to be as a nation and how we want to get there. Think about the debate about liberalisation, economic reforms, redistributive policies, the poverty line, the welfare state, affirmative action, casteism, rising Islamophobia—all of these fundamentally Indian debates are anchored in data collected by the State. Access to this data has empowered ordinary citizens to engage with and agitate against the State; public-spirited economists and activists have taken this data from the pages of government reports to the streets.

Data has been transformational for India. We need to build a future with more and better data that's more widely available and easier to understand. Without it, we are in danger of hollowing out democracy.

NOTES

I. How India Tangles with Cops and Courts

1. Girija Borker, 'Avoiding #MeToo: Harassment Risk and Women's College Choice', World Bank, 6 December 2017, https://blogs.worldbank.org/impactevaluations/avoiding-metoo-harassment-risk-and-women-s-college-choice-guest-post-girija-borker.
2. Rukmini S., 'India officially undercounts all crimes including rape', *The Hindu*, 13 September 2013, https://www.thehindu.com/news/national/india-officially-undercounts-all-crimes-including-rape/article5121114.ece.
3. https://ncrb.gov.in/sites/default/files/disclaimer2013.pdf.
4. 'Despite Collecting It, NCRB Hasn't Published 2017 Data on Lynchings', *The Wire*, 22 October 2019, https://thewire.in/government/despite-collecting-it-ncrb-hasnt-published-2017-data-on-lynchings-religious-murders.
5. Anubhav Vashishtha and Abhay Pachauri, 'Mob Lynching: A Crime That Exonerates The Offenders In India?', *Outlook*, 5 August 2020, https://www.outlookindia.com/website/story/opinion-mob-lynching-a-crime-that-exonerates-the-offenders-in-india/358031.
6. Kamaljit Kaur Sandhu, 'Will change laws to check mob lynching, govt talking to states: Amit Shah in Rajya Sabha',

India Today, 4 December 2019, https://www.indiatoday.in/india/story/amit-shah-says-govt-will-change-laws-to-check-mob-lynching-1625018-2019-12-04.

7. 'Delhi ranks first in crimes against women', *The Hindu*, 2 October 2020, https://www.thehindu.com/news/cities/Delhi/capital-ranks-first-in-crimes-against-women/article32749130.ece.

8. Rukmini S., 'The many shades of rape cases in Delhi', *The Hindu*, 29 July 2014, https://www.thehindu.com/data/the-many-shades-of-rape-cases-in-delhi/article6261042.ece.

9. Geetanjali Gangoli and Martin Rew, 'Continuities and Change: The Law Commission and Sexual Violence', *Journal of Indian Law and Society*, vol. 6, no. 3 (2018): 112–124, https://core.ac.uk/download/pdf/151188201.pdf.

10. Rukmini S., 'Why the FIR doesn't tell you the whole story', *The Hindu*, 22 December 2015, https://www.thehindu.com/opinion/op-ed/rukmini-s-writes-about-the-mumbai-sessions-court-rulings-on-sexual-assault-during-2015-why-the-fir-doesnt-tell-you-the-whole-story/article8014815.ece.

11. Rukmini S., 'Mumbai police and the curious case of meow meow', *HuffPost India*, 2018.

12. United Nations Crime Trends Survey (2020), United Nations Office on Drugs and Crime.

13. Abhijit Banerjee et al., 'Can Institutions be Reformed from Within?: Evidence from a Randomized Experiment with the Rajasthan Police' Working Department of Economics MIT, Working Paper, http://economics.mit.edu/files/7783.

14. *Crime Victimisation and Safety Perception: A Public Survey of Delhi and Mumbai*, Commonwealth Human Rights Initiative, 2015, https://www.humanrightsinitiative.org/download/1461662128Crime%20Victimisation_Soft%20File_distribution.pdf.

15. Abhijit Banerjee et al., 'Can Institutions be Reformed from Within?: Evidence from a Randomized Experiment with the

Rajasthan Police' Working Department of Economics MIT, Working Paper, http://economics.mit.edu/files/7783.

16. Kislaya Prasad, 'A Comparison of Victim-Reported and Police-Recorded Crime in India', *Economic and Political Weekly*, vol. 48, no. 33 (2013): http://www.india-ava.org/fileadmin/docs/pubs/external-research/Prasad__Victim_and_police_reported_crime__2014.pdf.

17. Interview to author.

18. Aashish Gupta, 'Reporting and incidence of violence against women in India', Rice Institute Working Paper, 2014, https://riceinstitute.org/research/reporting-and-incidence-of-violence-against-women-in-india/.

19. 'UP safer for women than many big states: NCRB report', *Times of India*, 11 January 2021, https://timesofindia.indiatimes.com/city/lucknow/up-safer-for-women-than-many-big-states/articleshow/80204684.cms.

20. National Family Health Survey (2019-20).

21. Abhijit Banerjee et al., 'Can Institutions be Reformed from Within?: Evidence from a Randomized Experiment with the Rajasthan Police' Working Department of Economics MIT, Working Paper, http://economics.mit.edu/files/7783.

22. Lakshmi Iyer et al., 'The Power of Political Voice: Women's Political Representation and Crime in India', *American Economic Journal: Applied Economics*, vol. 4, no. 4 (2012): 165–193, https://www.aeaweb.org/articles?id=10.1257/app.4.4.165.

23. Sofia Amaral et al., 'Gender, Crime and Punishment: Evidence from Women Police Stations in India', Department of Economics, Boston University, Working Paper (2019), http://barrett.dyson.cornell.edu/NEUDC/paper_32.pdf.

II. What India Thinks, Feels and Believes

1. R. Inglehart et al. (eds), World Values Survey: Round Six—Country-Pooled Datafile. Madrid, Spain and Vienna, Austria: JD Systems Institute and WVSA Secretariat, 2018.

2. Richard Wike and Shannon Schumacher, 'Democratic Rights Popular Globally but Commitment to Them Not Always Strong', Pew Research Center, February 2020, https://www.pewresearch.org/global/wp-content/uploads/sites/2/2020/02/PG_2020.02.27_global-democracy_REPORT.pdf.

3. Ibid.

4. Ibid.

5. Ibid.

6. *Society and Politics Between Elections: A Report*, Bangalore: Aziz Premji University, 2017, https://azimpremjiuniversity.edu.in/SitePages/pdf/Azim_Premji_Univ_PSBE_2017.pdf.

7. Ibid.

8. *Religion in India: Tolerance and Segregation*, Pew Research Centre, 29 June 2021, https://www.pewforum.org/2021/06/29/religion-in-india-tolerance-and-segregation/.

9. Richard Wike and Shannon Schumacher, 'Democratic Rights Popular Globally but Commitment to Them Not Always Strong', Pew Research Center, February 2020, https://www.pewresearch.org/global/wp-content/uploads/sites/2/2020/02/PG_2020.02.27_global-democracy_REPORT.pdf.

10. Pew 2021.

11. Ibid.

12. *Society and Politics Between Elections: A Report*, Bangalore: Aziz Premji University, 2017, https://azimpremjiuniversity.edu.in/SitePages/pdf/Azim_Premji_Univ_PSBE_2017.pdf.

13. Pew 2021.

14. Ibid.

15. Anuradha Banerjee et al., 'Urban Rental Housing Market: Caste and Religion Matters in Access', *Economic and Political Weekly*, vol. 50, no. 26–27 (2015), https://www.epw.in/journal/2015/26-27/housing-discrimination/urban-rental-housing-market.html.

16. Lok Foundation-Oxford University survey by the Centre for the Monitoring of the Indian Economy, Pulse II.

17. Pew 2021.

18. 'Key highlights from the CSDS-KAS Report "Attitudes, anxieties and aspirations of India's youth: changing patterns"', Lokniti, https://www.lokniti.org/media/upload_files/KeyfindingsfromtheYouthStudy.pdf.

19. Ibid.

20. Ibid.

21. Lok Foundation-Oxford University survey by the Centre for the Monitoring of the Indian Economy, Pulse V.

22. *Society and Politics Between Elections: A Report*, Bangalore: Aziz Premji University, 2017, https://azimpremjiuniversity.edu.in/SitePages/pdf/Azim_Premji_Univ_PSBE_2017.pdf.

23. 'Key highlights from the CSDS-KAS Report "Attitudes, anxieties and aspirations of India's youth: changing patterns"', Lokniti, https://www.lokniti.org/media/upload_files/KeyfindingsfromtheYouthStudy.pdf.

24. Neelanjan Sircar and Megan Reed, 'Choosing thy neighbour', *The Hindu*, 10 January 2015, https://www.thehindu.com/opinion/op-ed/comment-article-choosing-thy-neighbour/article6772534.ece.

25. Lok Foundation-Oxford University survey by the Centre for the Monitoring of the Indian Economy, Pulse I.

26. 'Key highlights from the CSDS-KAS Report "Attitudes, anxieties and aspirations of India's youth: changing patterns"', Lokniti, https://www.lokniti.org/media/upload_files/KeyfindingsfromtheYouthStudy.pdf.

27. Amit Thorat and Omkar Joshi, 'The Continuing Practice of Untouchability in India: Patterns and Mitigating Influences', *Economic and Political Weekly*, vol. 55, no. 2 (2020), https://www.epw.in/journal/2020/2/special-articles/continuing-practice-untouchability-india.html.

28. Diane Coffey et al., 'Explicit Prejudice: Evidence from a New Survey', *Economic and Political Weekly*, vol. 53, no. 1 (2018), https://www.epw.in/journal/2018/1/special-articles/explicit-prejudice.html.

29. Lok Survey Pulse II.

30. Pew 2021.

31. Lok Survey Pulse II.

32. 'Key highlights from the CSDS-KAS Report "Attitudes, anxieties and aspirations of India's youth: changing patterns"', Lokniti, https://www.lokniti.org/media/upload_files/ KeyfindingsfromtheYouthStudy.pdf.

33. Richard Wike and Shannon Schumacher, 'Democratic Rights Popular Globally but Commitment to Them Not Always Strong', Pew Research Center, February 2020, https://www. pewresearch.org/global/wp-content/uploads/sites/2/2020/02/ PG_2020.02.27_global-democracy_REPORT.pdf.

34. Lok Survey.

35. *Society and Politics Between Elections: A Report*, Bangalore: Aziz Premji University, 2017, https://azimpremjiuniversity.edu.in/ SitePages/pdf/Azim_Premji_Univ_PSBE_2017.pdf.

36. Lok Survey Pulse I.

37. 'Key highlights from the CSDS-KAS Report "Attitudes, anxieties and aspirations of India's youth: changing patterns"', Lokniti, https://www.lokniti.org/media/upload_files/ KeyfindingsfromtheYouthStudy.pdf.

38. *Society and Politics Between Elections: A Report*, Bangalore: Aziz Premji University, 2017, https://azimpremjiuniversity.edu.in/ SitePages/pdf/Azim_Premji_Univ_PSBE_2017.pdf.

39. Lok Foundation-Oxford University survey by the Centre for the Monitoring of the Indian Economy, Pulse VI.

40. *Society and Politics Between Elections: A Report*, Bangalore: Aziz Premji University, 2017, https://azimpremjiuniversity.edu.in/ SitePages/pdf/Azim_Premji_Univ_PSBE_2017.pdf.

41. Lok Survey Pulse I (2014)

42. 'Key highlights from the CSDS-KAS Report "Attitudes, anxieties and aspirations of India's youth: changing patterns"', Lokniti, https://www.lokniti.org/media/upload_files/ KeyfindingsfromtheYouthStudy.pdf.

43. World Values Survey, various rounds.

44. Ibid.

45. Ibid.

46. Ibid.

47. Jacob Poushter and Nicholas Kent, 'The Global Divide on Homosexuality Persists', Pew Research Center, 25 June 2020, https://www.pewresearch.org/global/2020/06/25/global-divide-on-homosexuality-persists/.

48. Based on data from CSDS-KAS 2007 and 2017. See, Roshan Kishore, 'Has the rise of BJP made India's youth less liberal?', *LiveMint*, 9 May 2017, https://www.livemint.com/Politics/R0eujsnVtHNdxwgtf3uDxM/Has-BJPs-rise-made-Indias-youth-less-liberal.html.

49. Lok Survey Pulse II.

50. Neelanjan Sircar and Megan Reed, 'Choosing thy neighbour', *The Hindu*, 10 January 2015, https://www.thehindu.com/opinion/op-ed/comment-article-choosing-thy-neighbour/article6772534.ece.

51. R. Banerjee and N. Datta Gupta, 'Awareness Programs and Change in Taste-Based Caste Prejudice', *PLoS ONE*, vol. 10, no. 4 (2015): e0118546, https://journals.plos.org/plosone/article?id=10.1371/journal.pone.0118546.

52. Matt Lowe, 'Unity in cricket: Integrated leagues and caste divisions', *Ideas for India*, 23 May 2018, https://www.ideasforindia.in/topics/social-identity/unity-in-cricket-integrated-leagues-and-caste-divisions.html.

53. Payal Hathi, 'Can more education reduce opposition to intermarriage? Comparing India and the US', r.i.c.e., 2 August 2018, https://riceinstitute.org/research/can-more-education-reduce-opposition-to-intermarriage-comparing-india-and-the-us/.

54. B.R. Ambedkar, *Annihilation of Caste*, 1936.

III. How India (Really) Votes

1. Daniel Stockemer, 'Turnout in developed and developing countries', *Political Science*, vol. 67, no. 1 (2017): 3–20, doi: 10.1177/0032318715585033.

2. International Institute for Democracy and Electoral Assistance Voter Turnout Database, idea.int, https://www.idea.int/data-tools/data/voter-turnout.

3. '2020 November General Election Turnout Rates', United States Election Project, http://www.electproject.org/2020g.

4. Rekha Diwakar, 'Voter Turnout in the Indian States: An Empirical Analysis', *Journal of Elections Public Opinion and Parties*, vol. 18, no. 1(2008): 75–100, https://www.researchgate. net/publication/233083087_Voter_Turnout_in_the_Indian_States_An_Empirical_Analysis.

5. Amit Ahuja and Pradeep K. Chhibber, 'Why the Poor Vote in India: "If I Don't Vote, I Am Dead to the State"', *Studies in Comparative International Development*, vol. 47, no. 4 (2012): 389–410, https://papers.ssrn.com/sol3/papers.cfm?abstract_id=2273322.

6. Turnout data from the Election Commission. Constituency-wise poverty rates from R. Kim et al., 2019. 'Parliamentary Constituency Factsheet for Indicators of Nutrition, Health and Development in India', HCPDS Working Paper, vol. 18, no. 4, https://www.hsph.harvard.edu/population-development/indiapcfactsheets/.

7. Kanchan Chandra and Alan Potter, 'Do Urban Voters in India Vote Less?', *Economic and Political Weekly*, vol. 51, no. 39 (2016): 58–69, https://as.nyu.edu/content/dam/nyu-as/faculty/documents/Chandra_Potter_EPW_UrbanVoters.pdf.

8. *Survey on the Quality of Voter Lists in Delhi: Summary of Research Findings*, Janaagraha, 2015, http://www.janaagraha. org/files/publications/Quality-of-Lists-Delhi-2015-Summary. pdf.

9. Pradeep Chhibber and Rahul Verma, *Ideology and Identity: The Changing Party Systems of India*, US: Oxford University Press (2018).

10. CVoter December 2019 tracker poll.

11. India Today-Axis My India exit poll. 'Delhi election 2020: Muslim voters prefer AAP over Congress, shows India Today exit poll', *India Today*, 8 February 2020, https://www.indiatoday. in/elections/delhi-assembly-polls-2020/story/delhi-election-2020-muslim-voters-prefer-aap-over-congress-shows-india-today-exit-poll-1644587-2020-02-08.

12. Tora Agarwala, '104-yr-old in Assam dies a "foreigner", hoping "CAA will solve all"', *The Indian Express*, 15 December 2020, https://indianexpress.com/article/north-east-india/assam/104-yr-old-in-assam-dies-a-foreigner-hoping-caa-will-solve-all-7105123/.

13. Interview with Rahul Verma.

14. Rahul Verma and Pranav Gupta, 'Facts and Fiction about How Muslims Vote in India', *Economic and Political Weekly*, vol. 51, no. 53 (2016), https://www.epw.in/journal/2016/53/uttar-pradesh%E2%80%94vortex-change/facts-and-fiction-about-how-muslims-vote-india.html.

15. Author's analysis using ECI data on outcomes, names analysis, and Datanet India estimates of Muslim population by PC.

16. *Society and Politics Between Elections: A Report*, Bangalore: Aziz Premji University, 2017, https://azimpremjiuniversity.edu.in/SitePages/pdf/Azim_Premji_Univ_PSBE_2017.pdf.

17. Rahul Verma and Pranav Gupta, 'Facts and Fiction about How Muslims Vote in India', *Economic and Political Weekly*, vol. 51, no. 53 (2016), https://www.epw.in/journal/2016/53/uttar-pradesh%E2%80%94vortex-change/facts-and-fiction-about-how-muslims-vote-india.html.

18. Shreyas Sardesai and Vibha Attri, 'The verdict is a manifestation of the deepening religious divide in India', *The Hindu*, 30 May 2019, https://www.thehindu.com/elections/lok-sabha-2019/the-

verdict-is-a-manifestation-of-the-deepening-religious-divide-in-india/article27297239.ece.

19. Lokniti-CSDS National Election Studies.

20. Gareth Nellis et al., 'Do Parties Matter for Ethnic Violence? Evidence From India', *Quarterly Journal of Political Science*, vol. 11, no. 3 (2016): 249–277, https://www.researchgate. net/publication/309601467_Do_Parties_Matter_for_Ethnic_ Violence_Evidence_From_India; Rohit Ticku, 'Riot Rewards? Religious Conflict and Electoral Outcomes', Graduate Institute of International and Development Studies, working paper no. 19/2015 (2016), https://papers.ssrn.com/sol3/papers. cfm?abstract_id=2803978.

21. Based on data from the Trivedi Centre for Political Data, Ashoka University.

22. Lok Foundation/Lok Foundation-Oxford University Survey administered by the CMIE, Pre-election Survey.

23. *Society and Politics Between Elections: A Report*, Bangalore: Aziz Premji University, 2017, https://azimpremjiuniversity.edu.in/ SitePages/pdf/Azim_Premji_Univ_PSBE_2017.pdf

24. Interview with author.

25. Francesca R. Jensenius, 'Development from Representation? A Study of Quotas for the Scheduled Castes in India', *American Economic Journal: Applied Economics*, vol. 7, no. 3 (2015): 196–220, https://www.francesca.no/wp-content/2015/12/ Development_reservations_postprint.pdf.

26. Yuko Mori and Takashi Kurosaki, 'Does Political Reservation Affect Voting Behaviour?', *Economic and Political Weekly*, vol. 51, no. 20 (2016), https://www.epw.in/journal/2016/20/special-articles/does-political-reservation-affect-voting-behaviour.html.

27. 'Karnataka: Dalit BJP MP stopped from entering village', *The Indian Express*, 18 September 2019, https://indianexpress.com/ article/india/karnataka-dalit-bjp-mp-stopped-from-entering-village-6004746/.

28. Kiran Parashar, 'Ground Zero of untouchability, this village

still lives in the past', *Times of India*, 19 September 2019, https://timesofindia.indiatimes.com/city/mysuru/ground-zero-of-untouchability-this-village-still-lives-in-the-past/articleshow/71195230.cms.

29. Interview with author.

30. Francesca R. Jensenius, *Social Justice Through Inclusion: Consequences of Electoral Quotas in India*, Canada: Oxford University Press (2017).

31. Ibid.

32. Ibid.

33. Simon Chauchard, *Why Representation Matters: The Meaning of Ethnic Quotas in Rural India*, US: Cambridge University Press.

34. Rahul Verma and P. Ramajayam, 'Lokniti-CSDS Post-poll Analysis: Women bought Jaya her return ticket', *The Indian Express*, 24 May 2016, https://indianexpress.com/article/india/india-news-india/jayalalithaa-aiadmk-dmk-tamil-nadu-assembly-elections-2016-results2815867/.

35. Lokniti-Centre for the Study of Developing Societies National Election Studies.

36. Lok Pre-election Survey.

37. Neelanjan Sircar, 'The Bengal model to counter the BJP', *Hindustan Times*, 2 May 2021, https://www.hindustantimes.com/opinion/the-bengal-model-to-counter-the-bjp-101619971740348.html.

38. Dhrubo Jyoti, '"Our caste won't change, that doesn't mean we can't progress"', *Hindustan Times*, 13 February 2019, https://www.hindustantimes.com/india-news/our-caste-won-t-change-that-doesn-t-mean-we-can-t-progress/story-VIKLOuWdNG0myM6mujEZXJ.html.

39. Aarefa Johari, 'Half the Vote: A Muslim woman in Godhra says she's proud that a man from her state is prime minister', *Scroll*, 12 April 2019, https://scroll.in/article/919406/half-the-vote-a-muslim-woman-in-godhra-says-shes-proud-that-a-man-from-her-state-is-prime-minister.

40. Nayantara Narayanan, 'Half the Vote: This farmer wants to protect her land – but will vote for the party her village picks', *Scroll*, 10 April 2019, https://scroll.in/article/919238/half-the-vote-this-farmer-wants-to-protect-her-land-but-will-vote-for-the-party-her-village-picks.

41. Sanjay Kumar, 'The Youth Vote Made a Difference for the Victory of the BJP', *Research Journal Social Sciences*, vol. 22, no. 2 (2014).

42. Deepankar Basu and Kartik Misra, 'BJP's Demographic Dividend in the 2014 General Elections: An Empirical Analysis', *Economics Department Working Paper Series*, 172, University of Massachusetts (2014), https://scholarworks.umass.edu/cgi/viewcontent.cgi?article=1172&context=econ_workingpaper.

43. Lok Pre-election Survey.

44. Key highlights from the CSDS-KAS Report. *Attitudes, anxieties and aspirations of India's youth: changing patterns*, Lokniti, https://www.lokniti.org/media/upload_files/KeyfindingsfromtheYouthStudy.pdf.

45. Lok Post-election Survey.

46. Ibid.

47. Lokniti-CSDS National Election Study 2014.

48. Rajeshwari Deshpande, Louise Tillin, and K.K. Kailash, 'The BJP's Welfare Schemes: Did They Make a Difference in the 2019 Elections?', *Studies in Indian Politics*, vol. 7, no. 2 (2019), https://journals.sagepub.com/doi/abs/10.1177/2321023019874911.

49. Sonalde Desai, 'The politics of perceptions', *The Hindu*, 9 November 2016, https://www.thehindu.com/opinion/lead/The-politics-of-perceptions/article16229245.ece.

50. Daniel de Kadt and Evan S. Lieberman, 'Nuanced Accountability: Voter Responses to Service Delivery in Southern Africa', *British Journal of Political Science*, vol. 50, no. 1 (2020): 185–215, https://www.cambridge.org/core/journals/british-journal-of-political-science/article/abs/nuanced-accountability-voter-responses-to-

service-delivery-in-southern-africa/506FC2E11C84ED2424B28 8201A22F389.

51. Christopher Blattman, Mathilde Emeriau, and Nathan Fiala, 'Do Anti-Poverty Programs Sway Voters? Experimental Evidence from Uganda', 2016, https://www.povertyactionlab.org/sites/ default/files/publications/5184_Do-Anti-Poverty-Programs-Sway-Voters_CBlattman_Dec2016.pdf.

52. Lok Pre-election and Post-election Survey.

53. CVoter.

54. Lokniti-CSDS National Election Studies.

55. Centre for Media Studies.

56. Lokniti-CSDS National Election Studies.

57. Spring 2017 Global Attitudes Survey, Pew Research Centre.

58. Lakshmi Iyer and Maya Reddy, 'Redrawing the Lines: Did Political Incumbents Influence Electoral Redistricting in the World's Largest Democracy?', Harvard Business School, Working Paper 14-051 (2013), https://www.hbs.edu/ris/ Publication%20Files/14-051_6beba5c6-4c63-455d-9f02-0f6bd9364877.pdf.

59. Neelanjan Sircar and Milan Vaishnav, 'Exploiting Survey Data', Carnegie Endowment for International Peace, 31 August 2016, https://carnegieendowment.org/2016/08/31/exploiting-survey-data-pub-64448.

IV. Eat, Pray, Enjoy, Love, Marry—How India Lives Life

1. National Sample Survey Office (2011-12), 'Household Consumption Expenditure', pp. 21-22, https://mospi. gov.in/documents/213904/301563//Report_no558_ rou68_30june141602588747485.pdf/8f8b3dda-26f4-788a-a386-d561e74774a6.

2. Balmurli Natrajan and Suraj Jacob, '"Provincialising" Vegetarianism: Putting Indian Food Habits in Their Place',

Economic and Political Weekly, vol. 53, no. 9 (2018), https://www.academia.edu/36065250/Provincialising_Vegetarianism_Putting_Indian_Food_Habits_in_Their_Place.

3. Derek D. Headey and Giordano Palloni, 'Stunting and Wasting Among Indian Preschoolers have Moderate but Significant Associations with the Vegetarian Status of their Mothers', *The Journal of Nutrition*, vol. 150, no. 6 (2020): 1579–1589, https://academic.oup.com/jn/article/150/6/1579/5805455.

4. National Sample Survey Office (2011-12), 'Level and Pattern of Consumer Expenditure', https://mospi.gov.in/documents/213904/301563//nss_rep_5551602588341368.pdf/c128687d-9151-59e4-30c8-963b11b783b2.

5. 'E. Sreedharan doesn't "like anybody eating meat", opposes love jihad', *The Week*, 20 February 2021, https://www.theweek.in/news/india/2021/02/20/e-sreedharan-doesnt-like-anybody-eating-meat-opposes-love-jihad.html.

6. C. Sathyamala, 'Meat-eating in India: Whose food, whose politics, and whose rights?', *Policy Futures in Education*, vol. 17, no. 7 (2019), https://journals.sagepub.com/doi/full/10.1177/1478210318780553.

7. Jahnavi Uppuleti, 'I Like My Beef and I Cannot Lie', *Vice*, 2 March 2021, https://www.vice.com/en/article/y3g9x5/india-marginalised-dalits-beef-food-identity-history-culture.

8. Angus Deaton and Jean Dreze, 'Food and Nutrition in India: Facts and Interpretations', *Economic and Political Weekly*, vol. 44, no. 7 (2009), https://www.epw.in/journal/2009/07/special-articles/food-and-nutrition-india-facts-and-interpretations.html.

9. Angus Deaton and Jean Dreze, 'Nutrition, Poverty and Calorie Fundamentalism: Response to Utsa Patnaik', *Economic and Political Weekly*, vol. 45, no. 14 (2010), https://www.epw.in/journal/2010/14/discussion/nutrition-poverty-and-calorie-fundamentalism-response-utsa-patnaik.html.

10. National Sample Survey Office (2011-12), 'Household Consumption Expenditure', https://mospi.gov.in/documents/213904/301563//Report_no558_rou68_30june 141602588747485.pdf/8f8b3dda-26f4-788a-a386-d561e74774a6.

11. Walter Willett et al., 'Food in the Anthropocene: the EAT–Lancet Commission on healthy diets from sustainable food systems', *The Lancet*, vol. 393, no.10170 (2019): P447–492, https://www.thelancet.com/journals/lancet/article/PIIS0140-6736(18)31788-4/fulltext.

12. National Sample Survey Office (2011-12), 'Household Consumption Expenditure', https://mospi.gov.in/documents/213904/301563//Report_no558_rou68_30june141602588747485.pdf/8f8b3dda-26f4-788a-a386-d561e74774a6.

13. Pew 2021.

14. Ibid.

15. Ibid.

16. Key highlights from the CSDS-KAS Report. *Attitudes, anxieties and aspirations of India's youth: changing patterns*, Lokniti, https://www.lokniti.org/media/upload_files/KeyfindingsfromtheYouthStudy.pdf.

17. Pew 2021.

18. Ibid.

19. Sanjay Kumar and Pranav Gupta, 'Why India's political parties are embracing Hindu rituals', *Mint*, 9 March 2020, https://www.livemint.com/news/india/why-india-s-political-parties-are-embracing-hindu-rituals-11583733286805.html.

20. Pew Research Center, *Religion in India: Tolerance and Segregation* (2021).

21. Lokniti-CSDS 2015 survey on religious practices. See, Sanjay Kumar and Pranav Gupta, 'Why India's political parties are embracing Hindu rituals', *Mint*, 9 March 2020, https://www.livemint.com/news/india/why-india-s-political-parties-are-embracing-hindu-rituals-11583733286805.html.

22. Pew 2021.

23. Arun Pratap Singh and Girishwar Misra, 'Pattern of leisure-lifestyles among Indian school adolescents: Contextual influences and implications for emerging health concerns', *Cogent Psychology*, vol. 2, no. 1 (2015), https://www.tandfonline.com/doi/full/10.1080/23311908.2015.1050779.

24. Key highlights from the CSDS-KAS Report. *Attitudes, anxieties and aspirations of India's youth: changing patterns*, Lokniti, https://www.lokniti.org/media/upload_files/KeyfindingsfromtheYouthStudy.pdf.

25. Lok Survey Pulse VI.

26. Ibid.

27. National Council for Applied Economic Research and University of Maryland, 'India Human Development Survey' Round 2, 2011-12

28. Lok Survey Pulse II.

29. Amit Ahuja and Susan Ostermann, 'Crossing Caste Boundaries in the Modern Indian Marriage Market', *Studies in Comparative International Development* (2015), https://papers.ssrn.com/sol3/papers.cfm?abstract_id=2626656.

30. Key highlights from the CSDS-KAS Report. *Attitudes, anxieties and aspirations of India's youth: changing patterns*, Lokniti, https://www.lokniti.org/media/upload_files/KeyfindingsfromtheYouthStudy.pdf.

31. Apurva Vishwanath, '30-day notice period not mandatory under Special Marriage Act: Allahabad High Court', *The Indian Express*, 14 January 2021, https://indianexpress.com/article/india/30-day-notice-period-not-mandatory-under-special-marriage-act-allahabad-high-court-7145476/.

32. National Family Health Survey (2015-16).

33. Key highlights from the CSDS-KAS Report. *Attitudes, anxieties and aspirations of India's youth: changing patterns*, Lokniti, https://www.lokniti.org/media/upload_files/KeyfindingsfromtheYouthStudy.pdf.

34. Demographic and Health Surveys (DHS).

35. National Family Health Survey (2015-16).

36. Z. Lin et al., 'The Emergence of Educational Hypogamy in India', *Demography*, vol. 57 (2020): 1215–1240, https://link.springer.com/article/10.1007/s13524-020-00888-2.

37. Rukmini S., 'Instead of a task force, delaying marriage needs more education', *Mint*, 17 February 2020, https://www.livemint.com/news/india/instead-of-a-task-force-delaying-marriage-needs-more-education-11581958682675.html.

38. Ibid.

39. Carolina Castilla, 'Political role models and child marriage in India', *Review of Development Economics*, vol. 22, no. 4 (2018): 1409–1431, https://onlinelibrary.wiley.com/doi/full/10.1111/rode.12513.

40. Tanushree Goyal and Sam Van Noort, 'The power of enforcement: State capacity and child marriage in India', *Ideas for India*, 24 October 2017, https://www.ideasforindia.in/topics/governance/the-power-of-enforcement-state-capacity-and-child-marriage-in-india.html.

41. *Key Indicators of Household Social consumption in Educatio in India*, NSS 75th round, Central Statistics Office, Ministry of Statistics and Programme Implementation, Government of India, 2019, https://mospi.gov.in/documents/213904/301563//KI_Education_75th_Final1602590967945.pdf/4d0dcdc4-a8f0-0795-df06-be25f2b3a6f7.

42. IHDS 2011-12

43. Abhijit Banerjee et al., (2018), 'Marry For What?: Caste and Mate Selection in Modern India', *American Economic Journal: Microeconomics*, vol. 5, no. 2 (2013): 33–72, https://economics.mit.edu/files/8979.

44. Ibid.

45. *Report on The Formal and Informal Barriers in the Implementation of the Hindu Succession (Amendment) Act 2005: In the context of Women Agricultural Producers of Andhra Pradesh, Bihar*

and Madhya Pradesh, Landesa Rural Development Institute and UN Women, 2013, https://cdn.landesa.org/wp-content/uploads/hsaa-study-report.pdf.

V. How Much Money Do Indians Make?

1. Lok Foundation-Oxford University survey by the Centre for the Monitoring of the Indian Economy, Pulse I.

2. IT Returns Statistics Assessment for 2018-19, https://www.incometaxindia.gov.in/Documents/Direct%20Tax%20Data/IT-Return-Statistics-Assessment-Year-2018-19.pdf.

3. *Key Indicators of Household Consumption Expenditure in India 2017-18*, NSS 75th Round, National Sample Survey Office, Ministry of Statistics and Programme Implementation, Government of India, 2019.

4. Ibid.

5. National Council for Applied Economic Research and University of Maryland, 'IHDS' Round 2, 2011-12.

6. Socio Economic and Caste Census, Ministry of Rural Development, Government of India, 2011.

7. Employment and Unemployment Situation in India 2011-12, NSS 68th Round, National Sample Survey Office, Ministry of Statistics and Programme Implementation, Government of India, 2014.

8. Rachel M. Gisselquist and Anustup Kundu, 'Horizontal inequality, COVID-19, and lockdown readiness: Evidence from India', UNU-WIDER, Working Paper 2020/156 (2020), https://www.wider.unu.edu/sites/default/files/Publications/Working-paper/PDF/wp2020-156.pdf.

9. Rakesh Kochhar, 'In the pandemic, India's middle class shrinks and poverty spreads while China sees smaller changes', Pew Research Center, 2021, https://www.pewresearch.org/fact-tank/2021/03/18/in-the-pandemic-indias-middle-class-shrinks-and-poverty-spreads-while-china-sees-smaller-changes/.

10. IHDS 2011-12; Mehtabul Azam, 'Income Inequality in India 2004-2012: Role of Alternative Income sources', *Economics Bulletin*, vol. 36, no. 2 (2016): 1160–1169, http://www. accessecon.com/Pubs/EB/2016/Volume36/EB-16-V36-I2-P113. pdf.

11. https://www.gc.cuny.edu/CUNY_GC/media/LISCenter/ Workshop%202017/Income-and-Employment-in-India.pdf.

12. Sonalde Desai, 'Rethinking Social Safety Nets in an Era of Declining Poverty', IHDS, https://cpb-us-e1.wpmucdn. com/blogs.gwu.edu/dist/5/1304/files/2018/05/Desai-GWU-conference-26omsbd.pdf.

13. National Council for Applied Economic Research and University of Maryland, 'India Human Development Survey' Round 2, 2011-12.

14. Nitin Kumar Bharti, using a wealth index from the National Family Health Survey (NFHS) 2005-06. See, Nitin Kumar Bharti, 'Wealth Inequality, Class and Caste in India,1951-2012', master's thesis, Paris School of Economics, 2018, http://piketty.pse.ens. fr/files/Bharti2018.pdf.

15. A Mint analysis of NFHS 2015-16 data; Tadit Kundu and Pramit Bhattacharya, 'Where India's affluent classes live', *Mint*, 8 August 2018, https://www.livemint.com/Politics/ DymS22taK4EyAbSYRx0rSO/Where-Indias-affluent-classes-live.html.

16. National Council for Applied Economic Research and University of Maryland, 'India Human Development Survey' Round 2, 2011-12.

17. Sam Asher, et al., 'Intergenerational Mobility in India: New Methods and Estimates Across Time, Space, and Communities' (2021), https://paulnovosad.com/pdf/anr-india-mobility.pdf.

18. Hai-Anh Dang and Peter Lanjouw, 'Welfare dynamics in India over a quarter century: Poverty, vulnerability, and mobility, 1987–2012', UNU-WIDER, Working Paper 2018/175 (2018), https://www.wider.unu.edu/sites/default/files/Publications/ Working-paper/PDF/wp2018-175.pdf.

19. National Council for Applied Economic Research and University of Maryland, 'India Human Development Survey' Round 2, 2011-12.

20. S. Singh and A .Thorat, 'Caste Restricted Occupational Mobility: Have Reforms Compelled Employers to Be Caste Blind?', *Himalayan Journal of Contemporary Research*, vol 3, no. 2 (2014): 2319–3174.

21. Sukhadeo Thorat and Katherine S. Neuman (ed.), Blocked by Caste: Economic Discrimination in Modern India, Oxford University Press, 2012.

22. Guilhem Cassan, 'Affirmative action, education and gender: Evidence from India', Journal of Development Economics, vol. 136 (2019): 51–70, https://ideas.repec.org/a/eee/deveco/v136y2019icp51-70.html.

23. Sam Asher, et al., 'Intergenerational Mobility in India: New Methods and Estimates Across Time, Space, and Communities' (2021), https://paulnovosad.com/pdf/anr-india-mobility.pdf.

24. Vani Borooah et al., 'The Effectiveness of Jobs Reservation: Caste, Religion and Economic Status in India', *Development and Change*, vol. 38, no. 3 (2007), https://onlinelibrary.wiley.com/doi/abs/10.1111/j.1467-7660.2007.00418.x.

25. Ashwini Deshpande and Thomas E. Weisskopf, 'Does Affirmative Action Reduce Productivity? A Case Study of the Indian Railways', *World Development*, vol. 64 (2014):169–180, https://www.researchgate.net/publication/263427329_Does_Affirmative_Action_Reduce_Productivity_A_Case_Study_of_the_Indian_Railways.

26. 'Earth's poor set to swell as World Bank moves poverty line', *Financial Times*, https://www.ft.com/content/81b0ac66-61e5-11e5-9846-de406ccb37f2.

27. Interview to Manasa R, who provided research assistance to the author.

28. Social Protection for a Changing India, vol. 2, Washington D.C.: World Bank, 2011, http://documents1.

worldbank.org/curated/en/155941468050952595/pdf/612750v20ESW0P11SP0Report0Volume0II.pdf.

29. Deepa Narayan et al., 'Moving Out of Poverty: Success From The Bottom Up', World Bank, 2009 https://openknowledge.worldbank.org/bitstream/handle/10986/11838/48104.pdf.

30. Jean Dreze et al., 'Casting the Net: India's Public Distribution System after the Food Security Act', vol. 54, no. 6 (2019), https://www.epw.in/journal/2019/6/special-articles/casting-net.html.

31. Seema Gaur and N. Srinivasa Rao, 'Poverty Measurement in India: A Status Update', Ministry of Rural Development, Working Paper No. 1/2020, 2020, https://rural.nic.in/sites/default/files/WorkingPaper_Poverty_DoRD_Sept_2020.pdf.

32. Basant Kumar Mohanty, 'Caste data hole in first meet on census update', The Telegraph, 4 March 2021, https://www.telegraphindia.com/india/caste-data-hole-in-first-meet-on-census-update/cid/1808420.

33. Shanmughasundaram J., 'Tamil Nadu: 9.11 lakh more BPL families to come under govt's housing scheme', 17 June 2020, Times of India, https://timesofindia.indiatimes.com/city/chennai/tamil-nadu-9-11-lakh-more-bpl-families-to-come-under-govts-housing-scheme/articleshow/76422535.cms.

34. Angus Deaton, 'Price indexes, inequality, and the measurement of world poverty', 2010, http://www.princeton.edu/~deaton/downloads/presidential%20address%2019january%202010%20all.

35. National Council for Applied Economic Research and University of Maryland, 'India Human Development Survey' Round 2, 2011-12.

36. Planning Commission of India, Government of India, 2013.

37. National Council for Applied Economic Research and University of Maryland, 'India Human Development Survey' Round 2, 2011-12.

38. National Council for Applied Economic Research and University of Maryland, 'India Human Development Survey' Round 2, 2011-12.

39. Ibid.

40. Ibid.

41. Lok Foundation-Oxford University survey by the Centre for the Monitoring of the Indian Economy, Pulse VIII.

42. Nancy Birdsall, 'The (Indispensable) Middle Class in Developing Countries; or, The Rich and the Rest, Not the Poor and the Rest' in *Equity in a Globalizing World*, edited by Ravi Kanbur and Michael Spence, World Bank, 2010.

43. Rakesh Kochhar, 'A Global Middle Class Is More Promise than Reality', Pew Research Center, 2015.

44. Devesh Kapur et al., 'The Importance of Being Middle Class in India', in *The New Middle Class in India and Brazil: Green Perspectives?*, edited by Dawid Danilo Bartelt and Axel Harneit-Sievers, Academic Foundation and Heinrich Böll Foundation.

45. Ibid.

46. Pradeep Chhibber and Rahul Verma, *Ideology and Identity: The Changing Party Systems of India*, Oxford University Press, 2018.

47. Himanshu, 'Why the picture on poverty is incomplete', *Mint*, 20 November 2019, https://www.livemint.com/news/india/why-the-picture-on-poverty-is-incomplete-11574269577580.html.

VI. How India Spends Its Money

1. Somesh Jha, 'NSO's consumer spend report showing first fall in 40 yrs won't be released', *Business Standard*, 18 February 2020, https://www.business-standard.com/article/economy-policy/national-statistical-commission-won-t-release-nso-s-consumer-spend-report-120021800045_1.html.

2. Ibid.

3. Menaka Rao, 'How To Live And Die On The New Dharavi Diet', Yahoo News, 2014.

4. Himanshu, 'Why the picture on poverty is incomplete', *Mint*,

20 November 2019, https://www.livemint.com/news/india/why-the-picture-on-poverty-is-incomplete-11574269577580.html.

5. Press Information Bureau, 'Household Consumer Expenditure Survey', Ministry of Statistics and Programme Implementation, 15 November 2019, https://pib.gov.in/Pressreleaseshare.aspx?PRID=1591792.

6. Surjit S. Bhalla and Karan Bhasin, 'Is the NSO's consumption data for 2017-18 beyond salvation?', *Mint*, 28 November 2019, https://www.livemint.com/opinion/online-views/is-the-nso-s-consumption-data-for-2017-18-beyond-salvation-11574962245323.html.

7. Angus Deaton and Valerie Kozel, 'Data and Dogma: The Great Indian Poverty Debate', *The World Bank Research Observer*, vol. 20, no. 2 (2005), https://www.princeton.edu/~deaton/downloads/deaton_kozel_great_indian_poverty_debate_wbro_2005.pdf.

8. 'Nobel laureate Angus Deaton: Open, uncensored data needed to support democracy', *The Hindu*, 16 October 2015, https://www.thehindu.com/news/national/statement-by-angus-deaton-to-the-indian-press/article7769880.ece.

9. Himanshu, 'Why the picture on poverty is incomplete', *Mint*, 20 November 2019, https://www.livemint.com/news/india/why-the-picture-on-poverty-is-incomplete-11574269577580.html.

10. Pramit Bhattacharya, 'New GDP series faces fresh questions after NSSO discovers holes', *Mint*, 10 May 2019, https://www.livemint.com/news/india/new-gdp-series-faces-fresh-questions-after-nsso-discovers-holes-1557250830351.html.

11. Pramit Bhattacharya and Nikita Kwatra, 'Fixing India's broken growth barometer key to revival', *Mint*, 25 July 2020, https://www.livemint.com/news/india/fixing-india-s-broken-growth-barometer-key-to-revival-11595634987337.html.

12. Rangarajan Commission report.

13. Pramit Bhattacharya, 'The battle to save India's statistical system',

Mint, 4 February 2020, https://www.livemint.com/news/india/the-battle-to-save-india-s-statistical-system-11580746495555.html.

14. Asit Ranjan Mishra, 'Why government has revamped the country's statistical system', *Mint*, 4 June 2019, https://www.livemint.com/news/india/why-government-has-revamped-the-country-s-statistical-system-1559667100886.html.

15. Pramit Bhattacharya, 'After junking report on consumption, NSO now looks for reasons', *Mint*, 22 November 2019, https://www.livemint.com/news/india/after-junking-report-on-consumption-nso-now-looks-for-reasons-11574361134927.html.

16. *Report of the Committee on Private Final Consumption Expenditure*, Central Statistics Office, Ministry of Statistics and Programme Implementation, Government of India, 2015, http://mospi.nic.in/sites/default/files/press_releases_statements/Adhikari_Committee_PFCE_22may15.pdf.

17. *Drinking Water, Sanitation, Hygiene and Housing Situation in India*, NSS 76th round, Central Statistics Office, Ministry of Statistics and Programme Implementation, Government of India, 2019, https://mospi.gov.in/documents/213904/301563//Report_584_final_01609135120775.pdf/4ed4d92a-19d9-0df1-548d-0f75bc0fc665.

18. Pramit Bhattacharya, 'Why India needs another statistical revolution', *Mint*, 22 May 2017, https://www.livemint.com/Opinion/aMKJ70TknavlOziQEg0SKL/Why-India-needs-another-statistical-revolution.html.

VII. How India Works

1. Full text of debate in Parliament, Lok Sabha, 7 February 2019, http://loksabhadocs.nic.in/newdebatemk/16/17/07022019/Fullday.pdf.

2. Census 2011.

3. Periodic Labour Force Survey 2018-19, National Sample Survey Office, Ministry of Statistics and Programme Implementation, GoI; and International Labour Organisation statistics.

4. *Teen Age Girls report*, Nanhi Kali, https://www.nanhikali.org/pdf/TAG-Report.pdf.

5. Periodic Labour Force Survey 2018-19, National Sample Survey Office, Ministry of Statistics and Programme Implementation, GoI.

6. *Employment and Unemployment Situation in India*, NSS 68th round, National Sample Survey Office, Ministry of Statistics and Programme Implementation, Government of India, 2014, p. A-373, https://mospi.gov.in/documents/213904/301563//nss_report_554_31jan141602150741128.pdf/3940f7c3-b843-ee94-66a3-0ddd837f20a8.

7. D. Coffey et al., 'Explicit prejudice: Evidence from a new survey', *Economic and Political Weekly*, vol. 53, no. 1 (2018): 46–54, https://www.researchgate.net/publication/322492420_Explicit_prejudice_Evidence_from_a_new_survey.

8. Ratna M. Sudarshan and Shrayana Bhattacharya, 'Through the Magnifying Glass: Women's Work and Labour Force Participation in Urban Delhi', *Economic and Political Weekly*, vol. 44, no. 48 (2009), https://www.epw.in/journal/2009/48/special-articles/through-magnifying-glass-womens-work-and-labour-force-participation.

9. Ashwini Deshpande, 'The Visible and Invisible Barriers to Indian Women Working', *The India Forum*, 1 August 2019, https://www.theindiaforum.in/article/visible-and-invisible-barriers-women-working-india.

10. S. Kapsos et al., 'Decline of women's labour force participation in India: Explaining the puzzling trend', in S. Dasgupta and S. Verick (eds.), *Transformation of Women at Work in Asia: An Unfinished Development Agenda*, Delhi: SAGE, 2016, pp. 75–102.

11. Ashwini Deshpande, 'The Visible and Invisible Barriers to Indian

Women Working', *The India Forum*, 1 August 2019, https://www.theindiaforum.in/article/visible-and-invisible-barriers-women-working-india.

12. Ashwini Deshpande and Jitendra Singh, 'Dropping Out, Being Pushed out or Can't Get In? Decoding Declining Labour Force Participation of Indian Women', Ashoka University Economics, Discussion Paper 65 (2021), https://dp.ashoka.edu.in/ash/wpaper/paper65.pdf.

13. Periodic Labour Force Survey 2018-19, National Sample Survey Office, Ministry of Statistics and Programme Implementation, GoI.

14. International Labour Organisation Statistics on Working Time, accessed February 2021.

15. According to data aggregated by the Centre for Diet and Activity Research, a research unit at the University of Cambridge.

16. Robert Joyce and Agnes Norris Keiller, 'The "gender commuting gap" widens considerably in the first decade after childbirth', Institute for Fiscal Studies, 7 November 2018, https://www.ifs.org.uk/publications/13673.

17. Anvita Anand and Geetam Tiwari, 'A Gendered Perspective of the Shelter–Transport–Livelihood Link: The Case of Poor Women in Delhi', *Transport Reviews*, vol. 26, no. 1 (2006): 63–80, https://www.tandfonline.com/doi/abs/10.1080/01441640500175615.

18. *A Gender Assessment of Mumbai's Public Transport*, World Bank, 2011, http://documents1.world bank.org/curated/en/857731468269134420/pdf/681950ESW0WHIT0nalReport00June02011.pdf.

19. 'Global Wage Report 2020-21: Wages and minimum wages in the time of COVID-19', International Labour Organisation, 2020, https://www.ilo.org/global/publications/books/WCMS_762534/lang--en/index.htm.

20. Periodic Labour Force Survey 2018-19, National Sample Survey Office, Ministry of Statistics and Programme Implementation, GoI.

21. Bidisha Mondal et al., 'Women workers in India: Labour Force Trends, Occupational Diversification and Wage Gaps', Centre for Sustainable Employment, Azim Premji University https://cse.azimpremjiuniversity.edu.in/wp-content/uploads/2018/03/Mondal_et_al_Women_Workers.pdf.

22. Lok Foundation/Oxford/CMIE. Rukmini S., 'For voters in Urban India, government is the first resort', *Mint*, 18 December 2018, https://www.livemint.com/Politics/7xSCJGgswHOEkhhzz9jLCK/For-voters-in-Urban-India-government-is-the-first-resort.html.

23. Sanjay Kumar and Pranav Gupta, 'What Young India wants: "Sarkari Naukri"', *Mint*, 22 August 2018, https://www.livemint.com/Industry/Ic7wicj8vnoT9BMj0Mj5TJ/What-Young-India-wants-Sarkari-Naukri.html.

24. Key highlights from the CSDS-KAS Report. *Attitudes, anxieties and aspirations of India's youth: changing patterns*, Lokniti, https://www.lokniti.org/media/upload_files/KeyfindingsfromtheYouthStudy.pdf.

25. Ibid.

26. YouGov-Mint Millennial Survey, Jan-Feb 2019, https://www.livemint.com/elections/lok-sabha-elections/what-young-indians-want-from-their-government-1556698416949.html.

27. 'Indian Railways completes recruitment exercise for 127,000 vacancies', *Business Standard*, 7 November 2019, https://www.business-standard.com/article/pti-stories/railways-completes-recruitment-exercise-for-1-27-lakh-vacancies-119110701503_1.html.

28. *Teen Age Girls Report*, Nanhi Kali-Naandi Foundation, 2018.

29. *Annual Status of Education Report (Rural) 2017: Beyond Basics*, Delhi: ASER Centre, 2018, http://img.asercentre.org/docs/Publications/ASER%20Reports/ASER%202017/aser2017fullreportfinal.pdf.

30. *Employment and Unemployment Situation in India*, NSS 68th round, National Sample Survey Office, Ministry of Statistics

and Programme Implementation, Government of India, 2014, p. A-373, https://mospi.gov.in/documents/213904/301563// nss_report_554_31jan141602150741128.pdf/3940f7c3-b843-ee94-66a3-0ddd837f20a8.

31. Christophe Jaffrelot, 'Why Jats Want a Quota', Carnegie Endowment for International Peace, https://carnegieendowment. org/2016/02/23/why-jats-want-quota-pub-62848.

32. Socio Economic and Caste Census, Ministry of Rural Development, Government of India, 2011.

33. Sneha Alexander, 'Govt job outlook remains bleak', *Mint*, 3 February 2020, https://www.livemint.com/news/india/govt-job-outlook-remains-bleak-11580670999078.html.

34. Santosh Mehrotra and Jajati Parida, 'India's Employment Crisis: Rising Education Levels and Falling Non-agricultural Job Growth', Centre for Sustainable Employment, Azim Premji University, Working Paper 23 (2019), https://cse. azimpremjiuniversity.edu.in/publications/indias-employment-crisis-rising-education-levels-and-falling-non-agricultural-job-growth/.

35. R. Nagaraj, 'Public Sector Employment What has changed?', Indira Gandhi Institute of Development Research, 2014, http://www.igidr.ac.in/indiapolecon/Public%20Sector%20 Empployment%20by%20R%20Nagaraj.pdf.

36. National Council for Applied Economic Research and University of Maryland, 'India Human Development Survey' Round 2, 2011-12.

37. Christophe Jaffrelot, 'Why Jats Want a Quota', Carnegie Endowment for International Peace, https://carnegieendowment. org/2016/02/23/why-jats-want-quota-pub-62848.

38. Ashwini Deshpande and Rajesh Ramachandran, 'Traditional hierarchies and affirmative action in a globalising economy: Evidence from India', *Ideas for India*, 21 June 2019, https://www. ideasforindia.in/topics/social-identity/traditional-hierarchies-

and-affirmative-action-in-a-globalising-economy-evidence-
from-india.html.

39. National Council for Applied Economic Research and University
of Maryland, 'India Human Development Survey' Round 2,
2011-12.

40.   Paul Attewell and Sukhadeo Thorat, 'The Legacy of Social
Exclusion', *Economic and Political Weekly*, vol. 42, no. 41 (2007),
https://www.epw.in/journal/2007/41/caste-and-economic-
discrimination-special-issues/legacy-social-exclusion.html.

VIII. How India Is Growing and Ageing

1.   The phrase was coined in Salman Rushdie's book *Midnight's
Children*, to refer to children born on 15 August 1947, the day
of Indian independence.

2.   Paul Ehrlich, *The Population Bomb*, US: Ballantine Books (1968).

3.   World Population Prospects (2020), United Nations Population
Division.

4.   'Census Office population projections', https://nhm.gov.in/
New_Updates_2018/Report_Population_Projection_2019.pdf.

5.   Jonathan Abbamonte, 'Modi warned about a population
explosion – but demographic data show declining trend',
Scroll, 12 September 2019, https://scroll.in/article/936158/
modi-warned-about-a-population-explosion-but-demographic-
data-show-declining-trend.

6.   Nayantra Sheoran Appleton, 'Why the 2019 "Population
Regulation Bill" Has Dangerous Consequences for India', 18 July
2020, *The Wire*, https://science.thewire.in/health/india-2019-
population-regulation-bill-marginalisation-womens-rights/.

7.   Neelam Pandey, 'BJP MPs say "save India", urge Modi govt to
bring in population control law', *The Print*, 23 September 2020,
https://theprint.in/india/bjp-mps-say-save-india-urge-modi-
govt-to-bring-in-population-control-law/509248/.

8. Anuja Jaiswal, 'Union minister Giriraj Singh says one community responsible for India's population explosion', *Times of India*, 1 October 2018, https://timesofindia.indiatimes.com/india/union-minister-giriraj-singh-says-one-community-responsible-for-indias-population-explosion/articleshow/66032611.cms.

9. Sample Registration Survey (2018), Registrar General of India.

10. Kartik Kwatra, 'What a narrowing Hindu-Muslim fertility gap tells us', *Mint*, 21 February 2019, https://www.livemint.com/news/india/what-a-narrowing-hindu-muslim-fertility-gap-tells-us-1550686404387.html.

11. Saswata Ghosh, 'Hindu–Muslim Fertility Differentials in India: Indirect Estimation at the District Level from Census 2011', *Indian Journal of Human Development*, vol. 12, no. 1 (2018), https://journals.sagepub.com/doi/abs/10.1177/0973703018780155.

12. Census 2011.

13. Seeme Jayachandran, 'Fertility Decline and Missing Women', *American Economic Journal: Applied Economics*, vol. 9, no. 1 (2017): 118–39, https://www.aeaweb.org/articles?id=10.1257/app.20150576.

14. Arun Jaitley, 'Gender and Son Meta-Preference: Is Development Itself an Antidote?', 2018, https://mofapp.nic.in/economicsurvey/economicsurvey/pdf/102-118_Chapter_07_ENGLISH_Vol_01_2017-18.pdf.

15. Sonia Bhalotra and Tom Cochrane, 'Where Have All the Young Girls Gone?: Identification of Sex Selection in India', IZA, Discussion Paper No. 5381, 2010, http://ftp.iza.org/dp5381.pdf.

16. Avraham Ebenstein, 'The "Missing Girls" of China and the Unintended Consequences of the One Child Policy', *The Journal of Human Resources*, https://scholars.huji.ac.il/sites/default/files/avrahamebenstein/files/ebenstein_onechildpolicy_2010.pdf.

17. S. Anukriti, 'Financial Incentives and the Fertility-Sex Ratio Trade-Off', *American Economic Journal: Applied Economics*, vol. 10, no. 2 (2018) 27–57, https://www.jstor.org/stable/26528382.

18. Sonia Bhalotra, correspondence with the author.

19. S. Anukriti, 'Financial Incentives and the Fertility-Sex Ratio Trade-Off', *American Economic Journal: Applied Economics*, vol. 10, no. 2 (2018): 27–57, https://www.jstor.org/stable/26528382.

20. S. Anukriti and Abhishek Chakravarty, 'Democracy and Demography Societal Effects of Fertility Limits on Local Leaders', vol. 54, no. 1 (2019): 79–121, http://jhr.uwpress.org/content/54/1/79.

21. Milan Vaishnav and Jamie Hintson, 'India's Emerging Crisis of Representation', Carnegie Endowment for International Peace, 14 March 2019, https://carnegieendowment.org/2019/03/14/india-s-emerging-crisis-of-representation-pub-78588.

22. Alaka Basu and Sonalde Desai, 'Hopes, Dreams and Anxieties: India's One-Child Families', *Asian Population Studies*, vol. 12, no. 1 (2016): 4–27, https://www.ncbi.nlm.nih.gov/pmc/articles/PMC4869707/.

23. Rosanna Ledbetter, 'Thirty Years of Family Planning in India', *Asian Survey*, vol. 24, no. 7 (1984): 736–758, https://www.jstor.org/stable/2644186?seq=1.

24. Soutik Biswas, 'India's dark history of sterilisation', *BBC*, 14 November 2014, https://www.bbc.com/news/world-asia-india-30040790.

25. National Family Health Survey I (1992-93).

26. Debasis Barik et al., 'After the Dividend: Caring for a Greying India', *Economic Political Weekly*, vol. 50, no. 24, (2015): 108–112, https://www.ncbi.nlm.nih.gov/pmc/articles/PMC4847957/.

IX. How India Lives and Where

1. Census 2011.

2. *Drinking Water, Sanitation, Hygiene and Housing Situation in India*, NSS 76th round, Central Statistics Office, Ministry of Statistics and Programme Implementation, Government of

India, 2019, https://mospi.gov.in/documents/213904/301563//
Report_584_final_01609135120775.pdf/4ed4d92a-19d9-0df1-
548d-0f75bc0fc665.

3. Ibid.

4. Ibid.

5. Ibid.

6. Ibid.

7. Census 2011.

8. P. Deshingkar and E. Anderson, 'People on the Move: New
    Policy Challenges for Increasingly Mobile Populations', *Natural
    Resources Perspectives*, vol. 92 (2004): 1–4.

9. Chinmay Tumbe, 'Urbanisation, demographic transition, and
    the growth of cities in India, 1870-2020', International Growth
    Centre, Working Paper C-35205-INC-1, https://www.theigc.
    org/wp-content/uploads/2016/11/Tumbe-2016-Working-paper.
    pdf.

10. Ibid.

11. 'Rural Urban Distribution of Population', Census of India 2011,
    Government of India, https://censusindia.gov.in/2011-prov-
    results/paper2/data_files/india/Rural_Urban_2011.pdf.

12. Sriharsha Devulapalli, 'Migrant flows to Delhi, Mumbai ebbing',
    Mint, 20 September 2019, https://www.livemint.com/news/
    india/migrant-flows-to-delhi-mumbai-ebbing-1568981492505.
    html.

13. Economic Survey of India 2017-18, Ministry of Finance,
    Government of India.

14. National Council for Applied Economic Research and University
    of Maryland, 'India Human Development Survey' Round 2,
    2011-12.

15. 'Migration in India 2007-08', NSS 64th Round, National
    Sample Survey Office, Ministry of Statistics and Programme
    Implementation, Government of India.

16. Diane Coffey et al., 'Short-term Labor Migration from Rural
    North India: Evidence from New Survey Data', *Population*

Research and Policy Review (2014), https://drive.google.com/file/d/1nrHOYzVYBARmgR-QwhIbxZpP5_8d3Qul/view.

17. Sonalde Desai and Esha Chatterjee, 'Male Migration from Rural India: Divergent Pathways to Long-Term and Short-Term Migration', http://paa2019.populationassociation.org/uploads/192011.

18. Gaurav Nayyar and Kyoung Yang Kim, 'India's Internal Labor Migration Paradox: The Statistical and the Real', World Bank, Policy Research Working Paper 8356 (2018), http://documents1.worldbank.org/curated/en/429181519662555108/pdf/WPS8356.pdf.

19. Ajay Sharma, 'Exclusionary Urbanization and Changing Migration Pattern in India: Is commuting by workers a feasible alternative?', https://www.iussp.org/sites/default/files/event_call_for_papers/Draft_Ajay.pdf.

20. R.B Bhagat and Soumya Mohanty, 'Emerging pattern of urbanization and the contribution of migration in urban growth in India', *Asian Population Studies*, vol. 5, no. 1 (2009), https://www.researchgate.net/publication/228431591_Emerging_pattern_of_urbanization_and_the_contribution_of_migration_in_urban_growth_in_India.

21. Yu Zhu, 'In Situ Urbanization in Rural China: Case Studies from Fujian Province', *Development and Change*, vol. 31, no. 2 (2000), https://onlinelibrary.wiley.com/doi/abs/10.1111/1467-7660.00160.

22. R.B. Bhagat and Kunal Keshri, Internal Migration in India: Intensity, Flows and Impact', (2018), https://www.researchgate.net/publication/334494446_Internal_Migration_in_India_Intensity_Flows_and_Impact/link/5d2e0806a6fdcc2462e60f42/download.

23. 'Maharashtra State Level Background Paper', Mumbai: Urban India Reforms Facility (UIRF), School of Habitat Studies, Tata Institute of Social Sciences, 2011, https://urk.tiss.edu/

wp-content/uploads/2019/09/Maharashtra-State-Level-Background-Paper.pdf.

24. Partha Mukhopadhyay et al., 'Understanding India's Urban Frontier: What Is behind the Emergence of Census Towns in India?', World Bank, Policy Research Working Paper 7923, http://documents1.worldbank.org/curated/en/378351482172055283/pdf/WPS7923.pdf.

25. 'Maharashtra State Level Background Paper', Mumbai: Urban India Reforms Facility (UIRF), School of Habitat Studies, Tata Institute of Social Sciences, 2011, https://urk.tiss.edu/wp-content/uploads/2019/09/Maharashtra-State-Level-Background-Paper.pdf.

26. Sandhya Nair, 'In Vasai's villages, lengthy battle against urban tag loses steam', *The Times of India*, 5 July 2015, https://timesofindia.indiatimes.com/city/mumbai/in-vasais-villages-lengthy-battle-against-urban-tag-loses-steam/articleshow/47942357.cms.

27. Ibid.

28. *Population Projections for India and States 2011–2036*, Census of India 2011, Delhi: National Commission of Population (2019), https://nhm.gov.in/New_Updates_2018/Report_Population_Projection_2019.pdf.

29. Ankush Agrawal and Vikas Kumar, *Numbers in India's Periphery: The Political Economy of Government Statistics*, Cambridge University Press (2020), https://www.cambridge.org/core/books/numbers-in-indias-periphery/FE6168238548B42FE99CC6C7896CACE3.

30. J. David Brown et al., 'Predicting the Effect of Adding a Citizenship Question to the 2020 Census', Center for Economic Studies, US Census Bureau, Working Papers 19-18 (2019), https://www2.census.gov/ces/wp/2019/CES-WP-19-18.pdf.

X. How India Falls Sick and Gets Better

1. Economic Survey of India (2020-21).

2. Rukmini S., 'India May Be Reversing Decades Of Progress On Child Nutrition, New Govt Data Show', *IndiaSpend*, 13 December 2020, https://www.indiaspend.com/health/india-may-be-reversing-decades-of-progress-on-child-nutrition-new-govt-data-show-701363.

3. Ishan Anand and Anjana Thampi, 'Less than a third of Indians go to public hospitals for treatment', *Mint*, 4 May 2020, https://www.livemint.com/news/india/less-than-a-third-of-indians-go-to-public-hospitals-for-treatment-11588578426388.html.

4. https://www.cbhidghs.nic.in/showfile.php?lid=1155.

5. Debasis Barik et al., 'Economic Status and Adult Mortality in India: Is the Relationship Sensitive to Choice of Indicators?', *World Dev*, vol. 103 (2018): 176–187, https://www.ncbi.nlm.nih.gov/pmc/articles/PMC5828167/.

6. National Council for Applied Economic Research and University of Maryland, 'IHDS' Round 2, 2011-12.

7. Ragini Bhuyan, 'More women falling ill, but they have lower access to medical treatment', *Mint*, 28 April 2016, https://www.livemint.com/Opinion/7otVkJiz6SmG5TSG9yyIGN/More-women-falling-ill-but-they-have-lower-access-to-medica.html.

8. IHDS 2011-12; Rukmini S., 'India's poor suffer cough and cold routinely, making coronavirus detection difficult', *Mint*, 30 March 2020, https://www.livemint.com/news/india/india-s-poor-suffer-cough-and-cold-routinely-making-coronavirus-detection-difficult-11585544409496.html.

9. Global Burden of Disease Collaborative Network, 'Global Burden of Disease Study 2019 (GBD 2019)' Institute for Health Metrics and Evaluation (IHME), 2021.

10. 'Key Indicators of Social Consumption in India: Health', National Sample Survey 75th round, Ministry of Statsitics and Programme Implementation, GoI, 2019.

11. Mudit Kapoor et al., 'Missing female patients: an observational analysis of sex ratio among outpatients in a referral tertiary care public hospital in India', *BMJ Open* (2019), https://bmjopen. bmj.com/content/9/8/e026850.

12. Shraboni Patra and Mahadev Bhise, 'Gender differentials in prevalence of self-reported non-communicable diseases (NCDs) in India: evidence from recent NSSO survey', *Journal of Public Health*, vol. 24, no. 5 (2016): 375–385, https://www. researchgate.net/publication/303344658_Gender_differentials_ in_prevalence_of_self-reported_non-communicable_diseases_ NCDs_in_India_evidence_from_recent_NSSO_survey.

13. Akansha Batra et al., 'Does discrimination drive gender differences in health expenditure on adults: Evidence from Cancer patients in rural India', Indian Statistical Institute, Discussion Paper 2014-03 (2014), https://www.isid.ac.in/~pu/ dispapers/dp14-03.pdf.

14. National Council for Applied Economic Research and University of Maryland, 'IHDS' Round 2, 2011-12.

15. All India Debt and Investment Survey, National Sample Survey 77th Round, Ministry of Statistics and Programme Implementation, GoI, 2021.

16. Malaisamy Muniyandi et al., 'Association of Tuberculosis With Household Catastrophic Expenditure in South India', *JAMA Network Open*, vol. 3, no. 2 (2020):e1920973, https://jamanetwork. com/journals/jamanetworkopen/fullarticle/2760664.

17. 'Key Indicators of Social Consumption in India: Health', National Sample Survey 75th round, Ministry of Statsitics and Programme Implementation, GoI, 2019.

18. Ibid.

19. Tabassum Barnagarwala, 'Endless tragedy: Mother dies of Covid, missing grandma is found dead in Jalgaon hospital toilet', *Times of India*, 11 June 2020, https://indianexpress.com/article/india/ coronavirus-death-jalgaon-hospital-grandma-found-dead-in-toilet-6453264/.

20. Bibhudatta Pradhan and Vrishti Beniwal, 'Indians Already Ravaged By Virus Now Slammed With Medical Debt', *Bloomberg*, 10 June 2021, https://www.bloomberg.com/news/articles/2021-06-10/medical-debts-bankrupt-indians-already-ravaged-by-covid-19.

21. Jishnu Das et al., 'In Urban And Rural India, A Standardized Patient Study Showed Low Levels Of Provider Training And Huge Quality Gaps', *Health Aff*, vol. 31, no. 12 (2012): 2774–2784, https://www.ncbi.nlm.nih.gov/pmc/articles/PMC3730274/.

22. Sophie Huddart et al., 'Case fatality and recurrent tuberculosis among patients managed in the private sector: A cohort study in Patna, India', *PLoS One*, vol. 16 no. 3 (2021): 1–16, https://journals.plos.org/plosone/article/file?id=10.1371/journal.pone.0249225&type=printable.

23. Jishnu Das et al., 'Two Indias: The structure of primary health care markets in rural Indian villages with implications for policy', *Social Science and Medicine* (2020), https://www.sciencedirect.com/science/article/pii/S0277953620300186?via%3Dihub.

24. 'Laboratory surveillance for SARS-CoV-2 in India: Performance of testing & descriptive epidemiology of detected COVID-19, January 22 - April 30, 2020', *Indian Journal of Medical Research*, vol. 151, no. 5 (2020): 424–437, https://www.ijmr.org.in/article.asp?issn=0971-5916;year=2020;volume=151;issue=5;spage=424;epage=437;aulast=ICMR.

25. Bithika Chatterjee et al., 'The mortality due to COVID-19 in different nations is associated with the demographic character of nations and the prevalence of autoimmunity', *medRxiv* (2020), https://www.medrxiv.org/content/10.1101/2020.07.31.20165696v2.full.

26. Soutik Biswas, 'Coronavirus: Are Indians more immune to Covid-19?', *BBC*, 2 November 2020, https://www.bbc.com/news/world-asia-india-54730290.

27. E. Westly, 'Global health: One million deaths', *Nature*, vol. 504 (2013): 22–23, https://www.nature.com/news/global-health-one-million-deaths-1.14269.

28. Arunabh Saikia, 'Why Assam's Covid Fatality Rate is Lowest in India', *Scroll*, 9 September 2020, https://scroll.in/article/972578/why-assams-covid-fatality-rate-is-lowest-in-india-60-of-deaths-in-confirmed-cases-not-counted.

ACKNOWLEDGEMENTS

This book grew out of two separate sets of experiences—the fourteen years I spent reporting on India before I ever thought of a book, and a unique group of people who led me to the book.

Since I first started out as an intern in the Mumbai bureau of the *Times of India*, every working day has felt to me as if I were getting paid to understand the country. For his belief in me, its translation into resources, support and space in newsprint, and his continuing friendship, I owe a debt of gratitude to my first editor, Jaideep Bose. For recognising the value of the data reporting I was doing and giving me a huge platform to shine, I owe my heartfelt thanks to Siddharth Varadarajan. For continuing to support me, helping integrate data work into the broader newspaper, and creating the position of a data editor, my deep thanks to Malini Parthasarathy. For not just being my editor and supporter but also my dear friend, my endless thanks to Sruthijith K.K. Since I went freelance in 2018, my thanks to Supriya Sharma, Shekhar Gupta, Rama Lakshmi, Pramit Bhattacharya, Rahul Kanwal, Govindraj Ethiraj, Madhur Singh, Upmita Vajpai, Ravi Agarwal and other editors for commissioning my work. Ravish Kumar and Karan Thapar gave my work the visibility that comes as a result of the respect that their voices command.

I learnt everything I know about data journalism on the job, and so any knowledge or expertise that I may have acquired is thanks to my first editor on data stories, Shankar Raghuraman, who showed me all that I know about the political economy of data. Thanks also to my former colleague at The Times of India, Subodh Verma, for insight into how numbers operate. In an unlikely twist, the best data editor in India is also somehow the most generous and kind, and I was lucky to benefit from Pramit's meticulous editing and feedback on my stories, as well as from his knowledge of the Indian economy, and his friendship.

More than fifteen years after he turned my way of seeing the world upside down from his first class at Sophia Polytechnic where I was studying communications, P. Sainath has remained a mentor and a moral lode star—if I ever worry that I am 'reducing' people to numbers, I need look no further than Sainath's work to see how to allow them to grow to their fullest on my pages. I have benefited enormously from the people I met on the job whose expertise helped form my world view and whose friendship I am privileged to have earned— Jean Dreze, Reetika Khera, Nikhil Dey, Dean Spears, Diane Cofey, Aashish Gupta, Sonalde Desai, Ashwini Deshpande, Rahul Verma, Milan Vaishnav, Sanjay Kumar and Shamika Ravi have been generous with their time and thoughts over the years, and I am lucky to know them. For their friendship, and for conversations over the years over dining tables and Udupi restaurant tables that helped me put what I was seeing in the numbers in perspective, I thank Nick Robinson, Mihir Sharma, Raghu Karnad, SK, Supriya Nair, Arun Mohan Sukumar and M Rajshekhar.

Up until 2020, I had never thought I had a book idea in me. My deep thanks to Pratap Bhanu Mehta, who, despite having only a passing acquaintance with me, gave me such fulsome praise and encouragement that I took his suggestion to write a book seriously. Once the pandemic hit and the difficulties of working under lockdown took over, the book receded to the back of my mind. Anand Krishnamoorthi gave me his time, friendship and expertise to get *The Moving Curve* podcast off the ground and get me back into the world of thinking. Amit Varma gave my thoughts about data, the media and democracy such careful consideration on his remarkable podcast that it made me take myself seriously again. The supportive responses of my readers and of listeners of Amit's podcast made me take the plunge. SK responded to my book plan with his characteristic enthusiasm and put me in touch with Anish Chandy, who turned my vague idea into an actual book. Anish's respect of his time and mine, ambitious deadlines and relentless matter-of-factness are among the qualities that make him a wonderful agent. The work that he put into the book all through, his availability to answer every small question, and his championing of the book far beyond what I had first pictured are qualities that make him so much more.

My first meeting with Karthika V.K. was everything a first-time author could dream of—she radiated positivity, I felt as if she truly got me and the book idea, and I left her office beaming helplessly. All through the process, Karthika has remained improbably cheery, kind and sharp. Since she's the only publisher I've ever known, I can only assume that everyone in publishing is equally charming and no unkind words are ever exchanged. At Westland, my thanks also to Ajitha G.S. for her time and engagement, Dipanjali Chadha for kind and careful editing, and to Saurabh Garge for his helpful and generous inputs on design. Every time I bristled at a suggestion from Karthika and her team, ready to 'reject insertion' and 'delete comment', I'd reach the next line and realise how theirs was absolutely the right call. When a weakness in the book was gently hinted at, I felt found out— that was precisely the portion of the book that needed fixing. This book couldn't have found a better home than at Westland.

Nithya Subramanian's brilliance with design has lifted the book, both in its illustrations and in its cover, and for her enthusiasm from the beginning, for the exceptional talent she brings and for her kindness and friendship I thank her for being my collaborator.

Samanth Subramanian walked me through the process of planning a book and has been a source of inspiration and support. Aashish, Pramit, Rahul, Milan, Ashwini, Anish, Pratap and Madhukar gave me invaluable feedback on early drafts.

This book has benefited greatly from data that was made available to me, some of which has never been reported on before. My thanks to officials at the Office of the Registrar General of India, the National Statistical Office, the National Crime Records Bureau and the International Institute of Population Sciences for helping me with data access and interpretation. Thanks also to Rajiv Lall of the IDFC Institute and Mahesh Vyas of the Centre for the Monitoring of the Indian Economy for generously making the Lok Survey data available to me. Thank you to Sonalde Desai, Omkar Joshi and Debasis Barik for making India Human Development Survey data available to me. My deep gratitude to Sanjay Kumar and others at the Lokniti programme at the Centre for the Study of Developing Societies for opening up their data to me.

Finally, the book could only be written because of my own version of a writer's retreat—friends and family chipping in to watch my locked-down kids so I could write in peace. Janaki Fernandes heard the stress in my voice and left everything to fly in to Chennai and live with us, an act that would sound incredible only to people who don't know Janaki. Sowmiya Ashok gave me coffee and her dining table where most of this book was written. My parents got on a flight in the middle of the second wave of the pandemic to take the baton from Janaki, and my in-laws from them, so the summer of 2021 could be one long writing residency for me. This book is here thanks to them.

For all of their unwavering support and love, right from watching me come dead last in kindergarten races to meticulously listening to my pandemic podcast, I thank my parents, Mini and Kumar Shrinivasan. For their pride in me and their unquestioning support of every step I take, thanks to my remarkable parents-in-law Sarojini and R. Shunmuga Sundaram. Thank you to my aunt Gouri Dange and uncle Anjum Rajabali for my first introduction to journalism, and thank you to Gouri and Tatsat for the love, fun and food they have filled my life with. My brother Siddharth, sisters-in-law Beth and Chindhu and brother-in-law Arthish are my greatest cheerleaders. For the unmatched joy they bring me, and for asking me every few hours for the last year if the book is over yet, thank you to my kids, Nilavan and Kanali. But most of all, my gratitude to my husband Manu—my life has got richer, broader, deeper and happier every single day since I met him, and every thought in this book has passed through a conversation we've had some time in the last ten years.

A NOTE ON THE COVER

The cover brings out how data can be used to reveal and conceal truths about India, by suggesting a Pinocchio within a bar chart. Evoking the colours of the national flag, it adds a human face to impassive numbers as a reminder of what they ultimately represent. The face wraps around the book, but it is the spine that shows where this work truly lies: filling in the gaps between the data.